Religion, Social Practice, and Contested Hegemonies

Culture and Religion in International Relations

Series Editors:
Yosef Lapid and Friedrich Kratochwil

Published by Palgrave Macmillan:

Dialogue Among Civilizations: Some Exemplary Voices
By Fred Dallmayr

Religion in International Relations: The Return from Exile
Edited by Fabio Petito and Pavlos Hatzopoulos

Identity and Global Politics: Empirical and Theoretical Elaborations
Edited by Patricia M. Goff and Kevin C. Dunn

Reason, Culture, Religion: The Metaphysics of World Politics
By Ralph Pettman

Bringing Religion into International Relations
By Jonathan Fox and Shmuel Sandler

The Global Resurgence of Religion and the Transformation of International Relations
By Scott Thomas

Religion, Social Practice, and Contested Hegemonies: Reconstructing the Public Sphere in Muslim Majority Societies
Edited by Armando Salvatore and Mark LeVine

RELIGION, SOCIAL PRACTICE, AND CONTESTED HEGEMONIES

RECONSTRUCTING THE PUBLIC SPHERE IN MUSLIM MAJORITY SOCIETIES

Edited by

Armando Salvatore and Mark LeVine

First published in 2005 by
PALGRAVE MACMILLAN™
175 Fifth Avenue, New York, N.Y. 10010 and
Houndmills, Basingstoke, Hampshire, England RG21 6XS
Companies and representatives throughout the world.

PALGRAVE MACMILLAN is the global academic imprint of the Palgrave Macmillan division of St. Martin's Press, LLC and of Palgrave Macmillan Ltd. Macmillan® is a registered trademark in the United States, United Kingdom and other countries. Palgrave is a registered trademark in the European Union and other countries.

ISBN 1–4039–6865–9

Library of Congress Cataloging-in-Publication Data

Religion, social practice, and contested hegemonies : reconstructing the public sphere in Muslim majority societies / edited by Armando Salvatore and Mark LeVine.
p. cm.
Includes bibliographical references and index.
ISBN 1–4039–6865–9
1. Islam and state. 2. Islam and civil society. I. Salvatore, Armando.
II. LeVine, Mark, 1966–

JC49.R47 2005
306.6'97—dc22   2004062065

A catalogue record for this book is available from the British Library.

Design by Newgen Imaging Systems (P) Ltd., Chennai, India.

First edition: June 2005

10 9 8 7 6 5 4 3 2 1

Printed in the United States of America.

For Yasmin, Alessandro,
and
Francesca Bianca

CONTENTS

ACKNOWLEDGMENTS

This volume is the outcome of a working group on "Islamic Movements and Discourses and the Public Sphere" established by Armando Salvatore and Amr Hamzawy as a project of the Forum of Social Research. The editors of this volume owe thanks to Amr for his uniquely sensible conduction of discussions within the working group, especially during a workshop held in Montecatini, Italy, in March 2002, during which intermediate drafts of some of the chapters here included were presented.

The activities of the working group intersected thematically and chronologically with the work of a two-year Summer Institute, "The Public Sphere and Muslim Identities," that began in July 2001 and concluded in August 2002, funded by the Alexander von Humboldt Foundation (Bonn), administered by the Wissenschaftskolleg zu Berlin on behalf of an international consortium of institutes for advanced study in Europe and the United States and convened by Dale F. Eickelman and Armando Salvatore. Some participants in the working group were also fellows at the Summer Institute, including Schirin Amir-Moazami, whom we also thank for her particular engagement.

During the decisive year of work at the draft chapters of the volume, between the fall of 2002 and the summer 2004, we also benefited from exchanges with the members of a new working group instituted within the Forum of Social Research, on "Socio-Religious Movements and the Reconstruction of Political Community." We thank Bo Stråth and Peter Wagner for their support in the initial phase of this working group at the European University Institute, Florence, Italy; the History Department, School of Humanities, Critical Theory Institute, Humanities Research Institute, and Global Peace and Conflict Studies Center at the University of California, Irvine, for their funding of an October 2002 workshop organized by Mark LeVine and at which advanced versions of some of the papers included here were discussed; and the Social Science Research Council, New York (in particularly Seteney Shami), for granting to this working group an award within the 2002–2003 International Collaborative Research Grants Competition (ICRG) on "Reconceptualizing Public Spheres in the Middle East & North Africa." Among the participants in this working group, we particularly benefited from intensive and mutually enriching exchanges with Rema Hammami, May Jayyusi, Issam Aburaiya, Raja Bahlul, Sami Shalom Chetrit, Sarah Helman, Oren Yiftachel, and Walid Shomaly.

A special thanks is due to Cecelia Lynch for acting as a discussant of papers from both working groups and for bringing cohesiveness to the outcome of their combined work, as testified by the conclusion that she contributed to this volume. Georg Stauth has acted as a discussion partner on theoretical issues throughout the period of production of this work. The Kulturwissenschaftliches Institut (Institute for Advanced Studies in the Humanities), Essen, has provided a supporting and stimulating research environment during the last phase of work at the book.

Notes on Contributors

Raymond William Baker is College Professor of International Relations at Trinity College and Adjunct Professor at the American University in Cairo. Baker is the author of several books on the Arab-Islamic world, most recently *Islam Without Fear: Egypt and the New Islamists* (Cambridge, MA: Harvard University Press, 2003). He currently serves as president of the International Association of Middle East Studies and as cochair, with Tareq Ismael, of the committee to establish the International University of Baghdad.

Lara Deeb is Assistant Professor of Women's Studies at the University of California, Irvine. Between 2003 and 2004 she was an Academy Scholar at the Harvard Academy for International and Area Studies. She received her Ph.D. in 2002 from the Department of Anthropology, Emory University. Her main research focus is on cultural and historical anthropology, with a geographical focus on Lebanon. Her current manuscript explores the ways modernity, piety, and gender intersect in an Islamist Shi'i community in Lebanon. This work is based on her dissertation that was granted the 2004 Malcolm Kerr Dissertation Award in the Social Sciences by the Middle East Studies Association of North America (MESA).

Baudouin Dupret received his Ph.D. and his Habilitation from the Institut d'Etudes Politiques de Paris. He is currently Research Fellow at CNRS, based at the Institut Français du Proche-Orient (IFPO), Damascus. He has coedited several volumes, among which are *Legal Pluralism in the Arab World* (The Hague: Kluwer Law International, 1999), *Egypt and Its Laws* (The Hague: Kluwer Law International, 2002), and *Standing Trial: Law and the Person in the Modern Middle-East* (London: I.B. Tauris, 2004). He is the author of *Au nom de quel droit. Répertoires juridiques et référence religieuse dans la société égyptienne musulmane contemporaine* (Paris: Maison des sciences de l'homme, 2000). His second book concerns the issue of legal practices and sexual morality in the Egyptian judicial context.

Jean-Noël Ferrié received his Ph.D. in Political Science from the Institut d'Etudes Politiques d'Aix-en-Provence, France, and his Habilitation from the Institut d'Etudes Politiques de Paris. He is currently Senior Research Fellow at CEDEJ (Centre d'Etudes et de Documentation Economique, Juridique et Sociale), Cairo. He also teaches in the Department of Political Science at Cairo University (French programme) and is a visiting professor at the Department of Political Science of Saint-Joseph University, Beirut. His research focuses on the public sphere and the democratization process in the Middle East. He is the author of *La Religion de la vie quotidienne chez des Marocains musulmans. Règles et dilemmes* (Paris: Karthala, 2004) and *Le régime de la civilité. Public et réislamisation en Égypte* (Paris: CNRS Editions, 2004).

Dyala Hamzah is Junior Research Fellow at the Zentrum Moderner Orient, Berlin and an advanced Ph.D. candidate at the Free University of Berlin (Institut für Islamwissenschaft) and at the EHESS, Paris. She holds an *Agrégation* in philosophy and has published her MA thesis *Farabi, L'Épître sur l'Intellect*, Paris: l'Harmattan, 2001. She is a former chief editor of *Égypte/Monde Arabe*, for which she launched a new series and edited the volume *La Censure ou Comment la Contourner: Dire et Ne Pas Dire Aujourd'hui en Égypte*. She is also a Board Member of the Forum of Social Research. Her main research interest is in the history of ideas and the sociology of knowledge of the modern and contemporary Middle East, with a special focus on Egypt and Palestine.

Mark LeVine is Associate Professor of Modern Middle Eastern History, Culture, and Islamic Studies at the University of California, Irvine. He is the author of two books, *Overthrowing Geography: Jaffa, Tel Aviv and the Struggle for Palestine* (University of California Press, 2004), *Why They Don't Hate Us: Lifting the Veil of the Axis of Evil* (Oxford: Oneworld, 2005), and coeditor with Viggo Mortensen and Pilar Perez of *Twilight of Empire: Responses to Occupation* (Los Angeles: Perceval Press, 2003). He has authored numerous academic and journalistic articles and is a founding board member of the Forum for Social Research and contributing editor at *Tikkun* magazine.

Cecelia Lynch is Associate Professor of Political Science and International Studies at the University of California, Irvine. She obtained her Ph.D. from Columbia University, and taught previously at Northwestern University in Evanston, IL. She specializes in international relations theory, social movements and world politics, peace and security, international organization and law, and ethics and religion. She is the author of *Beyond Appeasement: Interpreting Interwar Peace Movements in World Politics* (Ithaca, NY: Cornell University Press, 1999), which won the Myrna Bernath Prize of the Society of Historians of American Foreign Relations, and the Edgar J. Furniss Prize for best first book on security from the Mershon Center at Ohio State University. She coedited, with Michael Loriaux, *Law and Moral Action in World Politics* (Minneapolis: University of Minnesota Press, 2000), and has written articles on the UN, the anti-globalization movement, peace movements and internationalism, religious perspectives on multiculturalism, and conceptual issues in International Relations theory. She is currently working on two book projects, one with Audie Klotz on "constructivism" in International Relations theory, and another, for which she was awarded a Social Science Research Council-MacArthur Foundation Fellowship on Peace and Security in a Changing World, on religion in world politics.

Setrag Manoukian received his Ph.D. in Anthropology and History from the University of Michigan. He is Assistant Professor of Cultural Anthropology at the University of Milano-Bicocca. His main research focus is on cultural and historical anthropology, with a geographical focus on modern Iran. His main theoretical interests concern the relationship between anthropology and history, the social construction of knowledge, and the relationship between orality, writing, and semiotics. He is completing a manuscript on the social history of the Iranian city of Shiraz, concentrating on the role of the intellectuals in the political and cultural history of the city and on how they dealt with issues of local history and poetics. He is the editor of *Etno-grafie: Testi oggetti immagini* (Rome: Meltemi, 2003).

Muhammad Khalid Masud was until 2003 the Academic Director of the International Institute for the Study of Islam in the Modern World (ISIM) in Leiden, The Netherlands. Until 1999, he was a professor at the Islamic Research Institute in Islamabad, Pakistan. Presently he is the chairman of the Council for Islamic Ideology, Islamabad. He received his Ph.D. in Islamic Studies from McGill University, Canada. His publications include *Shatibi's Philosophy of Law* (rev. ed. 1995), *Iqbal's Reconstruction of Ijtihad* (1995), *Islamic Legal Interpretation: The Muftis and their Fatwas* (coedited with Brinkley Messick and David S. Powers, 1996), and the edited volume *Travellers in Faith: Studies of the Tablighî Jamâ'at as a Transnational Islamic Movement for Faith Renewal* (2000). He has been an editor of the journal *Islamic Studies*.

Brinkley Messick is Professor of Anthropology at Columbia University. He holds a Ph.D. in anthropology from Princeton University. His publications include *The Calligraphic State: Textual Domination and History in a Muslim Society* (Berkeley: University of California Press, 1993); the edited volume, with Muhammad Khalid Masud and David S. Powers, *Islamic Legal Interpretation: The Muftis and their Fatwas* (Cambridge, MA: Harvard University Press, 1996), and numerous articles in leading scholarly journals.

Armando Salvatore is Senior Research Fellow at the Institute for Advanced Studies in the Humanities, Essen (Kulturwissenschaftliches Institut) and at the Institute of Social Science, Humboldt University, Berlin. He received his Ph.D. in Political and Social Sciences from the European University Institute, Florence, in 1994. His dissertation was granted the 1994 Malcolm Kerr Dissertation Award in the Social Sciences by the Middle East Studies Association of North America (MESA). It was later published as *Islam and the Political Discourse of Modernity* (1997). He has edited several volumes, including *Muslim Traditions and Modern Techniques of Power* (2001) and *Public Islam and the Common Good* (with Dale F. Eickelman, 2004). He has completed a manuscript on "The Public Sphere: An Axial Genealogy," which condenses his main research interests within Social and Political Theory. He is founder and board coordinator of the Forum of Social Research, and editor of the *Yearbook of Sociology of Islam* (with Georg Stauth).

INTRODUCTION

RECONSTRUCTING THE PUBLIC SPHERE IN MUSLIM MAJORITY SOCIETIES

Armando Salvatore and Mark LeVine

The collection of essays in this volume examines how modern public spheres reflect and mask—often simultaneously—discourses of order, contests for hegemony, and techniques of power in the Muslim world. Although the contributors examine various time periods and locations, each views modern and contemporary public spheres as crucial to the functioning, and thus understanding, of political and societal power in Muslim majority countries. Part I of this volume analyzes the various discourses and technologies operating within Muslim public spheres; part II investigates how they impact and interact with the construction of moral and legal arguments within Muslim societies.

The chapters that follow seek to open new horizons for the study of how public spheres are conceptualized, produced, and deployed, not just in the Muslim majority world but in all modern societies. Such a step forward is made possible by our examinations of how discourses and techniques of hegemony are deployed by socio-religious movements, and of how their expression transforms the manner in which public spheres are constructed, and their borders and norms contested. The contributions here explore the impact of such conceptualizations on the very notion of "civil society" and the practices it authorizes, on the ensuing dynamics of hegemony, and on the way secularity, as a set of practices, norms, and discourse, binds together hegemonic discourses.

Our engagement with the public sphere focuses on the horizontal ties that bind together participants in social movements and public communication, rather than on the more often discussed vertical, segmented ties mediated by the institutions and identities of the supposedly modern and secular nation-state. At the same time, however, we interrogate the disciplinary and governmental practices of political elites that constrict and shape the activities of these movements and the horizons of action of their members. In so doing we address Nancy Fraser's simple yet important critique of Habermas's seminal discussion of the public sphere, which in her view "stops short of developing a post-bourgeois model while leaving unproblematized the dubious assumptions of the original liberal/bourgeois model" (Fraser 1997: 71). We do so by delineating such post- (and sometimes non-) bourgeois public spheres as they have emerged and continue to develop in the Muslim majority world. We explore not only their capacity to relativize crucial norms such as those defining "normal" trajectories of secularization, privatization, and/or "progress," but also the extent to which their genealogies and functioning challenge the dominant narratives surrounding the etiology and configuration of modern public spheres more broadly.

Yet in seeking to expand the definition of the public sphere, we are cautious not to adopt either a liberal or a republican-Jacobin norm. For *sharia* notions such as *istislah* that are at the heart of Muslim understandings of the public sphere operate from a different orientation than the liberal or Jacobin European frameworks. *Istislah* is a crucial notion of method of Islamic legal philosophy that is geared toward finding good in each situation, by mediating between contending positions, and shepherding the larger process of achieving balanced solutions that constitute the common good for the involved parties. The resulting public sphere can potentially be seen as a positive-sum game, one that reflects a logic quite distinct from the scarcely plastic—if not zero-sum—notions of social justice based on standards of "pure reason," or, at least, from the zeroing formal culture— that is, the elision of specific cultural and even legal traditions—that often accompanies Western discourses of "the public." Such a singular kind of public reason silences other kinds of reason embodied by autonomous social actors, especially those grounded in a religious identity.

As the contribution by Masud reveals (chapter 7), legal and political reforms can often be justified as implementations of *sharia* when in fact they comprise new notions of equity and cooperation that force people to formulate new claims in the name of the good of the larger society. As important is the dynamic of cooperation and often tension between mechanisms of Islamic mediation and those of supposedly "secular" political systems and "modern" courts (which pose as the incarnation of civil justice and state power), in which both represent attempts to control people's bodies and disperse power within a secularized political landscape.

Given such a plural, contingent, and open understanding of the public sphere, our exploration of these phenomena seeks to accomplish several goals. The first is to develop a "praxiological" conception of the public sphere—that is, one oriented toward uncovering the logic of actual practice—according to which the "public" and the "private" are understood to be contingent categorizations, reposing on specific cultural traditions. From the perspective of ordinary people, these predicates are characterizing procedures that are always particular and contextualized. Second, as Dupret and Ferrié (chapter 6) demonstrate, we ground analyses of public spheres in accounts of "ordinary situations," or daily exchanges, that create moral characterizations that cumulatively work to delineate a complex spectrum ranging from domesticity to publicity, and where the latter crystallize by virtue of the consolidation of border-enforcing norms. We cannot grasp the public sphere without a background knowledge of these processes of interaction, and without accepting that, before being—under certain conditions—a space of freedom and fairness of reasoned exchange, the public sphere is always a space strictly delimited by moral norms that, however fluctuating, emerge from concrete patterns of interaction that can be replicated but not generalized. Third, as will become clear from our chapter 1, we hope to clarify the need for greater attention to the historical relationship between the evolution of the notions of "civil society" and the "public sphere" as being of a contingent and not of a necessary nature. It is clear that these terms are intimately related yet reflect specific and sometimes competing ways of coming to grips with the relationship among individuals, societies, and the governing structures that rule both. Finally, we believe that in order to accomplish the above goals, the dominant understanding of both secularity *and* the dynamics of hegemony needs to be challenged and reexamined, and that a fresh understanding of both needs to be developed and redeployed within the sociology of modernity and the societies it has engaged worldwide. We consider hegemony a particularly important concept because it cuts through the overlapping but distinct realms of civil society and the public sphere. Therefore, broadening the base for an analysis of hegemony as well as its relationship to the defining of the secular in political practice will facilitate a more accurate understanding of the functioning of, and possibilities of strengthening, public spheres and democratic cultures in the Middle East and the larger Muslim majority world.

To achieve these goals, the chapters making up part I examine the role of discourses and techniques of hegemony and related interpretive and practical struggles. The public sphere is considered by the authors here to be an arena where official, state-sponsored discourses are both challenged and carried to the wider public by social and more specifically socio-religious actors, particularly as linked to fields delimited by the notions of voluntary and legal action. And it is through the legal field that we move to part II, which focuses on examinations of the role of law as linked to everyday social practices and to the construction of public argument. In this half of the book the tension among Islamic notions of custom (*'urf* and *'adat*), diverse concepts of common sense, and the wider search for fairness and justice is investigated as essential to the reconstruction of the public sphere in Muslim majority societies during the last century.

The Leap from Civil Society to the Public Sphere

If one opens a book examining contemporary Middle Eastern societies written during the 1990s, the chances are fairly good that one of the primary means of investigating them will be through the lens of civil society, one of the most important methodological innovations for studying the

Middle East and the larger Muslim (and indeed, third) world to emerge in the post–Cold War era.[1] In introducing his seminal two volumes *Civil Society in the Middle East* (1995–1996), Norton defines civil society as the "icon" of democracy: "If democracy has a home, it is in civil society, where a mélange of associations, clubs, guilds, syndicates, federations, unions, parties and groups come together to provide a buffer between state and citizen . . . The functioning of civil society is literally and plainly at the heart of participant political systems" (1995: 7).

In the latter part of the 1990s, and especially in the new decade, explorations of the public sphere have achieved similar importance as a framework for exploring the modern histories and contemporary dynamics of Muslim societies. Whether it is articulated or not, there would seem to be an emerging consensus among scholars of Islam and the Middle East that the "public sphere" offers a problematic field for investigating the thematic area of democratic development in the region that possesses greater analytical clarity and depth than has been achieved utilizing the civil society framework.[2] Significant research has already been undertaken demonstrating the productiveness of a reflective and theoretically conscious use of the public sphere as an explanatory paradigm for analyzing social processes in the Muslim majority world and Muslim diaspora communities (cf. Salvatore 1997, 2001; Hefner 1998; Stauth 1998; Schulze 2000 [1994]; Werbner 2002; Burgat and Esposito 2003; Eickelman and Anderson 2003 [1999]; Salvatore and Eickelman 2004).

Although the notion of the public sphere is better able to catch the intersection between the problematic and the thematic dimensions of democratic development in the region, it runs the risk of suffering the same fate as civil society: overenthusiasm, a lack of the circumspection warranted by its historical trajectory and problematic character, cynical use (as in the vocabulary of giving and receiving NGOs), and the concomitant loss of an analytic grasp of empirical phenomena. But let us assume that the concept of the public sphere will have a better fate. It is indeed the purpose of this volume to help engender one.

As Nancy Fraser describes it:

> The idea of the public sphere designates a theater in modern societies in which political participation is enacted through the medium of talk. It is the space in which citizens deliberate about their common affairs, hence, an institutionalized arena of discursive interaction. This arena is conceptually distinct from the state; it is a site for the production and circulation of discourses that can in principle be critical of the state. The public sphere in Habermas's sense is also conceptually distinct from the official economy; it is not an arena of market relations but rather one of discursive relations, a theater for debating and deliberating rather than for buying and selling. (Fraser 1997: 70)

The goal of the supposedly "rational" and "open" deliberations taking place in the public sphere was the shaping of a public opinion approximating a rational consensus about the common good (Fraser 1997: 72). Yet as the work of feminist scholarship has well documented, the idealized bourgeois public sphere explored by Habermas was in fact characterized — indeed, to a significant extent, made possible — by several types of exclusion, particularly gender (and class as well). Thus the postrevolutionary republican public sphere in France was constructed in deliberate opposition to that of the more woman-friendly salon culture that was now deemed "unmanly" and "irrational" (Fraser 1997: 73). This feminization of alternative discursive patterns and sites, as is well known, was repeated precisely in the emasculating colonialist/Orientalist discourses deployed by European powers in the Middle East (cf. inter alia, Said 1978, 1993; Badran 1996; Mir-Hosseini 1999).

And, indeed, we can imagine that in the same way as the public sphere from the start was gendered masculine, it was also "nationalized" — better, "civilized" — as European. Yet we also know that however powerful the normative discourses within Europe or in the colonies, there were always innumerable "counter-civil societies" that attempted to work around the irony of a public sphere based on accessibility and rationality, but factually deployed as a primary strategy of distinction and exclusion (cf. Fraser 1997). And so to give voice to — and at the same time, properly contextualize — these politically and socially marginalized public spheres, we recognize that even where certain categories of people such as women, minorities, or colonized populations were excluded from the dominant public sphere they did not sit idly by, but rather they created alternative parallel public spheres that must be uncovered and investigated. Having recognized these larger dialectics, we must focus on yet another, even more complex phenomenon of the emergence of public spheres, namely on the "public Islam" that cuts across, challenges, and shapes governmental *and* oppositional public spheres in Muslim majority societies as part of the same process of producing and reproducing a sense of publicness and its norms (cf. Salvatore 2001; Salvatore and Eickelman 2004).

The reason "public Islam" cannot be reduced to Habermas's "public sphere" becomes apparent when analyzing his famous definition of the latter "above all as the sphere of private people come together as a public" (Habermas 1989 [1962]: 27). The prior constitution of bourgeois private individuals as a condition for access and contribution to the constitution of the public sphere cannot be universalized historically or culturally; nor did it function in practice as described (in its admittedly idealized state) by Habermas. At least one reason for this is that "the idea of the individual as unconditionality . . . was too demanding a principle, one that carried too much baggage" to be universalized across time and geography (Seligman 1997: 172). Habermas's *Öffentlichkeit* is therefore conceptually too limited to explain trajectories of formation of and access to public spheres — not only for the non-Western world, but for large parts of Europe as well. At the very least it cannot capture the actions for reclaiming the common good performed by various social (including socio-religious) movements that do not reflect or endorse the kind of secularity produced by the modern state by any variant of liberal, republican, or socialist (and, not to

6

forget, fascist) ideologies. The public sphere does not operate on the basis of primarily functionalist reasons dictated by power or economic interest in the framework of a capitalist liberal democracy. However, even in abandoning its bourgeois prototypical model of the public sphere in favor of a non-bourgeois notion there is still the risk of universalizing—however surreptitiously—this distinctive and historically situated kind of subject imagined by Habermas.

Habermas's theorizing met with a similar shortcoming when, answering some of his critics,[3] he conceded the possibility of "plebeian," alternative or counterpublics that, according to him, are basically "the periodically recurring violent revolt or a counterproject to the hierarchical world of domination with its official celebrations and everyday disciplines" (Habermas 1992: 427). We agree that there are popular movements that attempt to reformulate and implement discourses of common good aspiring to represent a politically legitimized public reason. However, we stress the importance of examining the extent to which they remain unbound by the strictures of liberal conceptions and norms of publicness. There is the risk—though this is not endorsed by Habermas—that counterpublics are conceived as mere resistance movements, challenging bourgeois hegemony but lacking an alternative notion of the political glue of society (cf. Castells 1996). Indeed, the notion of "counterpublic" itself incorporates this theoretical bias.

When not limited to modern secular settings, the public sphere can be understood as the site where contests take place over the definition of the obligations, rights, and especially notions of justice that members of society require for the common good to be realized (Eickelman and Salvatore 2004 [2002]: 5). The idea of the public sphere is thus a wider and at the same time more specific notion than that of civil society. As put by Shmuel N. Eisenstadt,

> Civil society entails a public sphere, but not every public sphere entails a civil society, whether of the economic or political variety, as defined in the contemporary discourse, or as it has developed in early modern Europe through direct participation in the political process of corporate bodies or a more or less restricted body of citizens in which private interests play a very important role. We do indeed expect that in every civilization of some complexity and literacy a public sphere will emerge, though not necessarily of the civil society type. (Eisenstadt 2002: 141)

Habermasian definitions of the public sphere are too rigidly premised on a notion of a civil society of private citizens. This limitation becomes a particular handicap to contemporary theorization when we confront two other problems inherent in the way the public sphere is often described: first, such definitions do not sufficiently consider the modalities through which modern states introduce disciplining and legitimizing projects into public sphere dynamics, and the tension between such activities and the public sphere's specific role as a site for solidarities against the discursive power of the state; second, public spheres interact continuously with popular cultures in a manner that allows nonelites to challenge and shape hegemonic public discourses (LeVine 2004). As we see in reconstructing a partial genealogy of the liberal view of the public sphere (chapter 1), the grounding of the latter in the interests, rights, and duties of the "private citizen" is just one—albeit historically powerful and largely hegemonic—practiced and theorized approach to the public sphere.

This book, then, marks an attempt to bring to the attention of the scholarly community some of these heretofore little analyzed configurations of the public sphere as they emerged and continue to take shape and function in the Muslim majority world. But although we argue that public spheres must be explored in a much broader and more complex framework than is normally utilized by scholars, our deployment of the concept, not surprisingly, remains rooted in a critical reading of Habermas's seminal *The Structural Transformation of the Public Sphere* (1989 [1962]). That is, we recognize the unique contribution of his work, yet understand the importance of filling fundamental lacunae in his account of what constitutes the public sphere, who participates in it, and most important, what is the genealogy of the specific notions of the common good underlying distinctive configurations of the public sphere.

A central problem is that most conceptions of the public sphere, including that of Habermas, consider secularly oriented rationality to be the normative terrain on which public life thrives. Therefore, it is critical to explore the different means through which social practices inspired by Islam interact and sometimes clash with different forms of secularity as incorporated in the ideologies and practices of most states within Muslim majority societies.

In other words, the idea of the public is culturally embedded. The way a sense of the public is built into social interactions varies considerably depending on modalities of transaction over the definition of the common good, of equitable solutions to collective problems, and of shifting boundaries of inclusion and exclusion, as well as on background notions of personality, responsibility, and justice (Salvatore and Eickelman 2004). It is inevitable, therefore, to compare examples of public Islam with notions of public sphere developed within Western social theory. In so doing, the contributions that follow reveal the public sphere to be more than just the prerogative of "modern," "Western" societies, or of democratic political systems based on formalized templates of individual rights and their attendant forms of civil society. We demonstrate that semiformal and informal articulations of Muslim traditions and identities can also trigger the emergence of public spheres; moreover, that the coercive and institutional power of the modern state may both further and limit this potential. However, in order to introduce adequately this exploration of contested hegemonies and reconstructions of the public sphere in the Muslim majority world, we need to evidence the layers of tension inherent in the Western notions themselves that provide the background to concrete, historic articulations of the public sphere and related hegemonic forms.

The Overlapping Dimensions of
the Civic and the Public

The public sphere and civil society are clearly overlapping concepts, but in good measure because of a clear transformation—bordering on misunderstanding—in the use of the latter term by scholars during the 20th century. Both terms owe their origins to Greek concepts but then more specifically to Roman notions of the *societas civilis*, civic virtue (with both terms emerging out of the Latin *civitas*, or people united in a city), *res publica*, and the concomitant development of the common good—that, as we explore, circumscribes a family of notions that also developed, in parallel, in the Muslim majority world, and largely through Islamic legal discourse. However overlapping in covering fields and meanings of social action, the "civil" and "public" do not coincide, and indeed, if viewed from within concrete genealogies of religious, political, and legal traditions, as also shown by chapter 1, they often create a field of tension.

If we return to the classical Greek use of these terms, Aristotle's focus on civic responsibility, or virtue, saw it as central to the perfection of human nature; a sentiment that was later picked up by Machiavelli and his contemporaries as they attempted to defend the independence of the postmedieval Italian city-states. For Machiavelli, the survival of these mini-republics depended upon the civic virtue of their citizens; however, like the Jacobins centuries later, he believed that only the institutions of the republic—and not any mediating institutions or individuals— had the right to act for the public good (Machiavelli 1991 [1517], III: 28; Foley and Hodgkinson 2003).

However, another strand took Aristotle in a different direction. Through Aquinas and other scholastics Aristotle's notion of the *polis*, or city state, was refashioned as a *societas civilis* (as Aquinas describes it in the *Summa theologiae*), founded on the dictates of reason and oriented, above all, toward ensuring peace and the development of virtue. Such a transformation was made possible through the reconsideration of human beings from being "political animals" in Aristotle's terminology to being "social" beings whose primary goal in life was communion with God, yet at the same time retaining the notion of that participation in the political community. Unlike the Greek *polis*, the *societas civilis* acquires in Aquinas a potentially universal scope, going well beyond a definite polity, and the concomitant communitarian ethos of civic virtue.

In such a context the highest priority of the state would be ensuring the peace that people needed to pursue this primary goal (Foley and Hodgkinson 2003). Yet Aristotle also argued—in a manner foreshadowing Foucault, if viewed from a certain angle—that the good citizen "must possess the knowledge and the capacity requisite for ruling as well as being ruled" (Aristotle 1958: 105). And in the process of ruling and being ruled happiness or perfection is achieved not by the exercise of virtue in private but rather through participating in the governing of society—"Hence, a person who acts for his or her own good must also act for the good of all fellow citizens" (ibid.; cf. Halper 1998).

At the same time, however, the *polis* whose government was the responsibility of free citizens was not considered by Aristotle (as it was for Plato) a singularly or unitary entity, but rather a "plurality" of segmented units or associations, with "an essential difference between these persons, and between the associations with which they are concerned" (Aristotle 1958: 1252, 1261). Thus we see a tension inherent in the earliest conceptions of political community and the various arenas and mechanisms for its proper functioning that would continually inform—and problematize—modern discussions of civil society or the public sphere: Is the *polis*/political society fundamentally unitary (in a Jacobin sense) or a conglomeration of diverse and potentially competing interests? How do its members interact with their political leaders: directly or through mediating mechanisms? What are the mechanisms of such interaction, pressure or informed consent when they occur? Such questions would be central to debates on the nature of modern politics throughout Eurasia in the modern period.

What is clear is that in the modern era the basis for establishing both civil society and the public sphere emerges through the Rousseauian social contract, which considered the common good the highest priority of citizens, who are supposed to place their right for the individual pursuit of happiness after that of the community's collective well-being. Yet if for Rousseau (still under the influence of Machiavelli) the state was the arena for defining the nature of the common good, with Adam Smith we see the turn toward what would become classic political and economic liberalism through the foregrounding of private morality predicated on public recognition by one's peers as the best method for achieving the common good.

Smith's "liberal" turn, the concomitant atomistic focus on the individual ego–alter relationship, was foregrounded by Adam Ferguson, whose *An Essay on the History of Civil Society* published in 1767 can perhaps be credited as the first deployment of the term "civil society" in English in a proto-sociological sense (Locke in fact used the term earlier, but with a connotation much more restricted to political theory). In this essay Ferguson describes civil society as developing specifically out of the dynamics of the emergent industrial capitalism in Scotland and England, in which the new division of labor made possible the establishment of social institutions independent of the state and allowed for the idea and possibility of a truly "free society" (Ferguson 1995 [1767]). Ferguson's civil society, derived from *societas civilis*, referred literally to a *civil* society, that is a well-ordered and peaceful society governed by laws. Ferguson believed that the wealth and refinement of a truly civil—that is, civilized—society would undermine its sense of civic virtue; in good measure because the essence of a civil society was not the holistic order of a *polis*, but a society that, though constituting the foundation of the state, is also, inevitably, in tension with it (Foley and Hodgkinson 2003: xiii), due to an irreducible pluralism grounded in a certain primacy of the private sphere (see chapter 1). Therefore, the emergence of civil society heralds a separation of public and private functions and spheres of a new, modern type.

Ferguson's separation of the public and private functions of society through civil society greatly influenced Kant through his translation into German, providing a basis for the argument that civil society was a foundation for the emerging notion of a liberal republic. With this goal in mind, Kant attempted to move beyond Smith's belief that self-interested or even selfish actions lead to general prosperity through an "invisible hand," arguing instead that people must treat other people as ends in themselves rather than means to the ends of others. Moreover, Kant argued that the ethics and morals that derived from the private sphere would also shape a public arena of rational, critical discourse, which in turn was crucial to shaping the political sphere.

In chapter 1, we trace this genealogy of the public sphere via the Scottish Enlightenment by linking it to the contributions of an author like Giambattista Vico who was more sensible toward the transformations of religious traditions. We highlight the importance of their arguments for analyzing not just the subsequent theorizing about civil society and the public sphere in Scotland, England, France, and Germany, but also for the much more recent interventions of Gramsci and Foucault. But for the purposes of introducing the reader to the main themes and debates surrounding these two concepts, Kant's contribution remains essential. By picking up where Ferguson leaves off, he conceived of the public arena of civil society as separate from the state while remaining crucial to its proper function. As he describes it in propositions 5–7 of his *Idea for a Universal History with a Cosmopolitan Purpose* and in the argument in *An Answer to the Question What is Enlightenment*, the relation and tension between civil society and the state led him to conclude that the realization of a proper civil society constituted both the "greatest problem of the human species" and yet also the culmination of human history (Kant 1970 [1784]: 45–49). That is, with Kant the development of a problematic of public sphere overlaying the thematic notion of civil society develops directly from his argument for the "freedom to make public use of one's reason in all matters" (cf. Chatterjee 1993 for this reading of Kant).[4]

It is at this point in the development of the conceptual pair that civil society begins to be understood more as a problem than a solution for issues of good governance. Hegel certainly understood it thus, and tried to solve it by putting the State back in the center of the equation via the claim that only it could both provide societal unity and the mooring necessary for the realization of Spirit in history (as opposed to civil society's potential for insurmountable particularistic divisions). The importance of the State becomes clear when we understand that with Hegel we see the beginnings of a use of the term civil society in which far from excluding self-interested activities, the term refers *only* to them. In his *Philosophy of Right*, Hegel noted that "individuals in their capacity as burghers in this state are private persons whose end is their own interest"; moreover, he characterized civil society as "the battleground where everyone's individual private interest meets everyone else's" (Hegel 1991 [1821]: 224–26).

The notion of civil society as a battle ground, of course, would differentiate it from the emerging notion of a public sphere, in Habermas's terminology, as a body of private persons assembling to discuss matters of public concern or common interest and whose public opinions would serve as a counterweight to the still absolutist state (a dynamic that, following Habermas and his teachers, Adorno and Horkheimer, we can describe as being equally relevant in combating the power of the mass culture economy generated by late capitalism and now globalization). The tension in Hegel between two understandings of civil society—first as a realm of divisions and inequalities, and second as a realm in which human beings shape themselves through ethical norms to master their environment and work together—anticipates the problematic dynamics of the bourgeois public sphere explored by Habermas.

It is important to note for the purposes of relating discussions of civil society and the public sphere to Middle Eastern and other Muslim majority societies that the contemporary interest in these concepts is tied to their reappropriation, often via Gramsci, by activists and scholars in places such as Latin America and Eastern Europe as a way to find space to resist powerful and oppressive states when a direct assault (i.e., "wars of manovre" in the Gramscian terminology) on the state was not feasible. It is well known that for Gramsci, in the context of states functioning through hegemony—consent backed by coercion—rather than pure domination, civil society was the arena in which the struggle for hegemony and the potential for achieving state power by the working class unfold. More specifically, Gramsci's focus on civil society highlights the importance of culture as an arena for struggle, as opposed to just economic or political strategies. In other words, Gramsci can be used to open up the public sphere not just to contestations of interests and identities, but of the concepts themselves— inevitably culturally embedded—that delimit and define the public sphere.

This is clear in his discussion of the "ethical state" that "educates consent" by "raising the great mass of the population to a particular cultural and moral level, the level which corresponds to the needs of the productive forces for development and hence to the interests of the ruling class. These initiatives and activities form the apparatus of the political and cultural hegemony of the ruling class" (Gramsci 1971: 258). Gramsci's notion of hegemony and the role of the citizen in its sustenance reminds us that the public sphere can never be as free as in Habermas's bourgeois model. Yet while Habermas misses Gramsci's understanding of the superstructural, that is, cultural dimension of civil society when he defines it via Hegel as a primarily economic sphere (in fact, he doesn't engage Gramsci at all on this issue) he seemingly understands the importance of the state's educative function within society when he argues that in the contemporary period the state and corporate economy have undermined the ability of citizens to frame independent judgments, assert their authority over their lives, and reconstruct community among themselves (Habermas 1989 [1962]).

Gramsci's idea of cultural hegemony is interesting in that it incorporates a tension or a paradox: that the hegemonized classes who follow the discourses and conceptions of the dominant classes despite the unjust social relations they mask, have a largely autonomous, embryonic conception of a just world (Kantner 1998: 58). This is a motive that goes back to Vico's prototypical account of the conflict between patricians and plebeians (as we explain in more detail in chapter 1). There is in this idea a tension between the Gramscian "good sense" as the sole way to rationally transcend given social situations and power relations, and a more optimistic outlook on the reflexive capacities of the subaltern and the "common sense" of survival philosophies, including religion. In a Gramscian perspective, this can only happen through the role of intellectuals and their communication with the subaltern, in order to trigger off a collective learning process. But if we read Gramsci through such authors like Connolly and Benhabib injustice can only be fought through participation in hegemonic struggles for the *definition* of what is just (Kantner 1998: 58).

Beyond both Gramsci and Habermas, the contributions to this volume point to a new notion of hegemony, one which transcends the overpoliticized concept developed by Gramsci as being engineered through the "education of consent" described above. Rather we see how, depending on the situation, the state and/or nongovernmental and noneconomic organizations take the lead in shaping the attitudes and actions of citizens toward their larger society and their perspective of their role and obligations in achieving the "common good." And, among those organizations, socio-religious actors, groups, and movements often play a major role.

In this framework we articulate an idea of contestation that departs from a notion of hegemony conceived of as still based primarily on class struggle and the capture of state power (though we still believe that class factors and the capturing of the state power build the "wings" of hegemonic games). At the same time we distance our analysis from the inflexible view of history and progress that often accompanies such a perspective. Instead, we move toward an idea of hegemony that places it in the center of the contested cultural understandings of the associational bond underlying society, which better reflects "cultural" issues than does Gramsci's discussion.

More specifically, we see as crucial the contest between notions of secularity versus religiously grounded public reason; and even more basically, we observe how secularity seems to clash with the "common sense" in Muslim majority societies (where there is often no consideration of the possibility of a secular "good sense," as Gramsci terms it—see our chapter 1 for a fuller discussion of this issue) according to which secularity is ultimately oppressive and alien rather than emancipatory and adaptable. As important, our revised notion of hegemony no longer limits the direction and scope of human and social creativity as it does in Marxist and Gramscian notions of history and society. We base this argument (as discussed in our chapter 1) on the Vichian notion of common sense as being the first hard ground of human creativity and institution building, as well as on Vico's view of religion as one of the main such vectors and products of human institution building based on common sense developed into a wider sense of the common good.

Whether we are examining Shiraz at the beginning of the Pahlavi era or Lebanon today, a trans-Arab controversy on a fatwa condemning suicide bombings or a Yemeni trajectory of empowering autonomous lawyers in their dealing with both state and religious forces (Manoukian, Deeb, Hamzah, and Messick, in chapters 2, 3, 7, and 8 respectively in this volume), it is clear that hegemony is an even broader process than Gramsci's discussion would suggest: it is more than just a competition between a presently dominant bourgeois class that controls the state and the working class that is trying to supplant it. Rather, as the chapters in part I make clear, it is necessary to examine how particular conglomerations of social actors and forces struggle to obtain and distribute social power in pursuance of larger ideological and political objectives—a context in which seizing state power is seldom the primary objective. And here, if the conceptual developments of civil society and the public sphere are impacted by the evolving norms of secularity, the resulting relationship, in which privateness is protected from the force of publicness, too often leaves the former without a determinative influence on the latter as well.

It is indeed on these limits of the private–public distinction, formulated on the basis of historical experience and through the theoretical lenses of a certain type of Euro-American thinker (the trajectory of which we explore below), that alternative hegemonic configurations of publicness in the Muslim majority world and elsewhere base their force and sometimes legitimacy. For example, we must recognize and explore the resourcefulness, resilience, and impact of grassroots public spheres developed by women or other politically disadvantaged groups, which often constitute a positive means of helping their larger societies resist the hegemony of neoliberalism. What's most important here, as Lara Deeb's discussion of women activists in Beirut in this volume clearly demonstrates (chapter 3), is that these grassroots movements accomplish this often, though not always, precisely by deploying "religious" or "traditional" notions of the common good that have been considered in the literature on the public sphere and civil society to be alien (or even threatening) to their proper functioning (as we show in our chapter 1).

Despite—and perhaps because of—the overlap between civil society and the public sphere, it should now be clear why the public sphere has become an important conceptual tool for scholars of Islam and the Middle East. The analytical confusion generated by the recent utilization of civil society to describe a so-called third sector, or buffer, between the state and citizens clearly constitutes a misunderstanding of—or at best, a radical change from—its earlier use by Kant, Hegel, or more recently, Habermas.

We can argue that this shift in usage accounts in part for the fact that analyses of civil society of the last decade, however incisive in some respects, have often muddied the waters more than they clarified them. Yet at the same time we recognize the immediate connotation of "civil society" as a potential generator of civility within the larger society, coming close to the notion of a self-regulating "civil society" in the idealized imagination of it through Ferguson's day. Such a conception made it a natural term to explore how societies could function through mutual consent rather than coercion, or even the empty hegemony of formally democratic but effectively depoliticized late capitalist consumer societies, which Habermas showed lack properly functioning public spheres.[5]

And since several of the contributions to this volume explore public spheres as they have developed and operate in contemporary late capitalist—in popular terms, "globalized" societies (LeVine and Salvatore, Deeb, Baker, Masud, Hamzah, and Messick, in chapters 1, 3, 4, 6, 7, and 8 respectively in this volume)—it is important to explain why in the global era the notion of the public is so crucial to constructing a proper sociology of Muslim societies. This is because one of the primary processes unleashed by globalization is the "disembedding," or "deterritorialization" of identities from their moorings in previously hegemonic national and/or religious fields. This process is realized through the intensification of not just capitalist relations with neoliberalism and flexible accumulation strategies, but also via the hypercommodification of cultural symbols and the consequent "culturalization" of political economies affecting all social relations (Tomlinson 1999). In such a situation the need for spheres of public discourse and communication that are relatively free of either economic or political power relations—that is, the public sphere as imagined by Habermas—becomes more readily apparent within societies. Yet as we discuss below, as long as we remain locked within a framework (indeed, a hegemonic one) of secularity, the public sphere will be understood as "a space of zero-degree culture, so utterly bereft of any specific ethos as to accommodate with perfect neutrality and equal ease interventions expressive of any and every cultural ethos" (Fraser 1997: 79). Such a culture free zone of discourse, we argue, does not exist in practice, since public spheres are not just the arenas for the formation and enactment of discursive opinion but of social identities as well (which makes them the "theatre" of a singularly cultural activity; cf. Fraser 1997: 85).

Secularity and Public Islam

In a recent edited volume, Salvatore and Eickelman argue that "advancing levels of education, greater ease of travel, and the rise of new communications media throughout the Muslim-majority world have contributed to the emergence of a public sphere in which large numbers of people, and not just an educated, political, and economic elite, want a say in political and religious issues," separately from the formal structure of political authority and the traditionally familiar places of kin, neighborhood, and immediate community (Salvatore and Eickelman 2004: xi). In this context, the expansion of the intellectual and discursive spaces in which a variety of actors could operate helped Muslims navigate social conditions such as the fragmentation of religious and political authority and the ability to have increasingly open (if uneven and often contradictory) discussions of issues related to the "common good" (*al-maslaha al-ʿamma*). What Salvatore and Eickelman term the emerging "public Islam" includes the participation of a wider spectrum of citizens than had heretofore had access to or helped to shape either the normative expressions of Islamic belief and practice or the larger political system.

Going one step further, the contributions to this volume evince a notion of hegemony that is rooted in the contested interplay of various nodes of interaction—all of them culturally informed—in which groups have the power and ability to use coercive disciplinary measures even when they do not control state apparatuses such as the police or related "services." Indeed, these nongovernmental centers of power both use coercion and more traditional practices of achieving hegemony, through schools, mosques, and public political ideologies, in practice and discourse.

Our specific contribution to the sociology of public spheres is to explore, in a manner Gramsci and those following his trajectory have not, how groups can achieve hegemony without necessarily targeting state power, through the deployment of techniques of coercion and disciplining, education, and persuasion on the one hand, and through the constant and variable interplay of various circles of interaction and meaning production by different social groupings. Based on recent research (cf. Salvatore 2001) we find public spheres to emerge in the manner suggested by Foucault's diagnosis of the microphysics of power creating networks or discourses from the bottom up until they cohere into "global or macrostrategies of domination" (Foucault 1980: 39, 158–59).

The resulting bottom-up approach is also important to tracing a genealogy of secularity as a defining moment of the hegemonic forms of modernity, one that can help us understand the role it has played in framing investigations into the public sphere. We can thus see secularity emerging in this manner, taking diverse trajectories in different spaces of contention and production, including in the Middle East. Specifically, Asad's recent work (2003) facilitates situating the idea that for a society to be modern it must be "secular"—that is, have a formal separation between religion and the state—as itself part of the hegemonic discourse of modernity, not least because of the uncritical manner in which scholars have utilized the idea of "secularity."

Indeed, Asad convincingly demonstrates how the very term "secular" was introduced by free thinkers in the 17th and 18th centuries to differentiate themselves from infidels and heretics—that is, to show that they were not being irreligious, but rather changing the parameters for the space and role of religion in emerging modern capitalist (and, we should point out, colonial) societies formed through the cauldron of the modern state. The conceptual and discursive cluster gravitating around the idea of secularity emerged in the context of early modern Europe's need to address problems such as the need to control increasingly mobile poor, to govern mutually hostile Christian sects within a sovereign territory, and to present a united identity to the peoples that Europe colonized (Asad 2003: 192). Secularity must be accordingly understood not as an ideology or as the simple separation of church and state—since medieval Christian and Muslim societies did have patterns of separation, while modern states still incorporate religion at various levels for legitimation—but as "an enactment by which a political medium (representation of citizenship) redefines and transcends particular and differentiating practices of the self that are articulated through class, gender and religion" (ibid.: 5).

In fact, with Asad we can declare a fundamental question to be not how we can account for a supposedly increasing structural differentiation of social spaces resulting in the separation of religion from politics, economy, and science, in its "privatization" within its own sphere, and in the supposedly declining social significance of religious belief. Given the problematic nature of these normative assumptions, we should question how and why, under which conditions religion becomes public under conditions of modernity—whether in the shipyards of communist Poland or the bazaars of Pahlavi Iran (Asad 2003: 182). If secularity is, in Asad's terminology, a "form of life" and a way to mediate between various identities of citizens (ibid.: 5), we can conclude with Fraser that crucial to the proper functioning of public spheres is the ability of all participants to "make others listen even if they would prefer not to hear." In order to be heard, Asad goes on, religious or other viewpoints may specifically have to actively disrupt existing assumptions and discourses to be heard, so creating a tension with the liberal norms of the public sphere (Fraser 1997: 185). This "disturbing of the peace," as we might call it, helps us take up Asad's implicit call simultaneously to provincialize (yet in so doing, in fact opening new spaces for understanding) "secular modernity" as a specific normative project affecting subjectivity and modes of communication, and to recognize that its basic conditions include the ability of state apparatuses to govern through the political authority of the larger "nation-state" discourses, the freedom of exchanges within and beyond the market proper, and even the moral authority of the family without whose complicity the shaping of secular life forms would not be possible (Asad 2003: 235).

These characteristics were shared by many state structures in the Middle East since almost the dawn of the modern era (as were many of the most important markers of capitalism as well: cf. LeVine 2005, building on Pomeranz 2001; Gunder Frank 1999). Therefore, the processes of reconstructing public spheres in Muslim majority societies explored in this volume build by necessity on the ongoing historical tension between the global unfolding of secular discourses and institutions especially since the 1950s, and those claims to the common good and to the legitimization of public action that also play with techniques of power but are rooted in different genealogies of authority and sociocultural values (cf. Salvatore 2001).

Our particular focus on the boundaries and dynamics of the public sphere achieves several important goals, as will become apparent in the chapters that follow. Historically, it enables a plural, contingent, and culturally informed understanding of how hegemony is contested and achieved. Sociologically, it displaces—at least partially—secularity/-ization (and concomitantly, embourgeoization) as the necessary frame enclosing modern public spheres. As stated by José Casanova, who has set a more open accent on the relation between liberal secularity and "public religions" than Asad's relatively pessimistic diagnosis:

> The very resurgence or reassertion of religious traditions may be viewed as a sign of the failure of the Enlightenment to redeem its own promises. Religious traditions are now confronting the differentiated secular spheres, challenging them to face their own obscurantist, ideological, and inauthentic claims. In many of these confrontations, it is religion which, as often as not, appears to be on the side of human enlightenment. (Casanova 1994: 233–34)

Summary of the Book and Individual Chapters

When considered in light of our discussion in this introduction (which we deepen in chapter 1), the research findings of this volume reveal certain transversal themes that can be a felicitous guide for future research on public spheres in the Muslim majority world, if not the world at large (see Lynch's Conclusion). Here we intend transversal to signify both the sense of revealing commonalities in the experience, dynamics, and descriptions of the public sphere cutting across the various case studies, and, as important, the constituting of an alternative reading to the hegemonic narratives that "work to circumscribe and maintain" existing arrangements of power, knowledge, and sociability. Instead, our theoretical approach and empirical findings seek to evoke a sense of the public sphere as at least potentially a "subjunctive space" (such as Lefebvre's "clandestine" or "representational" spaces—hypothetical spaces of both "as if" and "what if") in which new and exciting (if frightening) spheres of publicness can be imagined and actualized (cf. Lefebvre 1991 [1974]; Reynolds 2003).

At some level, all the experiences and understandings of the public sphere discussed in this volume involve such a process of subjectivizing—and subjunctifying—what until they became hegemonic were destabilizing technologies and discourses of personhood and community. Our reappraisal of concepts such as hegemony and secularity, or the relationship between civil society and public sphere, is intended to suggest several directions that new research can take based on the groundwork laid in this volume. To the extent that we achieve this goal the knowledge produced here will facilitate the exploration by scholars and activists working on, and in, public spheres of its role as the space for scrutinizing the myths of liberal politics and economics, which until today have concealed the complexity of structures of social, political, and economic inequality in modern societies.

Part I: Contested Hegemonies in the Public Sphere

In chapter 1, "Socio-Religious Movements and the Transformation of 'Common Sense' into a Politics of 'Common Good'," we explore the philosophical foundations of the variety of notions of the "public" utilized—explicitly and implicitly—by socio-religious movements to define and justify their ideologies and actions to achieve social power. We argue that contemporary Islamic socio-religious movements attempt to reformulate and implement discourses of common good that represent a politically legitimized public reason; yet such discourses are often in tension with modern liberal conceptions of the public sphere. This is in large part because socio-religious movements—Islamic and non-Islamic—remain unbound by the strictures of liberal conceptions and norms of publicness premised on atomistic views of the social agent, by the private–public dichotomy, and by the basing of public reason on a reconciliation of private interests. Instead socio-religious movements base their public actions primarily on a practical reason sanctified by religious tradition (however variably interpreted).

In order to explore how this reinterpretation of religious traditions enters hegemonic contests within non-Western public spheres, this chapter engages a critical discussion of how the concept of the "common good" entertained by many socio-religious movements is linked to notions of practice and "common sense." To accomplish this objective, we develop a combined reading of the Gramscian notion of "hegemony" and Foucault's embryonic idea of "political spirituality." We argue that an approach critically combining the insights of these two concepts sharpens our understanding of the potential of socio-religious movements to develop a politics of the common good through an upgrading of commonsensical practical reasoning, an operation that comes close to Gramsci's notion of "good sense" as the key to mobilize successfully subaltern sectors of society.

Setrag Manoukian's chapter 2, "Power, Religion, and the Effects of Publicness in 20th Century Shiraz," discusses three documents that represent different and evolving forms of association in the Iranian city of Shiraz. Each moment analyzed is connected to specific articulations of the relations between power, religion, and publicness. Together they chart a historiography of the public sphere in an evolving urban space. What makes Manoukian's analysis unique is his attention to the technologies of presentation of these forms of association and his reflection on the particular ways in which they affect the quality of the "public" produced.

This exploration reveals a transformation in each period away from a more secularized, Habermasian instance of a bourgeois public sphere of free autonomous subjects endowed with decisional power, toward the use of religious argumentations to sustain, challenge or ignore the new logic of governmentality, and finally toward a utopian realization of the Islamic revolutionary subject. Yet at the same time the author illustrates a trajectory that represents not a linear transformation or fixed set of oppositions, but instead particular systems of differences and links between religion, power, and publicness. These complex patterns of transformation and "movement" can only be understood as unfolding within zones of possible social action in which the horizons for alternative trajectories are circumscribed by the structure of hegemony in that social space.

Laura Deeb's chapter 3, " 'Doing Good, Like Sayyida Zaynab': Lebanese Shi'i Women's Participation in the Public Sphere" examines how pious Shi'i Muslim women's role in community service has taken shape in the southern suburbs of Beirut. This phenomenon reflects a strong commitment to public welfare in the area; a commitment linked to both the absence of the Lebanese state in the southern suburbs, and to the religious and political ideals of the Shi'i Islamic movement in Lebanon. Utilizing the empirical case of the emergence of volunteering as a "new" social norm for pious Shi'i women, Deeb examines what happens to notions of the public sphere when Islamist women's activities are scripted into it. In doing so, this chapter focuses primarily on the narrative reference that frames much of the discourse about community participation: the 'Ashura story.

Parallel with the increase in community service, 'Ashura—the commemoration of the martyrdom of Imam Husayn—has undergone a transformation from the "traditional" practices and meanings to newly "authenticated" ones. The reconfigured version of 'Ashura, based largely on a reinterpretation of the behavior of the Imam's sister, Sayyida Zaynab, has emerged prominently into public spaces and discourses, providing a salient role model for women volunteers. Deeb argues that, in part through the impact of these discourses, volunteering has been incorporated into a normative moral system for pious Shi'i women in Beirut. An interrogation of why this is a gender-specific form of participation in community welfare leads to a consideration of the implications of locating Islamist women's community work in the public sphere. Deeb's analysis highlights how volunteering, through the plastic and narrative religious imperative of "doing good like Sayyida's Zaynab," has been incorporated into hegemonic normative systems of pious Shi'i women in Beirut.

The final chapter in part I, Raymond Baker's chapter 4, " 'Building the World' in a Global Age", examines the political–intellectual discourse of the Egyptian New Islamist School and argues that their ideologies and writings reveal a mainstream, transnational Islam, the *wasatiya*, that lends itself to centrist interpretations particularly well suited to the new social and cultural conditions of globalization. The thinkers he discusses describe an Islam that has taken shape "at the edge of chaos," that is, at the intersection of a powerful and destructively penetrating neoliberal globalization and a still uncertain nationalism that is continuously challenged by potentially more fundamental(ist) religious identities that grow in power precisely because of the weakness of the nation-state against the neoliberal "invasion."

This tenuous but productive situation gives contemporary *wasatiya* Islam the character of a "difficult whole," delicately poised between the fixity of extremist Islam and the chaos that results when Muslims go so far in imitating Western models that they lose connection with their roots and undermine their identities. Moreover it responds creatively to the Islamist imperative of *istikhlaf*, that is, that Man acts as God's regent on earth, by opening an analysis of this discourse to the potential for innovative responses by Muslims to contemporary situations. Baker argues that openness to their environment is what makes it possible for centrists like the New Islamists to take advantage of feedback and "feed forward loops" in reshaping the public sphere in Egypt, and therefore in preparing a possible alternative hegemony that could strengthen rather than undermine the processes of democratization in Egypt and other Middle Eastern countries.

Part II: Practice, Communication, and the Public Construction of Legal Argument

Dupret's and Ferrié's chapter 5, "Constructing the Private/Public Distinction in Muslim Majority Societies: A Praxiological Approach," calls for a radical redefinition of what is meant by public sphere while it denies the very possibility of the existence of something called the "Islamic public sphere." This chapter takes as its starting point an understanding of the role of morality as an activity that consists in the normative characterization of preferences in the course of an interaction. In so doing it grounds its analysis in accounts of ordinary situations, yet at the same time focuses on the manner in which social and state institutions fix moral preferences through activating law as a vehicle for the reduction of moral indeterminacy. Most importantly, this clarification is based on a realization that the practices and exchanges of everyday life are steeped in ambiguity and contradictory discourses, values, and relations of power. This theoretically sophisticated chapter condenses the methodological suggestion—applied through poignant examples—that any discursive activity of defining the boundaries of "Islamic" references with regard to the "private–public" dichotomy can only be investigated through a praxis-oriented approach that is sensitive to such ambivalences of language-in-use.

Muhammad Khalid Masud's chapter 6, "Communicative Action and the Social Construction of Shariʿa in Pakistan," explores how the Shariʿa was significantly marginalized in the public sphere that emerged during the colonial period in 19th-century Muslim India, and how it has returned to be a dominant force in the postindependence public sphere of Pakistan. In the colonial period, most Western experts on Islamic law saw no future for shariʿa in a modern society, which was conceived of as essentially secular. The main theoretical focus of Masud's analysis of the restoration of shariʿa in the Pakistani public sphere in the post-colonial period is based on a critical but sympathetic discussion of Habermas's theory of communicative action, which underlies the approach to the public sphere of the German thinker.

Exploring three varieties in the social construction of shariʿa, modernist (1961–1971), Islamist (1979–1985), and the era of "public debates" (1990–2002),

Masud argues that the contemporary disputes on shari'a reveal the importance of the protection of personal interests through law reforms, and stresses the increasing role of communicativity and public consensus in such modern legal processes. Concluding that the social construction of the shari'a is not necessarily a modern phenomenon, Masud argues that the emerging public sphere in Muslim societies in general and in Pakistan in particular has made this social contruction more transparent. It has certainly opened it to a process of questioning and challenging the interpretations sanctioned by traditional religious and political authorities. He subsumes this process under a revised, realistic understanding of communicative action.

What happens in the Egyptian press when a Saudi legal pronouncement against suicide bombings is perceived as desecrating an icon of Palestinian resistance? Dyala Hamzah's chapter 7, "Is There an Arab Public Sphere? The Palestinian Intifada, a Saudi Fatwa, and the Egyptian Press," answers this question by analysing the problematic staging of an "Arab public opinion." In this case study of a subsumption of a jurisprudential controversy on the legitimacy of a fatwa under the much more complex rules of disputation and polemic in a wider public sphere with potentially transnational reach, the author explores the mechanisms through which the specialized opinion of the 'ulama is given precedence over nonspecialized opinion, just for being, on a second step, "secularized" and reappropriated as "public" and as "Arab." This case study is particularly representative since it is centered on the country, Egypt, that claims for itself the role of center of Arab public opinion, secular and religious, and it affects one of the most sensitive topics under discussion, the legitimacy of Palestinian suicide attacks against Israelis.

Hamzah further argues that the consensual (mis)representation of a fatwa issued by the Saudi Grand Mufti in the Egyptian press is proof not so much of the existence of an "Arab public opinion," and a fortiori, of an Arab transnational public sphere, but rather of its latency. Moreover, the chapter shows the mechanisms of appropriation of a legal expert discourse, the issuance of fatwas by muftis, by so-called secular and religious voices alike in the public sphere, in ways that convert the legal issue into a wider moral and political bone of contention: largely in spite of the intentions of the religious experts, the 'ulama, who are at a loss to reaffirm the purely legal and religious character of their expertise. Indeed, the chapter also shows that among the most successful actors in this peculiar secularization of Islamic legal pronouncements are a restricted number of 'ulama who act as public communicators, like the ubiquitous Yusuf al-Qaradawi. They play astutely and competently on the multimediatic scene and re-politicize in a discursively consensual way the legal content of fatwas, so making them legitimate stakes in public disputes.

Brinkley Messick's chapter 8, "Cover Stories: A Genealogy of the Legal-Public Sphere in Yemen," provides an analysis of specific, new legal institutions and discourses that reveal a changing public conception of the legal sphere in republican Yemen. Messick approaches the character of the current legal situation in Yemen through the pages of a new Yemeni monthly legal magazine, *al-Qistas*, "The Scales," which as a nongovernmental and nonpartisan publication engages in an education and political program of what it terms "legal culturation" (*barnamaj al-tathqif al-qanuni*). Messick argues that this journal represents a new public discourse of the "legal," which he explores by first sketching the antecedent and the contemporary conditions for the emergence of such a publication and then assessing its character and agenda.

Messick locates the roots of this complex legal and interpretive field to the first law books published early in the 20th century and subsequently to the postrevolutionary efforts (i.e., taking place after 1962 in the Yemen People's Democratic Republic) to issue several types of legal publications by such state organs as the Ministry of Justice. Without yet relying on a slick media-savvy orientation like that of *al-Qistas*, these older publications nevertheless envisioned a new type of informed readership associated with the newly created status of citizen. Messick concludes by arguing that *al-Qistas* may represent a phenomenon relatively unique in the Arab world: one delimiting a field where intellectuals working in the legal field employ categories such as public sphere and civil society not just as a general rhetoric of public discourse, but as part of their practical-political agenda. What *al-Qistas* informs us is that if Habermas's categories cannot be directly transferred to non-Western cases, a genealogical account nevertheless may be inspired by his rich historical and social analyses of Western cases, and in particular by his emphasis on the transformative role of the press and print media in general.

The concluding chapter by Cecelia Lynch explores the implications of the findings in this volume for the globalized academic discourse on the concepts of public sphere and civil society. Lynch first summarizes the empirical and theoretical insights focusing on translating the relationship between the notions of "common sense" and "common good" into the theological discourse on "casuistry" (i.e., the process of ethical reasoning that pays close "attention to the specific details of particular moral cases and circumstances": Jonsen and Toulmin 1988: 2). She also discusses how the empirical and conceptual contributions in this volume relate to work being done on public spheres and civil society elsewhere in the world. This analysis is based on a critical examination of the stakes involved in distinguishing the concepts of public sphere and civil society (as is done in chapter 1) versus considering them as inseparably related components (conceptually and substantively) of the task of breaking down the secularist and modernist assumptions so ingrained in different branches of social theory.

Notes

We thank Cecelia Lynch for her comments on an earlier draft of the Introduction.

1. For a good bibliography of the literature on civil society in the Middle East during this period, see Norton 1995.

2. Following Chatterjee's useful discussion of the dialectical relationship between thematic and problematic, the former is the basic epistemological principle or goal of an ideological system—e.g., "civil society is important"—and the latter comprises the concrete statements about actions that should be taken, based on and in order to realize the thematic (Chatterjee 1993).
3. Here we are referring mainly to historians, who remain uneasy with the abstract character of Habermas's model.
4. Here it is worth noting that Kant's cosmopolitan politics necessitated a global political order—a "Federation of States"—to ensure the "peace and regular policy" described by Ferguson. Such a political arrangement bears some sympathy to the modern Muslim imaginations of the worldwide *umma* (Kant 1970 [1784]: 45–47).
5. We should point out here that Habermas's critique of late capitalism consumer society was gradually encumbered by qualifications and revisions of the argument during the 1990s, not least because he was influenced or mesmerized by the ephemeral Havel's wave in Eastern Europe.

References

Aristotle. 1958. *The Politics of Aristotle*, ed. and trans. Ernest Barker, Oxford: Oxford University Press.

Asad, Talal. 2003. *Formations of the Secular: Christianity, Islam, Modernity*. Stanford: Stanford University Press.

Badran, Margot. 1996. *Feminists, Islam and the Nation: Gender and the Making of Modern Egypt*. Princeton: Princeton University Press.

Burgat, Francois, and John Esposito. 2003. *Modernizing Islam: Religion and the Public Sphere in the Middle East and Europe*. New Brunswick, NJ: Rutgers University Press.

Casanova, José. 1994. *Public Religions in the Modern World*. Chicago: University of Chicago Press.

Castells, Manuel. 1996. *The Power of Identity*. London: Blackwell.

Chatterjee, Partha. 1993. *Nationalist Thought and the Colonial World: A Derivative Discourse*. Minneapolis: University of Minnesota Press.

Eickelman, Dale F., and Jon W. Anderson. 2003 [1999]. *New Media in the Muslim World: The Emerging Public Sphere*. Bloomington, IN: Indiana University Press.

Eickelman, Dale F., and Armando Salvatore. 2004 [2002]. "Muslim Publics." In *Public Islam and Common Good*, ed. Armando Salvatore and Dale F. Eickelman, Leiden and Boston: Brill, 3–27.

Eisenstadt, Shmuel N. 2002. "Concluding Remarks: Public Sphere, Civil Society, and Political Dynamics in Islamic Societies." In *The Public Sphere in Muslim Societies*, ed. Miriam Hoexter, Shmuel N. Eisenstadt, and Nehemia Levtzion, Albany, NY: SUNY Press, 139–161.

Ferguson, Adam. 1995 [1767]. *An Essay on the History of Civil Society*, ed. Fania Oz-Salzberger, Cambridge: Cambridge University Press.

Foley, Michael W., and Virginia A. Hodgkinson. 2003. "Introduction." In *The Civil Society Reader*, ed. Virginia A. Hodgkinson and Michael W. Foley, Hanover, NH: Tufts University/University Press of New England.

Foucault, Michel. 1980. *Power/Knowledge: Selected Interviews and Other Writings, 1972–1977*, ed. Colin Gordon, trans. Colin Gordon et al., New York: Pantheon.

Fraser, Nancy. 1989. *Unruly Practices: Power, Discourse and Gender in Contemporary Social Theory*. Minneapolis: University of Minnesota Press.

Fraser, Nancy. 1997. *Justice Interruptus: Critical Reflections on the "Postsocialist" Condition*. New York: Routledge.

Gramsci, Antonio. 1971. *Selections from the Prison Notebooks*, ed. and trans. Quitnin Hoare and Geoffrey Nowell Smith, New York: International Publishers.

———. 1993. *La religione come senso comune*. ed. Tommaso La Rocca, Milano: EST.

———. 2001. *Quaderni del carcere*, 4 vols. Rome and Trento: Istituto Gramsci/Einaudi.

Gunder-Frank, Andre. 1999. *ReOrient: Global Economy in the Asian Age*. Berkeley: University of California Press.

Habermas, Jürgen. 1984 [1981]. *The Theory of Communicative Action*, vol. 1: *Reason and the Rationalization of Society*, trans. Thomas McCarthy, Boston: Beacon Press.

———. 1987 [1981]. *The Theory of Communicative Action*, vol. 2: *Lifeworld and System: A Critique of Functionalist Reason*, trans. Thomas McCarthy, Boston: Beacon Press.

———. 1989 [1962]. *The Structural Transformation of the Public Sphere*, trans. Thomas Burger, Cambridge: Polity Press.

———. 1992. "Further Reflections on the Public Sphere." In *Habermas and the Public Sphere*, ed. Craig Calhoun, Cambridge, MA: MIT Press, 421–462.

Halper, Edward. 1998. "Aristotle's Political Virtues." Paper presented at *Paideia*, 20th World Congress of Philosophy, Boston, August 15.

Hefner, Robert. 1998. "Introduction: On the History and Cross-Cultural Possibility of a Democratic Ideal." In *Democratic Civility: The History and Cross-Cultural Possibility of a Modern Political Ideal*, ed. Robert Hefner, New Brunswick, NJ: Transaction, 3–49.

Hegel, Georg Friedrich Wilhelm. 1991 [1821]. *Elements of the Philosophy of Right*, trans. H. B. Nisbet, New York: Cambridge University Press.

Jonsen, Albert R., and Stephen Toulmin. 1988. *The Abuse of Casuistry: A History of Moral Reasoning*. Berkeley and Los Angeles: University of California Press.

Kant, Immanuel. 1970 [1784/1795]. "Idea for a Universal History with a Cosmopolitan Purpose," "An Answer to the Question: What is Enlightenment?" and "To Perpetual Peace: A Philosophical Sketch." In *Kant's Political Writings*, ed. Hans Reiss, trans. H. B. Nisbet, Cambridge: Cambridge University Press.

Kantner, Cathleen. 1998. "Machtfrage und Diskursivität: Gramscis Hegemoniebegriff." *Berliner Debatte INITIAL* 9, 6: 54–62.

Lefebvre, Henri. 1991 [1974]. *The Production of Space*. London: Blackwell.

LeVine, Mark. 2004. "Popularizing the Public and Publicizing the Popular: Contesting Popular Cultures in Mandatory Jaffa and Tel Aviv." In *Popular Palestine: Palestine, Israel and the Politics of Popular Culture*, ed. Ted Swedenburg and Rebecca Stein, Durham, NC: Duke University Press.

———. 2005. *Overthrowing Geography: Jaffa, Tel Aviv and the Struggle for Palestine*. Berkeley: University of California Press.

Machiavelli, Niccolò. 1991 [1517]. *The Discourses of Niccolo Machiavelli*, 3 vols., trans. Leslie J. Walker, London: Routledge.

Mir-Hosseini, Ziba. 1999. *Islam and Gender*. Princeton: Princeton University Press.

Norton, Augustus Richard, ed. 1995–1996. *Civil Society in the Middle East*, 2 vols. Leiden: Brill.

Pomeranz, Kenneth. 2001. *The Great Divergence: China, Europe, and the Making of the Modern World Economy*. Princeton: Princeton University Press.

Reynolds, Bryan. 2003. *Performing Transversally: Reimagining Shakespeare and the Critical Future*. New York: Palgrave.

Said, Edward. 1978. *Orientalism*. New York: Pantheon.

———. 1993. *Culture and Imperialism*. New York: Knopf/Random House.

Salvatore Armando. 1997. *Islam and the Political Discourse of Modernity*. Reading, UK: Ithaca Press.

———, ed. 2001. *Muslim Traditions and Modern Techniques of Power*, vol. 3 of *Yearbook of the Sociology of Islam*. Hamburg: Lit; New Brunswick, NJ: Transaction.

Salvatore, Armando, and Dale F. Eickelman, eds. 2004. *Public Islam and the Common Good*, Leiden: Brill.

Schulze, Reinhard. 2000 [1994]. *A Modern History of the Islamic World*. New York: New York University Press.

Seligman, Adam. 1997. *The Problem of Trust*. Princeton: Princeton University Press.

Stauth, Georg, ed. 1998. *Islam, a Motor or Challenge of Modernity*, vol. 1 of *Yearbook of the Sociology of Islam*. Hamburg: Lit; New Brunswick, NJ: Transaction.

Tomlinson, John. 1999. *Globalization and Culture*. Chicago: University of Chicago Press.

Werbner, Pnina. 2002. *Imagined Diasporas among Manchester Muslims: The Public Performance of Transnational Identity Politics*. Santa Fé, NM: School of American Research.

PART I

CONTESTED HEGEMONIES IN THE PUBLIC SPHERE

CHAPTER I

SOCIO-RELIGIOUS MOVEMENTS AND THE TRANSFORMATION OF "COMMON SENSE" INTO A POLITICS OF "COMMON GOOD"

Mark LeVine and Armando Salvatore

Introduction: Contested Hegemonies over the Public Sphere

This chapter explores the philosophical and epistemological foundations of the variety of notions of the "public" utilized—explicitly and implicitly—by socio-religious movements to define and justify their ideologies and actions to achieve social power. Our hypothesis is that contemporary Muslim socio-religious movements attempt to formulate and implement discourses of common good that aspire to legitimate specific forms of political community, based on distinctive methods of public reasoning. These discourses are often in tension with modern liberal conceptions of the public sphere; specifically, they remain unbounded by the strictures of liberal norms of publicness premised on atomistic views of the social agent and contractually based notions of trust, by a strict interpretation of the dichotomy between private and public spheres, and by the ultimate basing of public reason on private interest. What socio-religious discourses and movements primarily base their public reason on is a practical reason sanctified by religious tradition, however variably interpreted. Such a perspective provides these discourses with a level of fluidity and adaptability that accounts in large measure for their success in mobilizing large numbers of people to their cause.

An analysis of some important recent contributions to the theoretical literature on "civil society," the "public sphere," and the role of religion therein (see Introduction and Conclusion) provides the starting point for a critical discussion of how the concept of the "common good" entertained by many socio-religious movements is linked to notions of practice and "common sense." Our deployment of a new approach to the Gramscian notion of "hegemony" and Foucault's embryonic idea of "political spirituality" helps to sharpen the understanding of how socio-religious movements can develop a politics of common good through an upgrading of commonsensical practical reasoning. Specifically, we argue that such an operation comes close to Gramsci's notion of "good sense" (*buon senso*) as the key to mobilize successfully subaltern sectors of society. Explored from this vantage point, however, it would be reductive to argue that socio-religious movements represent "subaltern," "counter-hegemonic" movements, since they play a crucial role in shaping the larger socio-political fields of their societies in a manner comparable to the role played by the *salafiyya* movement a century ago. Their relation to official, nation-state bound public spheres, is much more complex and ambivalent, and therefore doesn't easily fit the straitjacket of prepackaged political categories like "revolutionary," "reformist," "conservative," or "reactionary."

Socio-religious movements contribute to the constitution and contestation of norms of public life by providing services to their communities and articulating social justice claims that challenge the discourse of rights that is increasingly the daily bread of secular elites. A specific combination of "resistance" and "project" identities (Castells 1996) deployed by these movements impinge on the legitimacy of both state and (more recently) NGO elites, and through them, on the allocation of resources for development, welfare, and education. This dynamic demands an integrated analysis and reconceptualization of how socio-religious movements unsettle material and normative dimensions of public spheres in the Muslim world. We argue that they do so through the creation of historically novel lines of solidarity that, without being utopianly "horizontal," challenge state-centric, vertically defined, disciplinary discourses of the social.

Guiding our approach, then, is a broad, transcultural understanding of the public sphere as the communicative and legitimizing basis of potentially democratic political systems. Religious reformers and the public mobilization of religion have long played an important role in Muslim majority societies, not least through their functions as primary carriers of and/or challengers to national projects (Rudolph and Piscatori 1997; Salvatore 2001). Socio-religious movements of various kinds articulate collective identities and constitute public interactive spaces without assuming a grounding centrality of nation-state institutions. In this way, they reconstruct alternative models of the relationship between state institutions and the interests of grassroots communities, often based on their educational and welfare projects. Backed up by discourses of social justice, these projects have a wide impact on views of political community, citizenship, and legitimate authority among their constituencies.

It is clear that for groups as diverse as Hizbullah in Lebanon (Deeb, chapter 3, this volume; Kreidie 2002) or Hamas in Palestine (Roy 2000; Hammami 2002) the constitution of an "Islamic state" means a "just social order" as much as, if not more than, a "religious," that is, shari'a-based state, and thus a model of what we would define as a "parallel/alternative civil society-*cum*-public sphere" with its own distinctive forms of social control, political deliberation, and techniques of power and governance. As of late 2004, a similar discourse also transpires through the options and speeches of moderate Shi'a clerics in Iraq under occupation. At the same time, a more radical discourse has emerged from Sistani's more militant colleagues, especially those allied with the much younger Muqtada' al-Sadr. National and provincial elections in the majority Shi'a areas in Iraq and municipal elections in Gaza in January 2005 seem to confirm a prag-matic approach of Islamic movements and groups that fight against military occupations and their appeal to impressively large constituencies. Yet it is everyday practice and mobilization more than strategies of political survival that provide the main terrain of cultivation of such alternative visions.

We find empirical evidence for an alternative approach to the common good in the engagement with "development" by the Palestinian Hamas, particularly if we separate core social activities from its involvement in local and regional conflicts and their organized use of violence against the Israeli occupation—including terrorist activities (although we recognize their inseparability in many areas). As shown by Hammami (2002), instead of mapping the needy through the standard statistical measures and assessment of poverty lines, Islamists chart their social environment through active social knowledge, produced through the creation and mobilization of dense social networks and communal frameworks that largely depend on voluntary action. A similar process can be observed with Hizbullah-related voluntary associations (Deeb, chapter 3, this volume).

Thus, while secular NGOs abstractly and "scientifically" produce society as fundamentally different from themselves (and objectify it in a vertical relationship to the state) Islamists relate to the societies as an extension of their own discourses of justice, in a web of relationships that are imagined and partly practiced as horizontal, although still largely vertical and based on ties of imagined or effective authority. The basically egalitarian and largely voluntaristic modes of interaction make Islamist charities often effective and sometimes hegemonic within local communities. At the same time, these strategies are woven into larger, global Islamist networks. Islamists receive major material resources from the larger Muslim world and so improve on the model of the earlier global solidarity networks that have supported the secular nationalist movement for decades. Indeed, charity work, and the funding it secures, has been inseparable from resistance—supported by a variety of organized uses of violence—by these same groups to the Israeli military occupation of Palestinian and Lebanese territories. This has created major political backlashes whose long-term effect on contested hegemonies is difficult to predict, as shown by the fact that the EU has long refused to bow to pressure and classify Hizbullah as a terrorist organization yet has agreed to include "charities" tied to Hamas, though clearly nonmilitary in scope, in its list of groups whose sources of funding have to be undercut on allegation of contributing to terrorism. The latter decision was accompanied by the declared wish of the EU that Hamas be transformed into a normal political party—A realistic option if and when the military occupation is effectively terminated.

Below the level of organized violence the drive of socio-religious movements to achieve political, social, and cultural justice for their constituencies can be accompanied by an ambivalent and often suspicious and offensive stance toward those they view as external to their community. This position is informed significantly by class dynamics, which play a determinant but relatively underestimated role in identity formation through these movements. Such identification is almost always framed through ethno-religious discourses that may both support and undermine the dominant discourses of the state, depending on the situation and on the specific political game played in a given moment or context. Our main point, nonetheless, is that even when rhetorically supportive of larger nationalist projects these identities and the movements that foster them can undermine the legitimacy of those projects through alternative educational and social policies, political rhetoric, and violent activities.

In general, then, socio-religious movements reflect the crucial relationship between commitment to the community and mutual insurance among members that is a hallmark of contemporary socio-religious discourses—specifically in contrast to neoliberal ideologies. Such a view is supported by Berman's "club good" model, which emphasizes the function of voluntary religious organizations as efficient providers of local public goods in the absence of government provision (Berman 2003: 2–4, 25–27). With this understanding, we can explore socio-religious movements and the public spheres they create as rational responses to insufficient provision of crucial services (health, education, welfare, security) by either public or other private institutions. In the same context, we recognize the long-standing role of religion as both an organizing force in community provision of local public goods and a mechanism for redistributing wealth, particularly in a context where a government "behaves like a club, limiting public good provision to loyal members" (ibid.). And so popular desire for self-determination can be assumed to strengthen those "clubs"—in our case, socio-religious movements—which promise that public good.

This chapter, unlike other contributions to our volume, does not offer a case study of any particular socio-religious movement; neither does it aspire to provide a modelized framework for a comparative enquiry. Instead, it attempts to conceptualize the complex and conflicted background of movements' modalities of public action. Our guiding hypothesis should help the reader explore the case studies in the chapters that follow.

Religious Traditions and the Dialectic between Practices, Movements, and Institutions

The Notion of Religious Traditions

In a recent book examining the practices, discourses, and institutions of contemporary 'ulama M. Qasim Zaman describes Muslim religious authorities as "custodians of change" (Zaman 2002). This description only seems to be an oxymoron until we examine the actual workings of tradition rather than looking at the ideologically biased view of religious tradit- ions inherited from the Enlightenment discourse. The revised idea of tradition, which we derive primarily from Alasdair MacIntyre (1984 [1981], 1988) and Talal Asad (1993, 2003), to whom Zaman (2004) also refers, has to be developed and tested through a constant reciprocal engagement between actual analysis—in past and present social worlds—of the workings of traditions, and a reconceptualization of the notion of tradition itself.

The workings of tradition cannot be reduced to a cultural variable rigidly depending on structural transformations within social fields. One has to take account of the immanent search for coherence of traditions conceived as congruous and dynamic ensembles of discourses and arguments governing actual social practice. The engine of traditions, and of their adaptations and transformations, lies therefore in the collective effort to redress and improve the stock of practical and theoretical knowledge that allows for the pursuit of the social and transcendent goods defined as cen- tral by a given tradition. Social processes and the underlying conflicts (based especially on class and gender cleavages), however, produce and reproduce social power and related hegemonic forms, thereby influencing the extent of success or failure of attempts to adapt or transform traditions.

The most dynamic core of a tradition resides, however, not in codified procedures or established institutions, but rather in the anthropologically and sociologically more complex level of the "living tradition," which over- laps more institutionally grounded levels yet is nurtured by social practice. Living traditions and attending practices cannot be the sole object of formal communication and training, but are embedded in life narratives, and pre- suppose not simply a quest for "identity" but more deeply a collective *telos* of action that is necessarily transindividual and transgenerational. As important, the collective life-goal is usually projected into some formula of "common good," whereas the scale of the community of reference might go from the local to the universal. Theologically, the Islamic *umma* encom- passes the entirety of Muslims worldwide; what gives such a vast community concreteness is that Islam (not unlike other religions) considers the fellow human being the first instantiation of the "other" whom a religious imper- ative enjoins Muslims to consider—or, if necessary, turn into—a "brother" in faith. It is through this initial micro-link, which often takes the form of moral admonition and brotherly correction, that the *umma* is bound together and grows.

MacIntyre stresses that tradition so defined is an eminent part of the motivational prism of any social agent.[1] Focusing on tradition so defined helps highlighting the link between grassroots practice and the dimensions of governance and stratification that create and reproduce authority, placing it in the hands of "custodians" of the tradition. However, seeing a set of practices as part of a tradition makes authority contestable and contested through shifting socio-political configurations of state power, class, and gender, as well as through intergenerational change. Calhoun similarly observes that it is difficult to have a theory of practice without a theory of tradition, and that sociologists are not exempt from grasping a more historical sense of tradition (Calhoun 1993). This historical sense emerges through a permanent recourse to a transindividual and transgenerational signifying of human action, one that is activated through the kind of exhortatory discourse that can be administered but not monopolized by religious personnel.

The reason for this theoretical deficit has profound historical roots in the traumas of modern European history. Relations of tension and compromise between religious communities, confessions, and institutions, on the one hand, and the rising states (eventually nation-states), on the other, have been constitutive of modern European societies since the Reformation, Counter-Reformation, the Wars of Religion, during and after the age of the great revolutions, and not least in the colonial era. In this conflicted modern European experience, religion happened to be considered legitimate in the public sphere only if it helped to overcome discord and moralize public life while remaining compatible with the general framework of political and moral values of its society, or at the least, with the religion of the ruler. This historical and experiential trajectory generated the conceptual networks revolving around ideas of "civility" and "publicness," which lie at the heart of the European matrix of the public sphere. Because of this, moving outside this matrix would allow us to encounter other trajectories and experiences.

In so doing, the vicissitudes of religious traditions and those of notions, norms, and practices related to the ideas of civility and publicness as based on views of the "common good" can be seen as interrelated in a more positive—or at least in a more complex, certainly more open—way than if viewed through the lens of the conceptual and institutional strictures of modern European history and its various models of secularity. Investigating the complex and open nature of these other trajectories is essential to understanding modern socio-religious movements and their ingraining into the dynamics of social self-organization, and sometimes governance, of Muslim (but also Jewish, Christian, and post-Christian) majority societies.

Adding to what we highlighted in the Introduction, we therefore have to recall that the notion of public has a much older, complex, and plural genealogy within Europe and the larger "West" than it would be perceived by looking at the modern paradigms of "civil society" and the "public sphere." This complexity deepens if we look at the Muslim world, and also at the intersections and reciprocal impingement between European and Muslim traditions (cf. Höfert and Salvatore 2000).

Maslaha, *the Common Good, and Civil Society*

The discourse of the common good has a long genealogy and a complex legacy that cut across conventional borders of Europe or the West to encompass the heritage of Muslim societies. For its part, Islam provided a sophisticated version of Abrahamic traditions' construction of the common good, incorporating elements not only of Platonic and Greek speculation on the goods and their origin, but also of Roman law. The most important element for our purposes is the Islamic jurisprudential notion of *maslaha*, based on the root *s-l-h*, which denotes being and becoming good, specifically in the sense conveying the full scale of positive values from uncorrupted to right, honest, virtuous, up to just (Masud 2000 [1995]: 135; cf. also Masud, chapter 6, this volume). The foundation of the conceptual network gravitating around *maslaha* was laid by thinkers and discussions occurring between the 11th and 14th centuries and was revived by modern reformers, such as the early 20th-century public intellectual Rashid Rida and the contemporary "global" *'alim* Yusuf al-Qaradawi (Zaman 2004). It is useful to check this conceptual crystallization of the notion of common good by relating it to the theorization of "common sense."

The philosophy of the Neapolitan thinker Giambattista Vico (1668–1744) and his focus on *senso comune*, that is, "common sense," turns out to be crucial for establishing the nexus. Common sense is a stock of ordinary knowledge present in poetic discourse, and preceding the irruption of revelation into history. The *senso comune* placed myth squarely in the fundamental elements of the *civitas* (which, importantly, can mean the state, citizenship, a city-state, or a city—that is, various levels of political and social interaction and authority) (Mazzotta 1999: 147). Vico considered *senso comune* nothing less than the point of origin of any civilizational course. It animates the primordial religious, civic, and legal institutions, and in particular the unreflected ideas without which these institutions would not have come into existence. In a nutshell, "common sense is an unreflecting judgement shared by an entire social order, people, nation, or even humankind" (Vico 1999 [1744]: 80), and directed at discovering and making available utilities matching human necessities, material and immaterial. Common sense is the knowledge stock of "tradition" as a motor of history. Vico's notion of common sense was however not to hold sway. Instead, from the Scottish Enlightenment to Hume and Adam Smith, the proto-liberal thought that ushered the modern conceptualization of civil society pushed aside Vico's insistence on history and difference, and stultified the "common sense" into a transhistorical notion of a "moral sense." In so doing, liberal thought produced a highly simplified view of the human and social actor.

Hume and Smith focused mainly on the two passions of sympathy (altruism) and vanity (egoism) as the main articulations of the moral sense—and the roots of civil society. But by admitting (in particular with the later Adam Smith) that these passions were enough to warrant coordination and social order, they postulated a public realm, or a public sphere, grounded on the idea or fiction of an impartial observer, a moral force inhabiting the self ("the great inmate of our breast") and ensuring a congruous degree of cooperation, fairness, civility, and courtesy among individuals.

One main vector of social action and coordination so defined was seen in prudential calculus, indeed through a major transformation of a common-sensical "practical reason." This new configuration of the social actor was the platform for the rise and consolidation of the modern liberal discourse premised on the private–public dualism (cf. MacIntyre 1988).

The German-based critical reflection on this liberal conceptual network, from Kant to Habermas (see Introduction), did not over-come Eurocentrism's dualisms (cf. Eder 1985; Stauth and Turner 1988; Stauth 1994 [1991]); instead it ended up in reinforcing it. What diminished those attempts was partly a reduced, one-sided notion of religion, perhaps related to the traumatic intensity and lack of distance of Germany from the protestant reformation. German thinkers provided nonetheless a sig-nificant background to the two authors we refer to here, Gramsci, who built on Marx while coping with the Hegelianism of Croce (who also helped him to relate to Vico's notion of *sensus communis*) and Foucault, who inherited both Nietzsche's genealogical approach and an original Kantian reading of the idea of revolution.

From Common Sense to Political Spirituality: Gramsci and Foucault

Gramsci's Approach to Alternative Hegemonies

Like several South-Italian scholars who followed in his footsteps, the great 20th-century Marxist theoretician Antonio Gramsci was motivated by a mixture of respect and aversion toward religion. That is, he saw religion simultaneously as a token of antimodernity and as the possible key to an alternative modernity—one liberated from socio-economic and cultural domination. This ambivalence prompted him to analyze religion in terms of its capacity to develop a resistance to, and critique of hegemonic discourses that alienate the cultural worlds of the rural masses. Religion appeared to Gramsci as the ambivalent medium for the reconstruction of an alterna-tive hegemony based on notions of the common good liberated from the ideologies concealing class domination—including the domination of the high hierarchies of the Catholic Church.

Gramsci wrote in a social and cultural context—a fragile post-unitarian Italy between the two world wars, kept together by the rhetoric and repression of the Fascist regime—that had not yet met the facile moderniz-ing formulas of the post–World War II era, when the Parsonian sociol-ogist Edward C. Banfield prescribed to Southern Italy—so anticipating the more famous Robert Putnam (1993) by a third of a century—economic modernization-as-development as a recipe for furthering the commitment to common good via participation in voluntary associations and public life (Schneider 1998: 6–7). Gramsci's diagnosis was that in a still largely pre-capitalist country like Italy one could not destroy religion. What could be achieved was the establishment of "a new popular belief, that is, a new common sense and thus a new culture and a new philosophy that is rooted in the popular conscience with the same solidity and imperativeness as traditional belief" (Gramsci 2001: 1400).

This is exactly what was being attempted in several Muslim majority countries, via the formation of national public spheres at the cusp of independence. Given this power of religion, Gramsci believed that the proletariat could only succeed in becoming the dominant class by creating a system of alliances with other classes, especially the peasants. The "Catholic question" was ultimately a "peasant/rural/farmer question" (*questione contadina*) (cf. La Rocca 1997: 41), since in Italy one could not get to the peasants without dealing with the Church, which traditionally asserted hegemony over them (ibid.: 46). Making this alliance possible was the fact that the "church" as a community of believers had developed over the centuries in almost constant political-moral opposition to the Church as a clerical organization (Gramsci 1997: 133).

For both Gramsci and his heir, the post–world war anthropologist Ernesto De Martino, "the study of popular religion is a political act, or at least a prelude to that act." They called us to "understand popular religion because it is itself intrinsically political, though its politics are complex, fragmented and contradictory" (Saunders 1998: 188). And for Gramsci it was the "creative spirit of the people"—which we will shortly relate to Foucault's political spirituality—that is the source of this politics (Crehan 2002: 19).

While it is doubtful that Gramsci had a specific concept of religious tradition, he certainly produced a highly sophisticated and dynamic notion of intellectuals not only as a class, but also as a social function linked to common sense and popular practices in complex but vital ways. This function of intellectuality is intimately connected to the concept of tradition as defined above, linking social practice with communication and reasoning skills. Such a meaning we receive from Alisdair MacIntyre, whose starting point was—as one could argue for Gramsci—Marx's *Theses on Feuerbach* (MacIntyre 1994).

> Practices always have histories and . . . at any given moment what a practice is depends on a mode of understanding which has been transmitted often through many generations . . . But the traditions through which particular practices are transmitted and reshaped never exist in isolation from larger social traditions . . . For all reasoning takes place within the context of some traditional mode of thought, transcending through criticism and invention the limitations of what had hitherto been reasoned in that tradition: this is as true of modern physics as of medieval logic. (MacIntyre 1984 [1981]: 222)

Tradition in this sense has to fulfill the task of linking discourse and practice across time, and allowing for a balance between stability and change, as well as between the ideational-discursive, the institutional, and the practical layers of intervention on social worlds. The main operational formula of a tradition is therefore the "search of coherence" between all these levels and layers, in spite of a fair degree of consciousness—both among the "guardians" of traditions and their daily practitioners—of the existence of enduring tensions among them.

Gramsci's approach to religious traditions might appear at first glance theoretically less sophisticated—certainly less systematic—than in MacIntyre's account, yet it is far from the one-dimensional consideration given to it by most leading modern social theorists. The merit of Gramsci's approach consists in its ability to astutely penetrate religion's basis in practice and common sense (Fulton 1987).[2] For him "every religion . . . is in reality a multiplicity of distinct and often contradictory religions" (Gramsci 1971: 420). He was interested in religion via the complex relationship between politics and culture, as the unity of these two spheres was considered by him to be central to the formulation of a critical perception of a civil society that is not merely at the service of the state.

What is necessary, more than just a new discourse that remains the patrimony of only a small group of intellectuals, is a culture that becomes the "base for vital action" (Gramsci 2001: 1377–78). Gramsci looks at the historical role of the church in its noninstitutional dimension as a revolutionary force and sees in it an example of the kind of role it could play in contemporary (for him) Italian society, if a genuine intellectual and religious "reformation" occurred. His philosophy of praxis could therefore tackle—though not solve—the crux of the role of religion in social mobilization, as schematically expressed by "the nexus Protestant Reformation plus French Revolution" (ibid.: 1860). Here it is important not to reproduce the facile analogy between all calls, including Gramsci's, to a reformation-like process of metamorphosing traditional and popular religion. This is because Gramsci's view of the process, as De Martino after him, sharply differed from those of "Protestant polemicists, the liberal bourgeoisie, and the economicist left" (Saunders 1998: 179).

While some of Gramsci's early writings display an open hostility to organized religion, this position was transformed over time as he came to realize that all commitments pose an element of belief—that is, an active conviction and commitment—that one could interpret as religious (cf. Fulton 1987: 201). Despite such ambivalence—in fact, because of it— Gramsci's examinations of religion reflect both a richness of themes and a complexity and multiplicity of levels, epistemological, ideological, historical, social, and political (La Rocca 1997: 24). Indeed, there is in Gramsci a fair degree of ambivalence not just vis-à-vis the Catholic Church, but also toward Islam, about which he wrote several entries in the *Prison Notebooks*. From these passages, we can determine that Gramsci believed that Islam could be examined in comparison to Christianity only if one had the "courage" to question the ubiquitous equation of Christianity with "modern civilization." To the specific question of why Islam failed to follow in the modernizing footsteps of Christianity, Gramsci felt that however "torpid from centuries of isolation and a putrefied feudal regime," it was "absurd" to assume that Islam was not evolving. To the extent such evolution was slow, a major issue was the lack of a large-scale ecclesiastical structure that, by acting as a "collective intellectual," could facilitate the "adaptation" to modernity (Gramsci 2001: 247).

As important, Gramsci believed that Muslims saw the "great hypocrisy" in Europe of the Church adapting to modernity, which provided them with less incentive to pursue their own modernization. And even if Islam was compelled to "run dizzily" toward modernity, "in reality it is the same with Christianity," with both involving "grand heresies" that promoted "national sentiments" tied to a supposed return to a pure origin (ibid.). We have here a fundamental intuition, that was later developed by theorists of the like of Eric Voegelin and Shmuel N. Eisenstadt, according to which it is impossible to understand national liberation movements and other progressive movements without looking at the genesis itself of the idea of "social movement" in medieval heretic movements that contested (in fact both within Christianity and Islam) the monopolization and institutionalization of faith by established religious authorities (Eisenstadt 1982, 2000; Voegelin 1994).

Gramsci further observed the contemporary focus on origins by many in the Muslim world, and he explained this trend as being common to seemingly opposite discourses such as Wahhabism and Turkish republicanism; together they constituted a record of modern expression developed as that of Catholicism (Gramsci 2001: 247–48). In fact, if religion is politically central to the creation of the "historical bloc" that could challenge bourgeois hegemony: and for intellectuals to help put this bloc together one needs the skills of a good parish priest who, more than explaining religion, could "listen" and "understand" (Vinco 1983: 84–85), Gramsci believed that "the absence of a clear link that would serve as a *trait d'union* between theoretical Islam and popular belief," along with the "great space between the intellectuals and the people," would be a cause of the problematic modernization of Muslim countries in a manner similar to the situation of the Church in Italy. Thus, the "fanaticism" of some Muslim countries was in reality very similar to Christian fanaticism in history and in the years before World War I (Gramsci 2001: 621–23).

Considering his focus on the production of knowledge by intellectuals, it is not surprising that Gramsci urged close study of the theological importance of both the "clerical" structure and that of Islamic universities in these processes (ibid.). Given the similarities he believed to hold between Islam and Christianity, we can extrapolate Gramscian elements for approaching the problematic of the public sphere in Muslim majority societies through his strategy vis-à-vis the Church, which was the subject of the vast majority of his writings. What is important here is that Gramsci saw in the history of Christianity, particularly the early Church and the protestant Reformation, seminal examples of a cultural revolution of the masses that was also possible in the Muslim world (Vinco 1983: 10).

In this context, we should recall Gramsci's argument that in every country, including those of the Middle East, intellectuals are impacted by the specific local dynamics of capitalist development. What Gramsci's analysis calls us to do is to explore the specific relationship between emerging leading classes and the "organic" intellectuals they interacted with, who themselves led various styles of reform movements in the region that were crucial players in the political as well as public spheres. Moreover, the mediation of these relationships within the larger political and public spheres in which they played a role also requires exploration (cf. Crehan's discussion of various excerpts from the *Prison Notebooks* and *Political Writings*: 2002: 135–38; cf. also Watts 1999: 67).

Gramsci's argument is not without contradictions, since he sees the absence of a centralized ecclesiastical organization as a point of advantage for (Sunni) Islam, while he points out the mobilizing potential of such an organization in the case of Catholicism. The way out of these contradictions, which were rooted in his tendency to overpoliticize and overstrategize his diagnosis of the present, is to move to a more basic socio-anthropological terrain and to the analysis of practices and their relations to structures of domination. With both Catholicism and (though fragmentarily) Islam as examples, Gramsci attempts to unravel the power relations between historical religions and social structures through a reading of folklore, popular religion, the religion of the intellectuals, and most important, "common sense" (*senso comune*) and philosophy (Fulton 1987: 203). For Gramsci, the central dynamic that would determine the success of the venture of socialism was the extent to which the common sense incorporated in everyday religious belief and practice could be dialectically exalted, as it were, to the status of "good sense" (*buon senso*), a common sense turned reflective, and potentially hegemonic.

Common sense is a central concept in Gramsci's analysis of religion. Indeed, the relationship between religion and common sense is what leads to the ambiguity that Gramsci, more than most other Marxist philosophers, saw in the history and contemporary expressions of Christianity (La Rocca 1997: 110–29). How can we understand this term? Common sense here means a sense, experience, or consciousness in common, so coming close to Vico's meaning, which sensibly differs from how the term is commonly understood in English, in a way related to the above-mentioned understanding of "moral sense" defined by the Scottish Enlightenment. It is inevitably fragmentary, not unitary. It is disorganized and inconsistent, "realistic" and "superstitious" at the same time (Gramsci 2001: 1396–97). Religion is thereby the "principal element" of a larger body of disorganized common sense (ibid.: 1378, 1396, 1397), yet is never reducible to common sense because it constitutes a form of total social praxis (ibid.: 1396–97; Fulton 1987: 206).

We notice here a sophisticated view of a "living tradition" (though not named as such by Gramsci) where fragmentation prevails, just to be recondensed and integrated through the necessary search for coherence inherent in practice. Vico's influence here (mediated by Croce, or more probably by Antonio Labriola, a Neapolitan Marxist who had some influence on Croce) is clear. However, Gramsci's full step beyond Vico was his conviction that, to the extent that all people share in the common sense, all are philosophers, and thus have the potential to elaborate critically the cultural base to achieve transformative social praxis and thus turn "common sense" into "good" (La Rocca 1997: 11). "Good sense" is what enables "common sense" to be invested into the pursuit of "common good." It is a cultured sense of direction in the pursuit of socio-political goals of justice and welfare. We should deduce that according to Gramsci a pursuit of common good can only succeed if a popular philosophy becomes self-conscious and hegemonic. Without this step, common sense will be at the service of the hegemonic culture of the dominant classes.

What makes the elevation of common sense possible is its continual transformation through scientific and philosophical ideas to shape the range of the maxims through which principles are translated into moral guides for everyday life—a back and forth pendulum between universality and common knowledge (Gramsci 1971: 325–27). In one of the attempts to reconcile Gramsci with Anglo-American progressive pragmatism, Nadia Urbinati has written that "the movement from common sense to philosophy might be seen as a gradual (and revolving) move from a lesser to a greater level of generality in the expression of the moral principles that are already shared by a political community" (Urbinati 1998: 151). The problem with this attempt to conciliation is that common sense, unlike Gramsci's (and probably Vico's) view, is considered not a cultural expression of the ideology of subaltern classes but an epistemic foundation elaborated in the ideological terrain external to the masses that express it. Because neither religion nor the larger body of common sense in which it participates are reducible to a unity and coherence in either the individual or collective conscience, Gramsci did not support the view that a common sense grounded in religion could inherently provide the cultural material for constructing an intellectual order conducive to the cultural and political hegemony of the subaltern classes (Vinco 1983: 102; Gramsci 1997: 157). This is because he devoted much attention to analyzing the "structural" conditions for the hegemonic emergence of "good sense." Gramsci's pessimistic diagnosis of the predicament of the southern peasant masses was only rescued by the optimism of voluntary action, ultimately culminating in organized, revolutionary political action. This understanding of common and good sense becomes important when we turn to Foucault's analysis of the Iranian revolution, which from this perspective can be understood as a case where religion accomplished the transformation into "good sense," precisely because of what Foucault saw as the unity of will of the masses. As we see, for Foucault in Iran religion stopped being common sense, at least for a short while, and became organized voluntary action, in the Gramscian sense.

If Gramsci saw religion as "a need of the spirit," and even a key to the needed "public spirit," he was echoing Marx's belief—and anticipating Foucault's—that religion is the spirit of a spiritless time (Gramsci, quoted in Fulton 1987: 202). A metamorphosed religion has therefore the potential to unify the will of the masses, and as such is central to executing the philosophy of praxis, and is key to the "intellectual and moral Reformation" that must precede any revolution (cf. Vinco 1983: 48; Gramsci 2001: 1447). Gramsci believed that the philosophy of praxis could only substitute the common sense and the old conceptions of the world by reproducing the same formal organizational structure and retake the same methods of propagation of Catholicism (Gramsci 2001: 1380–81).

Reinterpreting Gramscian categories, one could dare to say that religion itself—not as a theoretical activity but as a stimulus to action and a source of mobilization—*is* a philosophy, and thus a potential stimulus for a philosophy of praxis—that is, the kind of "immanence" that Croce believed came from humans realizing their authorship of history, and the kind of willed action that Foucault saw as central to the realization of a "political spirituality." In fact, the concept of religion as the opium of people was one of the points of departure between Gramsci's thought and Marx's (cf. Vinco 1983: 57). That is, while religion can express an alienated and illusionary ideology, it can also be a stimulus for revolutionary action—at least a "passive revolution," when the power deployed by the state against the masses is too great for active resistance (Vinco 1983: 58; Gramsci 2001: 748).

Finally, Gramsci believed that cultural dependency is always an indication of political dependence. This realization has been shared by leading Muslim critics of the West and capitalist modernity for two centuries, including Iranian thinkers such as Shariati and Jalal Al-e Ahmad. In his approach to the revolutionary events in Iran, and in his wider work, Foucault, however, laid a privileged emphasis on the prism of agential motivation more than on the goal of building up an alternative hegemony based on ethical-political claims to the common good. He would explain that "my role . . . is to show people that they are much freer than they feel" when they accept as permanent and absolute political configurations and truth regimes that are of quite recent vintage (Foucault 1988a: 10).

Foucault's "Political Spirituality": Beyond the Post-Colonial Paradigm?

> When a colonial people tries to free itself of its colonizer, that is truly an act of liberation, in the strict sense of the word. But we also know that . . . this act of liberation is not sufficient to establish the practices of liberty that later on will be necessary for this people, this society and this individual to decide upon receivable and acceptable forms of their existence or political society. (Foucault 1988b: 2–3)

Foucault has been criticized by scholars, especially from a postcolonial perspective, as devoting little attention to the colonial situation. We would not defend Foucault on this count, but would like to point out, via the quote above, and through his direct engaging with the early Iranian revolution, that while the colonial was not a major theme in his work, he did frame it in specific situations. Chief among the insights he produced is that "liberation" cannot engender real liberty without a certain level of "discursive control" by the people of the regimes of governmentality produced by such liberation.

In this framework, "the enigma of revolt" in the Iranian revolutionary events of the latter part of 1978 was a crucial discovery for someone exploring the manner in which the revolt was being lived:

> [the revolution] was dreamt of as being as much religious as political . . . [staying] close to those old dreams which the West had known at another time, when it wanted to inscribe the figures of spirituality on the earth of politics . . . What else but religion could provide support for the distress and then the revolt of a population which had been traumatized by "development," "reform," "urbanization," and all the other failures of the regime. (Foucault 1999 [1979]: 132)

This celebration of the power of religion might seem strange to many readers of Foucault, yet religious themes are central to Foucault's oeuvre. Foucault's "lifelong project" has been described as an attempt to overcome the alienation from the soul by exploring how the human sciences and politics turned the soul into something lifeless, ghostly, and separate from the world (Bernauer 1999: xiii). His work can thus be seen as an attempt to identify the forces that control and shape the religious subject, and as an exercise to uncover the silenced and subjugated discourses of both religion and the Other (Carrette 2000: 25).

The active role Foucault assigns to religion is related to his insights into how the discourses underlying the formation of modern subjects force potentially transgressive dimensions of the person into modern disciplinary matrices. If the struggle for our selves constitutes a politics of our selves, the key campaign in that struggle, according to Foucault, will be a new mode of fashioning an "ethical way of being a self" (Bernauer and Mahon 1994: 151). Foucault's main direct consideration of a socio-religious movement is in his reporting from Iran in the pivotal period of the 1978 revolution. Although not an expert on Iran, he did significant preparatory readings based on a bibliography prepared by his Iranian and French friends, and had previously signed a petition to protest against the execution of political prisoners by the Shah. Thus, Foucault was familiar with the general outlines of modern Iranian history and politics, as well as with Shi'a theology and the writings of thinkers such as Ali Shariati.

He first arrived in Teheran just after Black Friday, September 8, 1978, when the Shah's army had shot into a crowd, killing upward of four thousand people. During his sojourns, he met with all strata of society, from SAVAK (the Shah's secret police) and CIA agents to students and high-ranking oppositional clergy. The series of articles he wrote on Iran proved to be very controversial in France, and led to criticism, among other things, that he had become an apologist for a "spirituality that punishes and disciplines," in a paradoxical inversion of the concerns of his earlier work (Broyelle and

Broyelle 1979: 13; Macey 1993: 410).[3] This might be a good description of the Khomeinist politics that took over the revolution, but it does not accurately reflect the dynamics of the early stages of the revolution that Foucault witnessed first hand.

Moreover, if his work on early Christian religion aims to reveal how the religious subject is constituted, his writings on the Iranian revolution help us open new questions about how the emerging Iranian religious subject was created and managed to end the thousand-year reign of the Shahs. He examines how religion engenders forms of subjection by developing new power relations, and thus the Iranian revolution was particularly interesting to him because of the transformation of subjectivity it brought about . . . to examine "different ways of governing oneself through a different way of dividing up true and false—that is what I would call political spirituality" (Foucault, quoted in Carrette 2000: 137). Feeding off his work on the history of sexuality, Foucault's dealing with the Iranian revolution repositioned the language of spirituality within a new politics of experience in which the body is located at the center of the "spiritual"—especially the bodies marching and dying in the streets of Teheran to sanctify the revolution (cf. Carrette 2000: 48).

Foucault's work on early Christian religion taught him, as he wrote only months before leaving for Teheran (and as Gramsci before him learned from working on the Catholic Church in Italy) that religion has always been a political force; a "superb instrument of power for itself; entirely woven through with elements that are imaginary, erotic, effective, corporal, sensual, and so on" (Foucault 1999 [1979]: 107). Such a description is particularly apposite for Iranian Shi'ism, with its highly emotive rituals of mourning and flagellation surrounding the martyrdom of Hussein, which can nonetheless provide the material for constructing new forms of modern power (cf. chapter 3 of this volume by Deeb). However, Foucault's approach to the Iranian revolution added to his previous interest for religion and power as a singular fascination, for plotting an "escape" from history: it was "irreducible . . . there is no explanation for the man who revolts. His action is necessarily a tearing that breaks the thread of history and its long chains of reason" (ibid.: 131). Even more so when the man revolting is Muslim, as "the problem of Islam is essentially a problem of our age and for the years to come" (Foucault 1978e: 26).[4]

Foucault was thus bothered by what he believed to be the inaccurate and unfair portrayal of the Iranian revolution in the West, and the comparative lack of sympathy it received vis-à-vis the Portuguese or Nicaraguan revolutions of 1975 and 1978 (Foucault 1979: 227). In Iran Foucault saw the symptoms through which one could "diagnose the present in which we live" (Foucault 1999 [1978]: 92). And to make this diagnosis Foucault believed that the ideas of ordinary people and minorities, rather than those of intellectuals and other elites, should be examined. As Miller explains, "more clearly than many foreign reporters, [Foucault] grasped the religious dimensions of the revolt," understanding how Shi'ism armed its followers with an "ardor that is simultaneously political and religious" and in which the idea of an "Islamic government" fed into new forms of political spirituality (Miller 1993: 308–09; Foucault 1978b: 11, 1978c: 1–2). In this context, Foucault interestingly uses the same phrase as did Ali Shariati (whom he greatly admired)—a "return to the self"—to describe one of the primary technologies of the self, one that for Foucault would signal an Islam that "introduces into political life a spiritual dimension: to establish that political life need not always be the obstacle to spirituality, but can secure its survival, its occurrence, its flourishing" (Foucault 1978d: 48–49; cf. Carrette 2000: 38).

It would be very useful to put Foucault and Shariati into a critical dialogue that unfortunately never took place.[5] Foucault felt that Shariati exemplified the possibility of the spiritual politics and enlightened mysticism enshrined in religious activism (Foucault 1978a, 1978c). Shariati's early politico-religious experiences as a member of the "movement of God-worshipping socialists" reveal precisely the type of revolutionary socio-political program, rooted in Islamic Iranian intellectual culture, that would appeal to Foucault. This is not surprising, since for Shariati, and indeed, for his father before him, the root of Iran's predicament was in significant part due to "the penetration of European values" in the country, which exacerbated the existing lack of faith and ignorance of the Qur'an (cf. Rahnema 1998: 14). The ideology of the group, as laid out in its platform, included the necessity of faith in God, the defense of the real rights of workers and peasants, and opposition of dictatorship, exploitation, and colonialism (ibid.: 30).

Shariati was especially fond of Fanon, who taught that the colonized must return to their "true selves" to defeat colonialism (Shariati 1982). For Foucault, of course, there was no "true self" that one could return to, but rather a return to a focus on the self as a project, a "complex microsocial structure, replete with foreign relations," and not the disengaged autonomous self of the modern self-imagination (Connolly 1993: 370). For both Shariati and Foucault, the project of self-realization involved the politicization of an ethical sensibility, one that like Nietzsche's calls to us to "think differently," that solicits us to join the quest for a different future. And if one considers this ethical sensibility on a political register, we understand the relationships it might establish with religiously motivated movements of resistance around the world.

Yet, if the Iranian revolution provides evidence of the utility of technologies of power from below against hegemonic systems of domination, Foucault's "revolt with bare hands" clearly lacked coherent long-term goals; positively, this reflected a "simplicity of will" that posed a direct challenge to established politics. Unfortunately, as we now know, that lack of a plan—in particularly by the leftist–student–intellectual coalition that led the early part of the revolution—proved to be its undoing against Khomeini's ruthlessly well thought out strategy (cf. Stauth 1994 [1991]: 393). Thus, Foucault wrote: "during the whole of my stay in Iran, I never once heard the word 'revolution.' But four times out of five, I got the answer 'an Islamic government'. . . ." (Foucault 1978b: 49, 1978d).

By combining a simplistic—if not naïve—view of the forces operating in Iran with his longing for a "political spirituality" that he perceived as exhausted in the West, Foucault interpreted the Iranian events not just as a rejection of the Shah and of the American interference and exploitation of Iran's resources, but more profoundly, a "cultural revolution"—at once a "more radical *denial*, a refusal by a people, not simply of the foreigner, but of everything that it had constituted, after years, centuries, his political destiny," and a radical *affirmation* of a new subjectivity (Foucault 1979: 231; emphasis added). Georg Stauth (1994 [1991]: 385) argues that Foucault understood the situation as one in which the people on the street had become increasingly conscious of the fact that the socio-political system had come to depend on their own active ideas for its sustenance. To use Gramsci's categories, we can say that they realized the need to become their own organic intellectuals, to forge the ideology for their own con-quest of the Iranian state based on a reformulation, or philosophizing, of religion from "common" to "good sense." The *organicità*, or organic quality of this discourse would have to be tied specifically to the larger social class and set of economic relations from which it emerged (Gramsci 1971: 12), thereby articulating and complexifying the notion of "common good."

Yet there was a further layer, or at least potential, in Foucault's analysis that is part and parcel of his larger, admittedly naïve approach, and that is, however, particularly useful for our investigation: the genealogy of the popular Islamic insurrection cannot be explained through motiva-tional prisms based on Western notions of power. Most of all, Foucault realized that motivating the revolution was a desire by the people to "change themselves," to affect a

> radical change . . . in their experience. Here is where I think Islam plays a role . . . Religion was the promise and guarantee of finding a radical change in their subjectivity . . . This was compatible with traditional Islamic prac-tice that already assured their identity; in this fashion that had brought to live Islam as a revolutionary force. (Foucault 1979: 234)

And here, crucially, he reminds the reader that in the sentence before Marx's famous line about religion being the opium of the people, Marx argues that religion is "the spirit of a world without spirit"—"Let us say, then, that in 1978 Islam was not the opium of the people precisely because it was the spirit of a world without spirit" (Foucault, quoted in Stauth 1994 [1991]: 398), that is, an affirmation of will unknown to technologies of power's workings within modern politics. Almost a non-biopolitical (and therefore "spiritual") form of power, yet one with a legitimate aspiration to modern credentials, therefore one with uncertain effects. Under this light, the dilemmas and the discursive breaches of Islamic reformers in the modern era, in Iran like in the Ottoman Empire and elsewhere, might no longer be assessed as a failed attempt at constructing an endogenous modernity, but as simply a variation in an effort of metamorphosing traditions—and so the "self"—under the structural conditions of modernity, an effort that is always painful and never fully successful, not even in such rare revolutionary eruptions as in the Iranian events.

Although it is too soon to speak definitively, events in Iraq surrounding the Shi'a insurrection of spring 2004 seem to support some of Foucault's readings of the "revolutionary power" of Shi'ism while challenging others. Based on field work and a review of literature produced and speeches by various Shi'a leaders during this period,[6] we can read the rebellion by mostly young Shi'a men in the southern regions of the country as part of a larger, culturally motivated revolt against both the old regime and against the new order being imposed by the United States and its allies. Interviews with senior Shi'a religious figures revealed that most saw the cultural aspect of the U.S. occupation and planning for the future of Iraq as equally if not more threatening to them than the military and economic aspects (LeVine 2005).

One can also read the support for a young figure like Muqtada' al-Sadr (whose movement's fate we don't dare to predict here) as related to a generational conflict in which the supposedly quietest senior ayatollahs had lost the pulse of the largely young and disenfranchised population. Indeed, one could see older religious authorities increasing the stridency of their rhetoric in order to retain their followings. Religion is clearly playing a role in shaping a response to the kind of neoliberal "developmental reform" sponsored by the Shah in the 1970s and the United States through the Coalition Provisional Authority and the interim government in 2003–2004. Yet, the lack of long-range strategic planning by the rebels and al-Sadr, along with the resort to large-scale violence rather than mass political mobilization (unlike in the period of the Iranian Revolution when Foucault was in Iraq) has thus far weakened the ability of the movement to achieve long-term goals. For Sadr's followers, as in Iran of 1978, this is probably similar to a khomeinist form of "Islamic government," though both one adapted to the political and ethno-religious shape of Iraq, and one committed to shape up government through elections and coalitions, and therefore with a more democratic method than the dualistic and only semi-open political system of the Islamic Republic of Iran. Thus far, it is perhaps the violence that has ultimately characterized the outbursts of Shi'a rebellion throughout Iraq under military occupation, as with the violence that ultimately consumed the revolution in Iran (both of them heavily influenced by the role played by foreign powers) that has made it difficult for non-elite, grassroots religious discourses to play the potentially positive role that Foucault laid out for them.

Conclusion: From Common Sense to Politicized Spirituality?

We have argued here that there are concepts of the common good deployed by contemporary Muslim socio-religious movements that do not adhere to the dynamics or norms—and, indeed, as we learn from Foucault, the techniques of power and subjectivity—of the main historical trajectories of European public spheres. These movements' practices reflect an intersection of class and political cleavages with religious discourses that becomes increasingly powerful as governments face chronic shortage of funds for social welfare and development. Thus at the same time they grapple with internal conflicts, these movements impinge on hegemonic secular identities and state practices and allocation of resources. Such policies have a potential to articulate alternative hegemonies that deploy an immanent critique of the political status quo through religiously grounded notions of social justice and welfare.

These dynamics point to the need for contemporary scholarship to account for the often simultaneous drive by socio-religious movements to achieve political, social, and cultural justice for their constituencies at the same time they exhibit a deeply intolerant stance toward those they view as outside their community. This involves at least three dynamics: a redefinition of the organizational and programmatic outlook of socio-religious movements vis-à-vis their class composition, a gender-related division of labor (see chapter 3 in this volume by Deeb), and their attitude toward national goals (see chapter 2 by Manoukian); a reschematization of the public sphere from the viewpoint of the grassroots reconstructions of ties of solidarity and communication generated by potentially counter-hegemonic activities (see chapter 4 by Baker); and an analysis of how these movements use their activities to further structures of justice, welfare, and solidarity within a dynamic of extreme exclusion and violence (see chapters 2, 3, and 4).

In this framework of theoretical reflection that we are developing with an eye to concrete empirical investigations, we can here first attempt to summarize what can be retained by the singular experience of Foucault as spectator-interpreter of what was certainly an epochal eruption of political will, and therefore an historical edge for evaluating the potential of socio-religious movement, but certainly *not* a plausible "model." In response to his Iranian experience Foucault called for a "hermeneutic of social action" that, if combined with the "rhetoric of authenticity" articulated by Iranian clerics, had the potential for engaging in the kind of praxic philosophy that Antonio Gramsci has famously advocated (cf. Dabashi 1993; Stauth 1994 [1991]: 387).[7] The importance of bringing these two seminal figures into dialog is clear if we consider Edward Said's critique of Foucault vis-à-vis Gramsci:

> Gramsci would find Foucault's [history] uncongenial. He would certainly appreciate the fineness of Foucault's archaeologies, but would find it odd that they make not even a nominal allowance for emergent movements, and none for revolutions, counter-hegemony or historical blocks. (Said 1984: 246–47)

It is not clear whether Said was aware of Foucault's writings on Iran, but neither is it clear whether they completely answer his criticism. Yet, it is true that if Gramsci more explicitly focused on how to develop strategies to facilitate the emergence of movements of resistance, like Foucault (if anticipating him by almost fifty years) Gramsci saw religious spirituality as an embryonic force of reform (if not of revolution), both a collective will and a lived idea. If Foucault argued that in the Iranian revolution there was a convergence of the individual need for personal transformation with traditional Islamic religion emerging as revolutionary practice, he too saw a similar possibility in a potential alliance between workers and peasants through a rejuvenated religious ideology-*cum*-praxis. This convergence may have secured people's identity in such a way that they were able to live religion as a "radically transformative" force (Foucault 1988b: 214; cf. Stauth 1994 [1991]: 394).

Political spirituality is a central concept in Foucault's understanding of the transformative potential of religion that he redeveloped through the lens of the Iranian revolution. For Foucault, to achieve this political spirituality is to struggle to overcome resentment against the paradoxical circumstances in which one is set, especially in the context of an institutionalized, routinized, governmentalized, normalized evil—ultimately, to overcome a "transcendentalized ethics of modernity" that inexorably rationalizes—and in so doing both desanctifies and removes from experience—political speech and action (cf. Connolly 1993).

When publicly criticized by a Muslim woman for believing that "Muslim spirituality" was preferable to the Shah, Foucault argued that the Iranian revolution should remind the West of something it had forgotten since the Renaissance and the Reformation—the possibility of a political spirituality that in Iran had created a

> unified collective will . . . perhaps the greatest ever insurrection against global systems, the most insane and the most modern form of revolt . . . the force that can make a whole people rise up (importantly, even "with no vanguard, no party"), not only against a sovereign and his police, but against a whole regime, a whole way of life, a whole world. (Foucault 1978e: 26)

This focus on insanity as a moment of resistance to the modern condition is clearly related to Foucault's desire to move beyond Kantian ethics and reminds us of the insights of Foucault's comrades Gilles Deleuze and Felix Guattari, who argued that schizophrenia was a response of the silenced to the iron cage of rational modernity (Deleuze and Guattari 1983 [1972], 1987 [1980]). In fact, if we revisit a lecture Foucault delivered as early as 1962 on religious deviations and medical knowledge, we see that he argued for a unity between aspects of madness and "religious territoriality" (Foucault 1999 [1962]: 56). In this manner we can understand the Iranian revolution as a direct reaction to the process of extreme modernization-as-Westernization undertaken by the Shah, and particularly his White Revolution of the 1960s, which had created a "culture of idleness" among the Iranian elite. This would ultimately stand no chance among a culture of "ultimate concern" among the confederation of social forces that toppled the regime (Ashraf 1995).

We unfortunately know that the spirit of martyrdom of the millions that took the street in September 1978 in Iran can turn into the madness of suicidal-homicidal sacrifice of militant *istishhadiyyun* (those who voluntarily commit martyrdom) if there is no space for either a truly revolutionary or a real reform-oriented and electoral process that can absorb and channel this "praxic" religious territoriality. It is clear to us—and it is even clearer now to several generations of Islamist leaders and cadres in various countries—that while reform and a democratic process is often the preferred alley, if secularist forces effectively prevents it, the only alternative becomes one between an unlikely revolution and a much more likely spiral of violence in which political repression and military aggression and occupation might endlessly beget the religious readiness to (suicidal-homicidal) sacrifice.

Foucault's exploration of the meaning of the Iranian revolution gives us a conceptual edge to understand how religiously motivated social action and interaction, up to the level of social movements, do not fall quietly (if at all) into modern discourses of internalized self-policing, the legitimization of the state's monopolistic violence and legislating force, and its capacity to count, classify and separate functionally different parts of the population. In other words, socio-religious movements can appear quietist if they only concentrate on social solidarity work or militant if they challenge the state or the occupant, but both positions reflect the same tense and ambivalent relationship with modern forms of power, or, to use Foucault's expression, "bio-politics." As for Gramsci, religion "*may* contain the potential for 'breaking' the hegemony of the historical bloc, and for creating new forms of consciousness on the part of the subaltern groups. But is also may not" (Saunders 1998: 187).

We must discount some naïve enthusiasm and even neo-Orientalism in Foucault's position and in the notion itself of "political spirituality" as ultimately nourished by a projection and displacement of subjectivity and will from the "West" to an "Orient" perceived as still uncontaminated by modernist ideologies (see Salvatore 1997: 146–55). On the other hand, the Gramscian approach to the socio-political potential of religious traditions and movements, if immune from such a neo-Orientalism, was trapped in a too rigidly secular notion of hegemony and accordingly of the role of intellectuals vis-à-vis the "ordinary people" or the "masses."

The key concept of *buon senso* required that intellectuals capitalize on the fact that the peasants' masses of Southern Italy, though lacking an ideology of liberation, nourish a latent passion for justice. In current jargon, we would say that while for Gramsci religion represents a defective source of "agency," for Foucault this source is potentially excessive and expressive—a combination of passions or aesthetics that Bataille and Deleuze have also pointed to as being one of the crucial, albeit problematic means by which those excluded from or opposed to modernity and its spheres of influence can attempt to escape its strictures.

Given his position in the political struggles of the 1930s and notwithstanding the obvious fact that from the prison he could produce neither ethnographies nor journalistic accounts (but at best rely on those of others), Gramsci's influence upon such authors of the second half of the 20th century like the Neapolitan anthropologist Ernesto De Martino remains seminal. Located between Gramsci and more contemporary "subaltern studies," De Martino has cleared a view of religion and the potentials for movements of transformation that avoid the problem of a too compactly functional view of "civic spirit" (in the sense used by Putnam 1993). Instead he saw religion as intrinsically disjunctured, yet vital, and inherently— though unpredictably—dislocating the power relationships between dominant and dominated classes, between colonizers and colonized. With these further conceptual elaborations in mind, Gramsci and Foucault force us to take Islamic movements seriously on their own terms as intrinsically complex and ambivalent yet vital movements, that while not "emancipatory" in the liberal progressive sense (which in any case is not extraneous to their genealogies and grammars of action) cannot be rubberstamped as "fanatical" and "fundamentalist" either.[8]

At the same time, if we unwind the absolutist categories of post-reformation and post-enlightenment discourse, we are reminded of the necessity of moving beyond a focus on "religion" as a separate category, and thus on "Muslim" public spheres. when all the "spheres" composing a society can only be understood in relation to each other, as permeable to change from a vast array of agents, and as undergoing perpetual osmosis with surrounding political, cultural, and ideological material.

It is thus clear that the vocabulary of social science (in turn influenced by the grammar of theories of civil society) cannot completely capture the rich and complex idiom of these movements. For example, conventional views of welfare and charity, and their differences, are not suitable to make sense of Islamic benevolent associations, since they presuppose a certain structure and division of labor between the state and civil society, but also between the state and the market, a structure that is not always strongly institutionalized in the societies where we do investigations. It is a presupposition based on the view that profit-oriented economic activity within the market does well to society but creates pockets of need and poverty: welfare is where the state or public authorities jump in, and charity is where privately funded voluntary associations intervene. Even in the most prominent, modern-like and state-conforming among the Islamic associations in Cairo in the last thirty years, which consciously adopted a modernizing vocabulary—the Mustafa Mahmud association— the conventional notions of welfare and charity are not suitable to make sense of the structure and goals of the association, and how its actors are motivated, from the founder, to the employees, to those who volunteer their work, beginning with the medical doctors (Salvatore 2001).

Instead of seeing socio-religious movements and their associational networks as either opposed to modernity, or merely instrumentalizing the technical aspect of modernity, or as constituting alternative modernities, one should see them as the continuation of a trajectory of ordering social relations according to notions of practical reason and the common good that has always been in fast motion in several civilizational areas, but was superseded by modern liberal and non-liberal currents.

Finally, we should recall Foucault's belief that

> European thought finds itself at a turning point. The turning point is none other than the end of imperialism. The crisis of western thought is identical to the end of imperialism . . . If a philosophy of the future exists, it must be born outside of Europe or equally born in consequence of meetings and impacts between Europe and non-Europe. (Foucault 1999 [1979]: 113)

Future analyses of hegemonic contention within public spheres and of the transformative potential of socio-religious movements must build on this insight, which in conjunction with Gramsci's philosophical-*cum*-religious praxis disturbs the sense of ontological necessity, historical inevitability, and purity of discrimination in the established dualities of identity/difference, normality/abnormality and public/private that continue to shape modern polities (what we could call, with Eric Voegelin, the "Aristotelian hangover" of Western social sciences). Such an enterprise must also develop a "generous sensibility," the basis for the very "conversation of civilizations" called for by many Muslims and westerners alive. It is through such dialogs that more dynamic and plural public spheres can be imagined and constructed (Connolly 1993: 367).

Notes

We thank Margot Badran, Lara Deeb, Cecelia Lynch, and Setrag Manoukian for their comments on earlier drafts of this chapter.

1. This view approaches the Wittgensteinian concept of life form/*Lebensform*.
2. Interestingly, even in Italian, most of the major work on Gramsci and religion seems to have been done in the 1970s and 1980s—at the very moment that liberation theologies were gaining theoretical and political force (La Rocca 1997).
3. Indeed, some critics have labeled Foucault an "infantile leftist" and his reporting "folly" because of his seeming support of the Iranian revolution and his belief that Khomeini would never assume power and violate the popular will of renewal. Foucault wrote that "Khomeini is not a politician. There will be no Khomeini party, there will be no Khomeini government. Khomeini is the point of fixation for a collective will" (Foucault, 1978f).
4. Foucault's writings on the Iranian revolution for the Italian newspaper *Corriere della Sera* and other publications, are collected in Foucault 1998.
5. While Foucault expressed admiration for Shariati, the latter did not seem to have been appealed by Foucault's writing, despite being in Paris during the mid-1960s when Foucault was developing his critical approach. Yet, it was in Paris that Shariati rediscovered Islam in the words and deeds of European intellectuals. After his return to Iran he combined this rediscovery with a mysticism, whose product was a "political spirituality" of the kind Foucault speaks of

(cf. Shariati 1982: 305–07; see Rahnema 1998 for an examination of Shariati's time in France and his mystical tendencies).
6. LeVine, fieldwork interviews in Iraq, March 2004.
7. Cf. Dabashi 1993, particularly the chapter on Jalal Al-e Ahmad, for a relevant discussion of how authenticity and discontent are tied together in the Iranian revolutionary approach.
8. This is something which contemporary postcolonial theory has yet to succeed in impressing on the larger academy (never mind the public).

References

Asad, Talal. 1993. *Genealogies of Religion: Discipline and Reasons of Power in Christianity and Islam*. Baltimore and London: Johns Hopkins University Press.
———. 2003. *Formations of the Secular: Christianity, Islam, Modernity*. Stanford: Stanford University Press.
Ashraf, Ahmad. 1995. "From the White Revolution to the Islamic Revolution." In *Iran After the Revolution: Crisis of an Islamic State*, ed. Saeed Rahnema and Sohrab Behdad, New York: I.B. Tauris, 21–44.
Berman, Eli. 2003. *Hamas, Taliban and the Jewish Underground: An Economist's View of Radical Religious Militias*, Working Paper, National Bureau of Economic Research.
Bernauer, James. 1999. "Cry of Spirit." Foreword to Michel Foucault, *Religion and Culture: Michel Foucault*, ed. Jeremy Carrette, New York: Routledge, xi–xx.
Bernauer, James, and Michael Mahon. 1994. "The Ethics of Michel Foucault." In *The Cambridge Companion to Foucault*, ed. Gary Gutting, New York: Cambridge University Press, 141–58.
Broyelle, Claudie, and Jacques Broyelle. 1979. "'A' quoi rêvent les philosophes?" *Le Matin*, March 24: 13.
Calhoun, Craig. 1993. "Habitus, Field and Capital: The Question of Historical Specificity." In *Bourdieu: Critical Perspectives*, ed. Craig Calhoun, Edward LiPuma and Moishe Postone, Cambridge: Polity Press, 61–88.
Carrette, Jeremy. 2000. *Foucault and Religion: Spiritual Corporality and Political Spirituality*. London: Routledge.
Castells, Manuel. 1996, *The Power of Identity*. Oxford: Blackwell.
Connolly, William. 1993. "Beyond Good and Evil: The Ethical Sensibility of Michel Foucault," *Political Theory* 21, 3: 365–89.
Crehan, Kate. 2002. *Gramsci, Culture and Anthropology*. Berkeley: University of California Press.
Dabashi, Hamid. 1993. *Theology of Discontent: The Ideological Foundation of the Islamic Revolution in Iran*. New York: New York University Press.
Deleuze, Gilles, and Pierre-Félix Guattari. 1983 [1972]. *Anti-Oedipus: Capitalism and Schizophrenia I*, trans. Robert Hurley, Mark Seem, and Helen R. Lane, Minneapolis: University of Minnesota Press.
———. 1987 [1980]. *A Thousand Plateaus: Capitalism and Schizophrenia II*, trans. Brian Massumi, Minneapolis: University of Minnesota Press.
Eder, Klaus. 1985. *Geschichte als Lernprozeß. Zur Pathogenese politischer Modernität in Deutschland*. Frankfurt: Suhrkamp.
Eisenstadt, Shmuel N. 1982. "Heterodoxies, Sectarianism and Dynamics of Civilizations," *Diogène* 120: 5–26.

Eisenstadt, Shmuel N. 2000. "Fundamentalist Movements in the Framework of Multiple Modernities." In *Between Europe and Islam: Shaping Modernity in a Transcultural Space*, ed. Almut Höfert and Armando Salvatore, Brussels: P.I.E.-Peter Lang, 175–96.

Foucault, Michel. 1978a. "Taccuino persiano: L' esercito, quando la terra trema," *Corriere della Sera*, September 28: 1–2.

——. 1978b. "Teheran: la fede contro lo Scià," *Corriere della Sera*, October 8: 11.

——. 1978c. "Taccuino persiano: Ritorno al profeta?" *Corriere della Sera*, October 22: 1–2.

——. 1978d. "A' quoi rêvent les Iraniens?" *Nouvel Observateur*, October 16–22: 48–49.

——. 1978e. "Réponse à une lectrice Iranienne," *Nouvel Observateur*, November 13–19: 26–27.

——. 1978f. "Il mitico capo della rivolta nell'Iran," *Corriere della Sera*, November 26: 1–2.

——. 1979. "L' esprit d'un monde sans esprit." Interview. In *Iran: la révolution an nom de Dieu*, ed. Claire Brière and Pierre Blachet, Paris: Seuil, 227–41.

——. 1988a. "Truth, Power, Self: An Interview with Michel Foucault." In *Technologies of the Self: A Seminar with Michel Foucault*, ed. Luther Martin, Huck Gutman, and Patrick Hutton, Amherst, MA: University of Massachusetts Press, 9–15.

——. 1988b. *Politics, Philosophy, Culture: Interviews and Other Writings, 1977–84*, trans. Alan Sheridan et al., New York: Routledge.

——. 1998. *Taccuino persiano*, Milan: Guerini.

——. 1999. *Religion and Culture: Michel Foucault*, ed. Jeremy Carrette, New York: Routledge.

Fulton, John. 1987. "Religion and Politics in Gramsci: An Introduction." *Sociological Analysis* 48, 3: 197–216.

Gramsci, Antonio. 1971. *Selections from the Prison Notebooks*, ed. and trans. Quintin Hoare and Geoffrey Nowell Smith, New York: International Publishers.

——. 1997. *La religione come senso comune*, ed. Tommaso La Rocca, Milan: EST.

——. 2001. *Quaderni del carcere*, 4 vols., Rome and Trento: Istituto Gramsci/Einaudi.

Hammami, Rema. 2002. *Palestinian NGOs, the Oslo Transition, and the Space of Development*. Paper presented at the workshop on "Socio-Religious Movements and the Transformation of Political Community: Israel, Palestine, & Beyond," University of California Irvine, Department of History, October 10–12.

Höfert, Almut, and Armando Salvatore. 2000. "Introduction: Beyond the Clash of Civilisations: The Transcultural Politics Between Europe and Islam." In *Between Europe and Islam: Shaping Modernity in a Transcultural Space*, ed. Almut Höfert and Armando Salvatore, Brussels: P.I.E.-Peter Lang, 13–35.

Kreidie, Lina. 2002. *Hizbullah and the Challenges of Modernism and Secularism*. Paper presented at the workshop on "Socio-Religious Movements and the Transformation of Political Community: Israel, Palestine, & Beyond," University of California Irvine, Department of History, October 10–12.

La Rocca, Tommaso. 1997. "Gramsci sulla religione." In Antonio Gramsci, *La religione come senso comune*, ed. with an Introduction by Tommaso La Rocca., Milan: EST.

LeVine, Mark. 2005. *Why They Don't Hate Us: Lifting the Veil on the Axis of Evil*. Oxford: Oneworld.

MacIntyre, Alasdair. 1984 [1981]. *After Virtue. A Study in Moral Theory.* Notre Dame, IN: University of Notre Dame Press.

———. 1988. *Whose Justice? Which Rationality?* London: Duckworth.

———. 1994. "The Theses on Feuerbach: A Road not Taken." In *Artifacts, Representations, and Social Practice: Essays for Marx Wartofsky*, ed. Carol C. Gould and Robert S. Cohen, Amsterdam: Kluwer, 223–34.

Macey, David. 1993. *The Lives of Michel Foucault.* London: Hutchinson.

Masud, Muhammad Khalid. 2000 [1995]. *Shatibi's Philosophy of Islamic Law.* Kuala Lumpur: Islamic Book Trust.

Mazzotta, Giuseppe. 1999. *The New Map of the World. The Poetic Philosophy of Giambattista Vico.* Princeton: Princeton University Press.

Miller, James. 1993. *The Passion of Michel Foucault.* New York: Simon and Schuster.

Putnam, Robert D. 1993. *Making Democracy Work: Civic Traditions in Modern Italy.* Princeton: Princeton University Press.

Rahnema, Ali. 1998. *An Islamic Utopian: A Political Biography of Ali Shari'ati.* New York: I.B. Tauris.

Roy, Sara. 2000. "The Transformation of Islamic NGOs in Palestine." *Middle East Report*, 214: 24–27.

Rudolph, Susanne Hoeber, and James Piscatori, eds. 1997. *Transnational Religion and Fading States.* Boulder, CO: Westview.

Said, Edward. 1984. *The Word, the Text and the Critic.* London: Faber and Faber.

Salvatore, Armando. 1997. *Islam and the Political Discourse of Modernity.* Reading, UK: Ithaca Press.

———. 2001. "Mustafa Mahmud: a Paradigm of Public Islamic Entrepreneurship?" In *Muslim Traditions and Modern Techniques of Power*, vol. 3 of *Yearbook of the Sociology of Islam*, ed. Armando Salvatore, Hamburg: Lit; New Brunswick, NJ: Transaction, 213–25.

Saunders, George R. 1998. "The Magic of the South: Popular Religion and Elite Catholicism in Italian Ethnology." In *Italy's "Southern Question": Orientalism in One Country*, ed. Jane Schneider, New York: Berg, 177–206.

Schneider, Jane. 1998. "Introduction: The Dynamics of Neo-Orientalism in Italy (1848–1995)." In *Italy's "Southern Question": Orientalism in One Country*, ed. Jane Schneider, New York: Berg, 1–23.

Shariati, Ali. 1982. "The Return to the Self." In *Islam in Transition: Muslim Perspectives*, ed. John Donohue and John Esposito, New York: Oxford University Press, 305–07.

Stauth, Georg. 1994 [1991]. "Revolution in Spiritless Times: An Essay on Michel Foucault's Enquiries into the Iranian Revolution." In *Michel Foucault: Critical Assessments*, ed. B. Smart, vol. 3, London: Routledge, 379–401.

Stauth, Georg, and Bryan S. Turner. 1988. *Nietzsche's Dance: Resentment, Reciprocity and Resistance in Social Life.* Oxford: Blackwell.

Urbinati, Nadia. 1998. "The Souths of Antonio Gramsci and the Concept of Hegemony." In *Italy's "Southern Question": Orientalism in One Country*, ed. Jane Schneider, New York: Berg, 135–56.

Vico, Giambattista. 1999 [1744]. *New Science. Principles of the New Science Concerning the Common Nature of the Nations*, 3 ed., trans. David Marsh, London: Penguin.

Vinco, Roberto. 1983. *Una fede senza futuro? Religione e mondo cattolico in Gramsci.* Verona: Mazziana.

Voegelin, Eric. 1994. *Das Volk Gottes.* München: Wilhelm Fink.

Watts, Michael. 1999. "Islamic Modernities? Citizenship, Civil Society, and Islamism in a Nigerian City." In *Cities and Citizenship*, ed. James Holston, Durham, NC: Duke University Press, 67–102.

Zaman, Muhammad Qasim. 2002. *The Ulama in Contemporary Islam: Custodians of Change*. Princeton: Princeton University Press.

———. 2004. "The 'Ulama of Contemporary Islam and their Conceptions of the Common Good." In *Public Islam and the Common Good*, ed. Armando Salvatore and Dale F. Eickelman, Leiden and Boston: Brill, 129–55.

CHAPTER 2

POWER, RELIGION, AND THE EFFECTS OF PUBLICNESS IN 20TH-CENTURY SHIRAZ

Setrag Manoukian

Introduction

The photos of people marching in the streets during the Iranian revolution of 1979 and the televised spectacle of masses of Iranians grieving at the funeral of Ayatollah Khomeini in 1989 remain in Western media central images to any discussion about the political relevance of Islam, especially in relation to its mass character. The compact, indistinct character of the mass and its emotional behavior is often framed as an implicit or explicit example of the "primordial" and "archaic" link between Islam and the population of Iran, projecting the country into a space of alterity where religion is the explanatory trope deployed for all occasions.

This chapter proposes an alternative interpretation of the manner in which Islam as a discursive tradition (Asad 1986) variously encroached upon and interacted with the political category of the "people" in 20th century Iran. If the accepted view often assumes a stable link between "Islam and the people," I present three case studies that demonstrate that the articulation of Islam in Iran is much more contingent and variable over time than is normally assumed.

My discussion describes the particular configurations of this articulation in different historical moments using three documents. The backdrop of this discussion is the cluster of social and economic transformations that took place in Iran during the 20th century and the intertwining shifts in the political imaginary of the country. Particularly relevant in this regard are the development of "print-capitalism" (Anderson 1991) and the contested reception of concepts of European political modernity. The three documents I describe are connected to three crucial moments in this process: the Constitutional Revolution (1906–1911), the struggles for the nationalization of oil (1951–1953), and the revolution of 1979. While I do not argue that the documents are particularly representative, they are fragments through which some of the dynamics of these events can be glimpsed at: they carry with them, frozen in their particular format, the limits and possibilities of those moments.

Historical and cultural contextualization would, however, only partially dislodge the supposedly natural link between Islam and the people in Iran (and would replace it with an equally stable social link) if it were not accompanied by an effort to question the analytical categories used in describing and organizing temporal narratives. Talal Asad has defined an approach to the social study of Islam in this context, insisting on the need to consider the particular framings of religious discourses, locating the normative constraints of their expressive styles and connecting them to social practice. I use description as a tool for interpreting the heterogeneous trajectories that make up specific social configurations. Neither the model of "a public coming together" (Habermas 1989 [1962]) nor the "public negotiation of meaning in social life" (Geertz 1973), are apt to describe the heterogeneity through which Islam is produced as social practice, because in my view both models posit a homogeneous stability of the components of the social world. The self-transforming discursive tradition of Islam should be viewed as only one of the trajectories of this process: its immanent developments being effected in different instances by external encounters that cannot be considered just concurring factors of its transformation. Other aspects, however much they have encroached upon and related to this tradition, are not isomorphic with it.

To focus on difference is particularly important when discussing Islam, an ostensibly totalizing constellation of discourses in the contemporary world that has the power to vanquish other trajectories and impose itself as the uniform structure of explanation. In my view, the social relevance of religion is best discussed by locating particular power dynamics that structure this relation, without assuming any inherent role of the religious dimension. In the three documents I discuss, the articulation of the link between Islam and the people cannot be considered by itself, but is always intertwined with, and thus reconfigured by other encroaching trajectories: the state, the British, the famine, and also education, charcoal, and money all come to play a role in the ways in which Islam is framed.

Moreover, the "people" too are not a uniform social subject but rather a relational one. I am interested in describing how, in the specific instances I discuss, the "people" are constructed as the primary political subject endowed with sovereignty, understood here as the absolute power to act. The articulation of power that results from the construction of the people as the sovereign effects particular social modalities of the state and society. In 20th-century Iran, particular articulations of this construction became crucial in structuring state power. The process of formation of a constitutional monarchy early in the century initiated the construction of the people as such a referent. Reza Shah's nationalist state structured them as the disciplined actors of "modernization." The people, understood in different ways, were the center of the self-emancipation rhetoric of the 1950s and the object of Pahlavi's state maneuvering in the 1960s and 1970s. With the failure of modernization the people "made the revolution" of 1979, and they figure centrally in one of the current slogans of the Islamic Republic (*millat va doulat*).[1]

I discuss the articulation between Islam and the people in the three documents through the category of publicness. While many analyses privilege spatial conceptualizations of the public, I prefer to consider publicness as the abstract quality of wholeness, openness, and availability described in the Oxford English Dictionary.[2] "Public" is something whole, that is shared and total, encompassing everything, or having the possibility to do so. It is open and available in the sense that it is "in view" and at somebody's disposal. The actualization of these characteristics is a matter of degree and depends on the particular situation and its means of implementation. Considered in such a broad and abstract way, publicness is a quality of people and things that cuts across distinctions such as state/society, because its articulation and its effectiveness are linked to the peculiar conjuncture in which it is produced.

The term correlated to publicness is secrecy (rather than privacy). Partiality, unavailability, and closeness characterize secrecy. Publicness and secrecy, though opposed, are in many ways complementary qualities of the documents I discuss and the relationship between the two is a crucial element in the construction of the people as a political subject in Iran. I will come back to this point in my conclusion.

In the three documents, publicness is brought into view by highlighting the ways in which specific modalities of representation construct the totalizing effect of the articulation of Islam and the people. I wish to draw attention to the degree to which effects of wholeness, openness, and availability are related to the particular possibilities of specific representational media. The published record, the photograph, and the diagram I analyze produce publicness in particular configurations that are connected to the particularities of each of these representational media. I will describe the specific rhetorical strategies put in place in each of the three documents and connect them to the expressive possibilities of published texts, photographs, and diagrams. The relation between Islam and publicness effected through specific technologies of presentation finds its realization in forms of socialization that are as much the cause as the effect of these concatenations.

Public Record

The first document I analyze is the published record of an assembly (*majlis*) summoned in Shiraz on November 6, 1917 by the then governor of the region of Fars, 'Abd ul-Husayn Mirza Farmanfarma.

Eleven years earlier, in 1906, the Constitutional Revolution had instituted a national assembly (Bayat 1991; Afary 1996). A period of intense political confrontations on the forms and scope of government began, marked by the invasive presence of British and Russian interests. The concept of the nation was reconfigured through the restructuring of political categories.

Several recent studies point out how the political vocabulary and its social articulations were profoundly affected in the process (Sohrabi 1999; Tavakoli-Targhi 2001). A new national discourse emerged. The word *millat* that earlier referred to the community of believers acquired a distinctive national character and became the main locus for the construction of political legitimacy, defining the Iranian collectivity. It retained however for some time what Tavakoli-Targhi calls an "ambiguous double articulation" that allowed for the inclusion of the Shi'i imaginary within the nationalist and constitutionalist project. As Tavakoli-Targhi argued, this double articulation soon transformed itself into open confrontation between the two opposed camps of the Constitutionalists and the Shari'atists and resulted in the victory of the former.

This opposition and momentary overtaking however did not dislodge the double bind of the question and the latent or more overt presence of Shi'i trajectories (on either side) continued to characterize the political imaginary in Iran throughout the 20th century. It is not a matter of secularized religion subsumed into nationalist discourse. Rather it is the unstable play and repositioning of religious discourse and its appropriation in different contexts that allowed for its continuing relevance in politics. In this dynamic publicness articulated the degree of visibility, comprehensiveness, and availability of the religious trajectory.

Beside discussions in the National Assembly, these different articulations were dispersed and recomposed in various venues, most notably in the councils and the press, two arenas that featured centrally in the transformation of politics. Councils (*anjuman*s) began to take shape in late 19th century and multiplied in the wake of the constitutional movement, also under the influence of the soviets of the Russian Revolution of 1905.[3]

*Anjuman*s combined forms of political discussion and representation with older forms of male sociability, such as poetic assemblies and mystical brotherhoods. These forms of male socialization comprised heterogeneous gathering practices. Sometimes they were (and are) based on competition among participants, such as in poetic contests; sometimes they were (and are) predicated on a "brotherly" communion in praying, eating, or playing music.[4] The fraternal link refers to a certain type of bond structured on shared feelings and exhibition of maleness. Social positioning was (and is) relevant, as gatherings tend to be homogeneous in terms of the economic stand of participants. Their location cuts across (and dilutes) the state/society/privateness borders: some were held at court, others in the bazaar, in the mosque, at people's houses.

The quantity and variety of *anjuman*s in the constitutional period (urban, rural, formed by intellectuals, merchants, students, shopkeepers of different political orientation, organized on ethnic, regional, or professional affiliation) is an indication of the climate of political and social engagement (Afary 1996: 37–39). *Anjuman*s were contexts for debating political issues and some of them worked as electoral councils for the national assembly and had executive and judicial powers. Some were also engaged in administering funds for schools, roads, and charitable activities (Afary 1996: 73–81). *Anjuman*s were at least in part contexts for the emergence of new political subjectivities: the production of socially and politically committed individuals working together for the country. The degree of "individualization" in the *anjuman*s was fairly high and though they were oriented toward a "general" commitment, their project remained a partial one, not fully public, sometimes secret.

During the period of the Constitutional Revolution, the role of the press expanded greatly. Newspapers and leaflets were crucial in the dissemination of those political ideas that formed the background of the revolutionary movement and the political struggles of the following years. Newspapers reported discussions in the parliament as well as political commentary and criticism. Although it would be exaggerated to locate the birth of a general reading public in these years given the relatively small number of people who could read, it is difficult to underestimate the role of the press in the political process and in the construction of a public opinion (Najmabadi 1998).

These transformations were taking place foremost in the capital Tehran, but in other cities significant forms of political mobilization were happening too. In Shiraz the struggle between the different tribal confederations, the city notables, and the governor that had characterized the articulation of power in the city during the 19th century was being reconfigured in new ways, through a changing balance of power between merchants and tribal leaders in the context of greatly increased British power, which became de facto occupation during World War I (Oberling 1974; Royce 1981; Bayat 1990; Beck 1990; Ruknzada-Adamiyat 1991; Iraji 1999). The British encouraged these transformations by envisaging a differential system of control that conceived the city of Shiraz as separate from the surrounding countryside. In the British vision, the city was the site of government and control, where power could be forcefully exercised but where at the same time a certain consensus had to be built—if not consensus on British presence, at least on the legitimacy of the governor. The countryside, instead, was to be controlled through punishment.[5] In the meantime, the different and often competing opponents of the British appropriated the discourse of the nation in various ways, defining their political imaginary and structuring the meanings and genealogy of the nation itself.

Throughout the summer and fall of 1917, the situation in Shiraz was very tense. The harvest was meager. The price of bread was rising sharply, as in the rest of the country, and discontent was growing in the city. There were a few protests and a policeman was shot. On November 5, a group of women took to the streets but were sent back home by an influential ayatollah.[6] On November 6, the governor convened a general assembly. The published record of this assembly is an interesting document for understanding how, in the tense context briefly described above, political legitimacy was reconfigured through the deployment of the "ambiguous double articulation" of religious and national discourses.

The record of the assembly was printed in the printing shop of the governor (*matb'-i iyalati*) and was probably part of a periodical publication.[7] In any case, the format of the chronicle clearly indicates its public aim and the official character of its preparation. As it becomes clear below, the assembly had a general and inclusive character, and the publication of its record doubles this public quality by making available to everybody the transcription of the event. The fact that the record was published at the time by the governor, highlights how part of this strategy relied on producing politics as a public event: the assembly was organized to be public and its political effectiveness was predicated on its publicness.

The published record of the assembly is similar to the lithographed editions that were published in those years (framing of the page, shape of the colophon). It is composed of different genres of texts: written announcements, letters, and transcriptions of speeches in summarized or verbatim form. Each of these different sections is introduced by titles in bold calligraphy. Each of these texts has stylistic peculiarities. There are different linguistic registers, spoken, written, colloquial, and formal. Some of the reported speeches retain in written form the interjections, repetitions, and suspended sentences typical of spoken language, while others seem to have been rewritten. Within the speeches, there are also striking differences in individual styles: some are direct, others allusive; some are blunt declarations, others subtle plays with rhetorical figures. The sentences that introduce these diverse texts or describe the proceedings of the assembly between the different speeches (such as the description of the voting procedure) combine this variety of textual genres in a coordinated whole. The result is a cohesive and convincing presentation of the event.

From a textual point of view the document is therefore in many ways an exemplification of a process of political exchange and participatory decision making: this effect stems as much from the chronicle of the assembly as from the textual strategies of its narrative. Its hybrid character also locates it in a sort of intermediary position in relation to the periodical press. If, taking the lead from Walter Benjamin (1968), the press is that form of communication that ensures the exclusion of the events it depicts from the experience of readers, this published record projects the event it describes into a differential space where government is enacted. On the other hand, for its formal characteristics as well as for reasons that will become clearer below, such as mentioning people's names, the distancing effect of the press is only partial and the record does tend to include its potential reader in the event itself: the participants in the assembly are also the potential readers of the record, and the account of the assembly is constructed in such a way that makes specific references to individual and recognizable members of the summoned "community."

The record opens with the "leaflet of invitation" (*surat-i da'vatnama*) sent out by the vice-governor to convene the assembly:

> The most important task today in the city is to provide tranquility (*asayish*) to the people (*'umum*) as far as bread is concerned, and to take care of the

poor and the weak. To obtain this good aim it is necessary to organize a consultative assembly (*majlis-i mashvirati*) with the presence of *hujjatulislam*[8]
and *'ulama*—be their benediction upon us—chiefs, experts in agriculture,
guilds (*asnaf*), merchants (*tujjar*), nobles (*a'yyan*), and landowners (*malikin*).
Through the consultations and the opinions of these well-intentioned people of this country this benevolent aim will be reached and implemented.
With this announcement we kindly ask all gentlemen to come to the
Governor's fort on Thursday, the 21th of Muharram three hours before noon,
ready to discuss, consult with each other, and vote, so that with such good
intentions they will fulfill their national (*milli*) duty. We ask for forgiveness if
the priority of names and titles has not been respected and if the seating
arrangement in the assembly will not follow the status of the person. Since
there is a lot to do we ask you not to be late. (2–3)

This announcement sets the tone of the whole document and presents the
conceptual characters that shape its rhetoric. There is famine and shortage
of bread in the city. People are dying as a result. The state of emergency is
a constitutive element of the assembly. It frames the ways in which power
is displayed and articulated in it. The exceptions that the state of emergency brings forth, such as the convocation of the assembly itself or
the neglect of perceived customary rules of etiquette reveal the transformations that are taking place in the configuration of power. The assembly
is an instance of such transformations and the whole event can be seen as
a moment of restructuring that concerns the scope and techniques of
government.

The announcement proposes a political model: the convocation of a
consultative assembly that aims at gathering the widest array of people in
order to take common decisions through consultation and effectively
counter the famine. The categories of people convoked correspond to the
six classes of voters that were designated for electing the national assembly (Afari 1996: 64),[9] reinforcing the representative character of the gathering. The announcement explicitly frames the event as a *milli* duty. By
1917 *milli* certainly refers to the constituting political collectivity of the
nation; however, in the record it still often carries with it reference to the
community of believers so that in several passages *milli* can be translated
"national" as well as "religious": it is through this ambiguity that "the people" are born as a subject, that sovereignty is bestowed upon them and they
are attributed the power to act.

While the record of the assembly emphasizes repeatedly the general
character of the meeting, summoned to find a "common" solution to the
famine through a process of consultation, it also posits a constant distinction
between the people present in the assembly, who are those who have to
consult, vote, and act, and those who are needy and absent. The distinction
between *khas* and *'amm*, between the "distinguished" and the "commoners"
that had been for centuries one of the main partitions of Iranian society, is
here proposed on new grounds.

The term *khas* used to refer to the elite as distinguished from the majority,
the group of the selected few who knew and constituted the ethical model

(Abedi and Fischer 1993: 223–24). Here however the *khas* are "the people" present in the assembly and exhibit the qualities of wholeness and openness of the majority. They are not however an indistinct crowd. At the end of the announcement there is a list of 158 names that, although not stated clearly, are probably the addressees of the invitation to the assembly. The present public is thus not an indistinct whole but a gathering of identifiable people with a social role and location. There is a hierarchy among them as their division by category in the announcement reveals, even if this hierarchy is denied in the assembly: the usual seating arrangement will not be observed. The absent, the unnamed and undistinguished who are sometimes called '*amm*, or more often the "poor," are the object of administration, those excluded from the assembly, and whose destiny is being discussed and taken care of.

After the announcement the document chronicles the event, recounting the arrival of four hundred or so people at the governor's residence. The first person to speak is not the governor, as it might have been expected, but the *hujjatulislam* Shaykh Murtiza Mujtahid Mahallati.[10] Shaykh Murtiza's speech, reported in a summarized way in the chronicle, makes clear why he intervened first:

> It is not my habit to participate in this kind of assemblies, however since I am here it is necessary for me to say a few things . . . Your highness Farmanfarma, are you head of the region? I do not know. Are you governor? I do not know. Are you powerful? I do not know. Are you great? I do not know. Today everybody is looking at you. Is it for your money or your power? I do not know. Do you have 500.000 *touman*? I do not know. You do not have anything? I do not know. I want one thing from you. I want help for these weak and poor people, my heart burns for them. Yesterday I was coming back from the house of Mirza Abu al-Fazl when I saw two poor women who were carrying a bowl on their head with blood in it. I was walking and all of a sudden I hear these women cry. I thought their children had died but when I looked I saw that the bowl one of them was carrying had fallen and the blood in it had spilled. I have nothing to do with the police nor with the administration nor with Farmanfarma.
>
> My heart grieves for these people (*mardum*). O people (*mardum*) don't you have honor, religion and humanity? Can you recognize God? Why is bread so expensive in this country? . . . Bread does not come all the way from Europe. I am a *mujtahid*, Praised be the Lord. I decree (*hukm*) that who will help in this question can account the expenses as *zakat* . . . Mr Farmafarma why you do not oppose the speculators? Farmanfarma if you practice virtue God will raise you. If you do not fulfill your duty, fear God. Farmanfarma, are you rich? I do not know. You do not have anything? I do not know, but save the people, the people are getting lost. Landowners, you people who are here, help! I will do what I can. Everybody knows I do not have anything, but I will sell my books and I will contribute a hundred *touman*s. (5–6)

As the record specifies, soon after this emotional speech, Shaykh Murtiza quits the assembly leaving two representatives in his place as if to express his ambivalent position toward the initiative. In his speech, through a very effective rhetoric that can be sensed even in the summarized transcription, Shaykh Murtiza positions himself outside the order of the assembly and does not fully legitimize it, while at the same time recognizing its relevance.

Shaykh Murtiza challenges the authority of the governor and asks for accountability. The attack is harsh, especially if juxtaposed to the respectful and complimentary way in which other religious scholars in the assembly address the governor. The series of direct and blunt questions, posed as coming from the voice of conscience, produce an ethical tension, a call to duty that while addressed primarily to the governor, is also directed at the people in the assembly, rising the question of collective responsibility.[11]

While Shaykh Murtiza does not put forth an alternative legitimacy or questions directly the initiatives of the governor, his suspicious attitude and his declarations of intent place him, and the religious authority he embodies in an ambivalent relation to political power. Within the production of publicness, his speech positions the religious at a peculiar juncture to the political. On the one hand, Shaykh Murtiza supports the assembly and the decisions it will take and significantly contributes to its effectiveness by issuing the decree by which offerings for the bread will be counted as *zakat*: fulfilling what had been called a "national obligation" the people present at the assembly are also, at the same time, obeying a religious duty. On the other hand, Shaykh Murtiza positions himself outside the political order ("I do not know"): his authority does not stem from any privileged relation with the political but originates from his religious knowledge and his ethical stance. The governor and the people in the assembly will have demonstrated their accountability and their humanity only when they will have done something. The distancing position of the religious ensures its authority. The governor's actions are not public (Shaykh Murtiza and the people "do not know" what he is doing), while publicness is firmly grounded in religious discourse: God knows what Farmanfarma is doing. Religion becomes the arena for the evaluation of the governor and the parallel accountability of the people (and the 'ulama) as a whole.[12]

Not all the religious scholars who intervene in the course of the assembly share Shaykh Murtiza's position. The differences between 'ulama have to be understood in political terms: while some like the Mahallati group forcefully locate themselves at a distance from the governor, others do not step outside his shadow. Religious discourse per se is not a differentiating element. Most of the people who intervene in the assembly or write letters afterwards resort to categories that refer to the discursive tradition of Islam. They do however modulate their approach in very different ways. The difference among the participants emerges in the ways in which these categories intersect with the rhetoric of the speech or the letter.

It is the turn of the governor to speak. Farmanfarma notes that since the assembly gathers representatives from every social group, it is as if he is addressing all the people of the region, thus reiterating the consultative and general character of the assembly. He defends his administration and argues that he never appropriated funds or bribed functionaries,[13] that he is a patriot, and that his profession is the art of government:

> My trade is government, I studied the art of war and, basically, I am a *mujtahid* of Iranian military art and I am sorry that up until now I could not practice my military skills in this country. For this reason and for the responsibility I have towards God and the nation it is my duty to explain to you the fundamental questions as far as I know them (11).[14]

The governor's positioning corresponds to a reconfiguration of power; government is here presented as a "trade," a profession that involves certain skills and certain responsibilities. The parallel with religious authority involves establishing a relation between government and knowledge. It is also a response to Shaykh Murtiza's declaration of authority. The art of government is military art, which Farmanfarma learned at the Austrian Military Mission in Tehran (Wright 2000: 107). But it is also the art of finding practical solutions.

The governor explains that the people convoked are not obliged to donate money, except paying the religious tax, which, being a "sacred (*muqaddas*) question" is not subject to his will but responds to a higher order. This, as other statements, produces the space of the assembly (as represented in the record) as a free association of individuals rather than as mandatory on the governor's summoning. This projection of will onto the people structures a process of recognition. The vision of authority proposed rests on mutual social obligation; an obligation that is of a moral and therefore religious order: it is this duty that brings the people together and makes them act toward a common goal. The governor is acting only on their behalf, realizing their will, thanks to his art of government. The relation between religious discourse and public here is quite different from that established in Shaykh Murtiza's speech. Though the sacred order (which is the funding element of the people as sovereign, what gives them the power to act) is placed atop the governor, in fact it becomes the basis for a reconfiguration of the legitimacy of the governor's power in the new consultative mode of the Constitutional Revolution.

The governor talks about the famine. He argues that "mindful" people should consider that "certain events have certain consequences: drought and grasshoppers effect famine and inflation." He also mentions fights between different tribes or sections of the same confederation as concomitant reasons, but he does not talk about the British. By invoking natural and political causes the governor is defending himself. The naturalization of the chain of causes and effects dislocates social conflict (and the British presence) while establishing a relation between rationality and government: only the people who do not reflect fail to understand that the famine has natural causes, that it does not depend on the market, on the war, or on the British.

The governor proposes the institution of temporary bakeries for producing bread at controlled price. These bakeries would be created with a government fund and with people's contributions. The record narrates that after the governor's speech people got up one by one and announced their participation in the relief effort. People cheer each time a person offers his contribution: "Among all the cheering that came from each corner, a wealthy individual named 'Abd ul-Khaliq Kirbala'i refused to offer his contribution, offering what others present clearly believed were unacceptable excuses." In response, "some people said we should cry 'down with him' and the people present, all together, cried 'down with him,' and they all laughed" (19).

The governor then proposes the election of a committee (*hay'at*) of representatives from the different groups present in the assembly, charged with overseeing the setting up of the temporary bakeries and the distribution of grain. Shaykh Murtiza who had been asked to participate in it had declined.

> The governor ordered that a great amount of barley and wheat-bread be brought along with cheese, saying that "since today everybody was equal, we are going to eat a common (*'umumi*) meal of bread, cheese and onion." Bread, cheese and onions were brought in sufficient quantity and everybody, the governor included ate with great satisfaction and after eating drank tea, smoked the water-pipe and white sheets of paper were distributed among those present to write their secret vote and choose the committee (22).

The communal meal seals the assembly that met to provide bread for the poor. Here the word *'umumi* refers both to the shared consumption of food and to its simplicity (there is no meat or rice). Even the governor ate people's food, poor people's food.

The production of a new form of power passes through a reformulation of the relation between the rulers and the ruled, or the creation of new political subjects. The assembly of November 6, 1917 can be read as such an instance. The production of this new form of power, the reformulation of the social pact, takes place through the production of a public form of welfare. It is public not only because it is based on collective participation but also because it establishes a form of visibility. In Shaykh Murtiza's provoking intervention the religious order is located outside the political and the relation between religion and public effects a partition (if not a fracture) between the governor and the people. In the speeches of the governor and the other religious leaders the relation established between religious discourse and public legitimizes a new form of power. The published chronicle of the assembly weaves together these conflicting positions by combining "national" responsibility and religious duty for the goal of reorganizing a community whose main bond is the administration of the poor. During the same assembly, the governor also announced the creation or renovation of seven "places for the poor, the weak and the orphans" (*mahal bara-yi fuqara zahifa va yatam*). These were houses where "the poor" could sleep and eat. The moment of the construction of a visibility of government and that of its public coincides with the institution of the separation between the participants and the excluded.

The Durkheimian effects of the published chronicle, its projection of a social collective ready to mobilize as an agent of transformation endowed with a "collective consciousness," contrasts vividly with the situation around the document. The struggles between the tribes (Qashqa'is in particular) the bazaaris, and the British mentioned above, continued and worsened by the end of the war when the Qashqa'is were defeated. The published chronicle should be read as a token in this struggle. A token that mobilizes qualities of wholeness, openness, and availability in an attempt to shift alliances and transform a challenge to the governor into a "natural" state of emergency, so that "the people" instead of taking up rifles set up bakeries and ate onion and bread.

Public Photograph

The second document I discuss is a photograph of a group of young men holding bicycles, taken in Shiraz in the 1950s.

The young men are disposed on two rows in the courtyard of a building. They are all dressed in trousers and coats; one of them, at the far left of the photograph wears a bow tie. Each of them (except one) holds a bicycle. All the bicycles appear in good conditions, all have mudguards, most of them have a light, at least one has a pump, and at least one has a rear mirror positioned on the handle. All the young men stare into the camera, oriented diagonally in relation to the group.[15] Although not martial, the posture of the young men is orderly. These young men belong to a bicycling club organized by an entrepreneurial ayatollah, Sayyid Nuriddin.

A charismatic figure, Sayyid Nuriddin (1894–1960)[16] had a great following among the merchants and artisans of the bazaar. Proposing an interpretation of Islam based on social activism, Nuriddin aimed at an "educational revolution," a movement of reform that would emancipate the "people" from poverty and ignorance. He was active in organizing welfare, distributing medicine, food, and coal to the people. He reconfigured the groups (*hay'at*) that organized the public mourning processions and prayer sessions on the occasion of religious holidays. These gatherings had a neighborhood base and were one of the main forms of male socialization. Run by older or more charismatic figures within the neighborhood, these groups were also means for social control and were often in competition with other neighborhoods. Sayyid Nuriddin reorganized these groups by creating an integrated network across the whole city of Shiraz, emphasizing the loyalty and mutual solidarity between the members of the groups.

These renewed *hay'at*s were venues for an array of social activities that beside processions and prayer sessions included initiatives such as the bicycling club. They were also the organizational core of a political party created by Sayyid Nuriddin, the Brothers' Party (*hizb-i baradaran*) that, as its name underlines, proposed a religiously connoted "fraternity" as the founding element of social cohesion. In the early 1950s the party had the majority of elected candidates to the national parliament from Shiraz and was, at the local level, the main opponent of the National Front led by Prime Minister Musaddiq. The party's supporters often organized punitive expeditions against their political opponents and were active in disrupting protests in favor of the oil nationalization policies of Musaddiq. The party had also several newspapers directly or indirectly connected to it. The newspapers circulated in the bazaar and carried articles by Nuriddin and his affiliates on the need to act "as Muslims" in daily and political life, exemplary tales on the Imams and other religious figures, as well as satirical poems attacking their political rivals.

The "people" played a crucial role in the political events of the 1950s. Emerged as a political subject during the Constitutional Revolution and consolidated into a "national mass" during the reign of Riza Shah, "the people" acquired new political relevance in the aftermath of Word War II, becoming the principal articulation through which different visions of the nation were constructed. Mass demonstrations became crucial moments of political recognition. By transforming oil into a national icon,

Prime Minister Musaddiq pushed for the idea of a self-determining people that could take their resources into their own hands. Musaddiq formed a coalition that included both the communist party (called, *tudah*, the mass) and sectors of the 'ulama. The coalition did not last long and was dismantled in 1953 by a CIA coup that was able to mobilize "the people" (or, rather, to simulate mobilization) deploying the same kind of rhetoric that had been implemented by Musaddiq himself. All these different appropriations and constructions of the people (as a violent mob, as an imagined proletariat, as the owners of the country's resources, as a community of believers) through their diverging trajectories solidified the people as the stable source of sovereignty, the one that had to be addressed and mobilized by whomever entered the political arena.

Within this national context, the activities of Nuriddin can be understood as efforts to construct the people as a political subject through a religious discourse that emphasized solidarity between individuals, under the watchful eye of a patriarchal figure. Transforming consolidated practices such as charitable activities or processions into constitutive moments of new forms of solidarity that centered on the construction of the people as the principal metaphor of aggregation, Nuriddin effectively established publicness as an important sign of the religious articulation. The implementation of his vision was much more connected to the set of practices described above than to a specific political position.

Not all Nuriddin's activities had the same degree of publicness: some of his initiatives like food distribution during religious holidays were oriented to everybody, others like the constitution of *hay'at*s or similar groups were more selective; they were however all guided by a celebration of fraternity based on communal practices such as prayer sessions, sport, and political demonstrations.

His detractors attacked him for selling off religion for food, for reducing participation to collective prayers and holidays to a mere trade-off between rice and expressions of religious piety. But this relation between food and piety, rather than revealing the mutual opportunistic relation between Nuriddin and his followers, exemplifies how the production of wholeness, openness, and availability took place in this case through the implementation of concrete acts and was connected to particular objects or services. Certainly Nuriddin's words were effectively public, but the ready availability of food, charcoal, and medicine gave to his public words a particularly realistic dimension that heightened publicness. Things were as important as words in this configuration.

The production of publicness relies here on a tautological structure: Nuriddin gives food to the people, thus they think he is for the people, and the people are for him, because he gives food to them. This circularity establishes "public" services and things as self-evident: their practice reinforces their availability, which makes them effective in turn.

The technology of public presentation that best inscribes tautology is photography. As Roland Barthes has noted in his classic discussion, the prominent indexical quality of the photograph carries with it a tautological aspect: the photograph always carries its referent with it, it shows what it is (Barthes 1980). Moreover, as theorists of different persuasions have stressed, an important element of the "photographic" genre is its reality-producing effect. These characteristics make photography a particularly apt medium for the representation of publicness. The photographic display enhances the public quality of people, things, and situations depicted, while the photograph itself is available for viewing by everybody.[17]

Photography in Iran spread in the second half of the 19th century: individual portraits, pictures of groups and public events (Adle and Zoka 1983; Afshar 1983). There is a remarkable quantity of photographs of the protagonists of the Constitutional Revolution and of its crucial moments (Afshar 1992: 103–55; 217–58). In Shiraz, several photographers were active since the late 19th century.[18] By the 1950s photography was no longer a novelty but an established genre of reproduction; at least since the early 1900s prominent 'ulama had their portraits taken. Nuriddin's use of photography in comparison with that of other religious leaders of the time is particularly extensive. While in fact there are portraits of all the major religious figures active in that period, Nuriddin's portraits are many and circulated widely among his followers: today there are still numerous shops in the city that have a portrait of Nuriddin hanging on the wall. There are also numerous photographs of the different associations he coordinated. One is the photograph of the bicycling group above.

The photograph is constructed as representing an orderly and "clean" group engaged in healthy bodily activities; modernity, signified by the bicycles, is the means through which a disciplined emancipation is achieved. The absence of an explicit hierarchy and the fact that each young man holds his personal bicycle (with both hands firmly on the handle) reinforces the representation of this brotherly and masculine order. While it is possible to speculate over the social location of the young men (by focusing for example on the differences in their dress and shoes),[19] the overall effect is one of cohesion and homogeneity. These are Nuriddin's men, his people. Because they are his group, this picture does not exhibit publicness as a general quality, but rather frames it within the orderly and closed community of the bikers: they are a whole and are available, though they are not open to everybody. The expressive force of the photograph lies in the cohesion of the image. Nuriddin's social projects conceived the needy people as the object of social action, but grounded this action on the mobilization of tightly knit groups of militants who would be ready to distribute food, mobilize for communal prayers but also use their clubs against opponents.

In the photograph there is however a young man who, although aligned with the others, does not hold a bike. Instead he has a notebook in his left hand and a pen in the front pocket of his coat. Why is he there then? He is 'Ali Asghar 'Arab, a young shopkeeper, journalist, and poet who was one of the closest associates of Nuriddin and coordinated several of the activities of the ayatollah. Whether he was responsible or not for ordering the group in front of the camera, his presence can be interpreted as indexing a different reading of the photograph. He signals the "staged" quality of the photograph, breaks the tautology of the indexical effect, and points to the prescriptive character of the bikers' association: the production of autonomous subjects riding toward modernity is an effect of the photograph itself.

The contextual reading of the photograph offers this different interpretation. However, rather than diffusing the photographic effect into the web of its context, I prefer to make the difference significant. There is nothing in this picture that refers to religion; it is only by knowing the context of the photograph that one knows of the link of the *hay'at* network with Nuriddin. Knowing the context, the absence of any overt religious sign is conspicuous. It suggests that the restricted public produced in this instance, though constituted through a network that articulated itself through religious practices, was not the carrier of an autonomous religious discourse that needed to be coded as such in order to be made public. It seems to suggest that this absence was not considered a lack of any kind in relation to the "sport" activity of the bicycling group. This does not imply that practices were not religiously coded, nor that every photograph related to Nuriddin and his followers does not have religious signs in it. Rather, it is possible to argue that in the photograph of the biking group the relation between religiosity and publicness is so firmly established that there is no need to visually inscribe it: the young men are holding their handles so firmly that there is no need to restate in which direction they will cycle.

Public Diagram

The third document I analyze is a diagram that accompanies a short booklet entitled: "Constitution of the Islamic Society of the Teachers of Shiraz" (*asasnama-yi jam'a-yi islami-yi mu'alliman-i shiraz*).

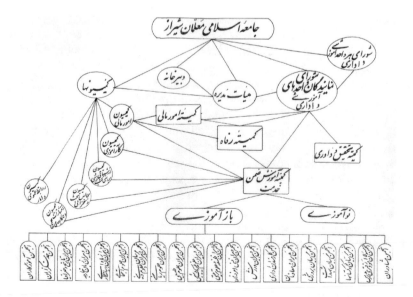

The booklet presents a project to institutionalize procedures of decision making and representation among the teachers of Shiraz by creating an assembly, a system of councils, and an executive committee. As its author told me in 1997, this project was approved in the summer of 1979 but was never implemented. He described it to me as a model that could be valid for different kinds of associations and indeed for any political structure. Infused with the language of the first days of the revolution, the document can be read as a utopian manifesto, as an idealized model of social relations based on cooperation and activism. Even if the constitution is to some extent specifically tailored for an organization of teachers, the kind of representative structure proposed is a general model of social organization.

The diagram that accompanies the Constitution presents the different organs of the Society and shows the relations between them through straight lines that connect them. Diagrams can be thought of as conceptualizations that emphasize the relational aspect. According to Charles S. Peirce, diagrams are iconic, they represent the object they refer to primarily in terms of similitude and emphasize the relations between the parts of the object represented. As schematic images, diagrams for Peirce give an idea of the object represented by reproducing analogous relations (Peirce 1998: 274). Relations are therefore central to the diagrammatic form of representation. As icons, diagrams are signs of possibility and in this sense, general.

Graphically, the diagram of the teachers' Society is the conjuncture of different traditions of knowledge and presentation. It bears resemblance to diagrams designed by Muslim mystics to describe the path of knowledge that the seeker must follow to reach complete cognizance of the Unity (*vahdat-i vujud*). In these diagrams, the related parts are usually either concepts (such as affection, love, etc.), figures (animals, animal-shaped constellation of stars), or characters (often prophets and imams, each embodying a specific quality).[20] At the same time the Society's diagram is also similar to diagrams used in Western social and political science to illustrate the workings of associations, the organization of a state, or to present conceptual models of society.

The graphics of the diagram combine rectangles, ovals, and circles with straight lines. The size of the different geometrical figures is, at least in part, proportional to the size of the unit they represent. The diagram has the form of a polycentric whole: a system of connected parts that balance each other. The collective body of the teachers, the Society itself, occupies the top of the diagram. The different organs of the association descend (rather than ascend, as one might expect in a structure based on representation) from this collective and undifferentiated whole: they appear as specifications deriving from a common, overarching source. The descending order of the diagram produces wholeness as a source of the organization proposed.[21]

Considered as a pure model of relations the diagram exemplifies from top to bottom a passage from an undivided collectivity to a coordinated multiplicity. The hierarchical relations are structured in such a way as to form a network that finds its resolution only in the top unit, toward which all the others converge.

The utopian vision of the diagram is transformed into law in the booklet that accompanies it. This balanced and suspended view is distant from the context in which it was produced, that is, in the months that followed the revolution of 1979, and carries with it little trace of the struggles that were taking place in the institutionalization process of the new state.

However, the teachers' constitution is deeply connected to the constitution of the Islamic Republic, written at about the same time. The adjective Islamic that defines the teachers' assembly is a specific reference to this origin and an ideological declaration that is substantiated in several of the articles of the Society.[22] The first of the listed goals of the association is: "to enrich the contents of teaching with ideological issues in such a way as to respond to the needs of a Muslim society (*jama'a-yi islami*)" (Art. 7, alif).

The word ideology (*iduluji*) recurs often in the text and refers to a systematized body of ideas that are to be made socially relevant. It is ideology that constructs the relation between religion and publicness. Although several articles of the teachers' constitution refer to Islam as *matkab* or as *din* (also used in the plural to refer to the religions of the book), as a legal and ethical school or as a system of reference and belief, it is the term ideology that relates Islam and the social collective of the teachers.

The Society is a professional association that gathers the employees of the Ministry of Education and from this point of view it could be considered as an integral part of state organization (the symbol of the Islamic Republic appears on the cover of the booklet). However the utopian space of the Society is constructed in such a way as to be completely autonomous. On the one hand it is possible to say that, in a revolutionary mode, the difference between society and the state is erased. On the other, the Society is not presented as being part of the state bureaucracy or to depend on some external authority. The state is subsumed within society as a self-governing entity in which there is no separation between the people and the government.

The vocabulary that defines the different units of the Society comes from the political experiences of 20th-century Iran, and is related to some of the forms of association discussed above. In contemporary Persian the word *jama'a* that names the Society as a whole has more or less the semantic spectrum of the word "society" in English, referring both to forms of association (by projecting a much stronger collective quality) and to society as a sociological concept (cf. also Abedi and Fischer 1993: 223). The indistinct will of the people is often evoked in revolutionary rhetoric as the original motor behind the revolution of 1979 and scenes of mass demonstrations are often chosen to depict the revolutionary order of the Islamic Republic. Michel Foucault in his newspaper reports from Tehran was impressed by what he felt was the realization of something akin to general will (cf. chapter 1 in this volume by LeVine and Salvatore). The collective and undifferentiated character of this general configuration of the teachers (indeed of "the people," or, may be more aptly, of the mass) is underscored by the fact that this unit of the organization is an abstract one, while all the others are effective organizational organs of the teachers.

The units that descend from the collectivity of the teachers are elected councils that have legislative and executive functions. The word *shura* (council) indicates consultative assemblies and is used in the Islamic Republic to refer to different kinds of councils with legislative powers (such as the Council of the Guardians). The teachers' constitution states that in order to be elected to the Councils of the Representatives a member has to:

1. Be a Muslim or profess one of the religions accepted by the Constitution [of the Islamic Republic];
2. Believe (*mu'taqid*) in the Constitution of the Islamic Republic of Iran and in *vilayat-i faqih*;
3. Do not belong to any of the parties, groups, associations, and fractions that are considered illegal according to the Constitution of the Islamic Republic of Iran;
4. Be committed to develop the aims of the Islamic Society of the Teachers (Art. 14).

The Constitution of the Islamic Republic and the concept of *vilayat-i faqih* are the conditions of possibility of the association: they structure the rules of accession to the consultative organs of the teachers. The conceptual space of the association coincides with these ideological boundaries. The first three points are however also specifically related to the context of the period. The first clause can be related to the Baha'i who are not recognized in the constitution. The second to those within the religious field who opposed the concept of *vilayat-i faqih* and argued for a different articulation of the religious within the instituting state. The third point refers to the increasing regimentation of the numerous political organizations of different kinds that had developed during the revolution and in its aftermath.

Among the five units that descend from the collectivity of the teachers, the Executive Committee (*hay'at-i mudiriyya*) has a central position. Today the word *hay'at* is used in this and other syntagmas to refer to small committees, such as the ministers' cabinet, that have legislative powers. However, its choice is also an evocation of the groups, called with the same name, which organize collective prayers and mourning rituals discussed above and are still existent today, in Shiraz and other cities.

The professional orientation of the Society makes it somewhat similar to artisans' guilds, especially in the scope of its activities. The web of units that descend from the Assembly of the Representatives and the Commissions cover three main areas of activities: administration, welfare, and education. The pragmatic function of many of these organs is expressed through the two words that designate them, *kumisiun* and *kumita* borrowed from French but by this date commonly used in Persian. The definition of specific units devoted to administration responds to organizational needs, but underlines a particular care for the operational level and a concern for the efficiency of the Society. The *kumita-yi rifah*, literally the committee for abundance, is the unit directly concerned with charitable activities, which are listed as one the principal aims of the Society (Art. 7); the committee is described as organized "through cooperatives." This corresponds to the early orientation of the revolutionary state that had set up cooperatives for all state employees.[23] Welfare, one of the cornerstones of religious practice and duty is here externalized into a collective concern to be administered bureaucratically.

The responsibility of the well-being of the people is part of the collective body of the Society, which as in all other matters, acts as a whole.[24] In this regard it is interesting to note that the Society fulfills some of the functions of a union but not through contract negotiations; it is the system of welfare that assists the members and absorbs possible conflicts by redistributing wealth and thus neutralizing fractures.

The educational dimension appears as the overarching activity of the association. There is equal concern devoted to teaching and to educating the teachers. The word *anjuman* is used to define the 20 units at the bottom of the diagram, which are groups for "continuing education" (*bazamuzi*) divided by subject matters and roles within the administration. *Anjuman* as noted above refers to different kinds of gatherings and is not restricted to politics, but its use here is a reference to the social and political activism pursued by those groups since the time of the Constitutional Revolution. There are also commissions for organizing conferences and discussions, for studying, writing, and publishing textbooks for teachers' training.

The emphasis on education is surely related to the specific project, but it is also indicative of a general pedagogical disposition, linked to the understanding of Islam as knowledge. More specifically, in the context of the Islamic Republic, especially in its early days, one should recall the debates on the role and scope of university and the fact that the theory of *vilayat-i faqih* implies the inscription of specialized religious knowledge at the very core of the political structure. Education as a societal model however does not refer only to a privileged relation to knowledge. It structures subjectivities on self-improvement. The discourse of *agahi* was central during the revolution (Khosrokhavar 1997: 37–65). *Agahi* refers to a movement toward self-awareness and realization.[25] It implies the conceptualization of a transformation of the self, oriented toward greater understanding and consciousness.

The relevance given to self-improvement has as its counterpoint a consideration of the perfectibility of present society that is always seen as not yet quite what it should be. This pedagogical mission combined with an emphasis on social activism results in a reforming posture that aims at the transformation of the present state of things and envisions a continuing education toward the bettering of society.

Islam is the frame of this process and is seen both as the essential condition of possibility for this movement and its guideline. On the one hand Islam is objectified as an ideology. On the other, as the diagram shows, this vision of Islam is marked by a participatory and consultative ideal: councils and debates are considered essential for its implementation. This solidarity is reinforced through the welfare system included in the organization. It is through this configuration that the effects of wholeness, openness, and availability are produced. In the utopian space of the diagram the relation between religion and publicness is structured upon ideology and coordination. As a utopia, the Constitution of the Teachers does not envision so much a revolutionary movement as the abstract realization of a social model, which in such a frozen form is deprived of the movement and engagement that it presupposes.

The diagram itself is the model for the relations between religion and publicness. An abstract social machine constituted of interconnected parts and regulated by "Islamic ideology," the Society produces perfectly attuned subjects that have a total commitment to the institution and work for the education of "the people." The Constitution of the Society was never implemented. A relation between religion and publicness severed from any tangential trajectory and projected into a social void found no way of effecting its project.

Conclusion: The Limits of Publicness

In the three documents analyzed, I focused on the relation between religion and publicness, exploring the particular ways in which the latter is effected in relation to specific technologies of presentation. While discussing some of the contextual information, I purposefully focused on the documents themselves and on the particularities of print, photographs, and diagrams. I also hinted at several clues within the documents that point toward different readings of the events, if matched with contextual information. These different readings are not an unveiling of a hidden truth behind the representational superficiality of the documents; rather, they show how the production of the quality of publicness is made possible through the structuring of a limit.

Beyond this limit is the opposite but correlate quality of secrecy, a trajectory that effects selection, partiality, and unavailability. The role of secrecy is uneven and, as publicness, varies in degrees and kind in the different instances that I discussed. However, this role is pervasive and constitutes an important feature of the social worlds I evoked through the three fragments. The thematization of secrecy in different forms and degrees is a recurrent trajectory in Iranian history, and in the 20th century seems to have accompanied the transformations of publicness. The role ascribed to freemasonry in social movements and coups, the recurring mobilization of "mobs" to stalemate "peoples' " demonstrations, the parallel organization of tight small groups of activists, the development of a covered opposition during the 1970s, and also the extremely refined political analyses that posit secrecy as the generative matrix of national and international politics and most of all the continued discussion around these themes, signal the relevance of secrecy as a correlate to publicness in Iranian politics.

The three documents analyzed here confirm the resilience of this dynamic of publicness and secrecy, especially when read through contextual information. The record of the consultative assembly of 1917 makes little reference to the British occupation of Shiraz. Constructed as a performative document to effect legitimation, it describes a constituent community engaged in debates over the form and scope of government and the administration of the poor. Without the British however there is no legitimacy of the governor and no money to set up temporary bakeries.[26] By masking the principal source of legitimacy of the governor, the published record constructs an autonomous arena of consultation in which dissenting opinions can be voiced. The production of this "public sphere" is made possible by the elusion of the colonial dependence of the assembly and the differential effect of colonial forms of governmentality. This does not mean that the assembly is just the governor's own projection, nor that the British colonial archive holds the truth that unmasks the fiction of the assembly.

While certainly the colonial trajectory cannot be underestimated (in terms of money and suggestions to the governor), its articulation does not exclude the production of a local conjuncture. Caught between British pressure and an emergent (and partially reactive) constituency of the people, the governor set up the assembly as a way to redirect the situation. Publicness and secrecy thus are simultaneously at work and not only from the governor's point of view. Mahallati's challenging speech too, is not only a hint in that direction, a coveted denunciation of the governor's political and economic position but also an indirect, implicit, and partial support for his initiative.

The public effects of the photograph of Nuriddin's bicycling group are predicated on the self-organized and autonomous character of the group, produced by the photograph itself. The partiality of the group, while limiting its availability, strengthens its cohesion. This limited and self-assured publicness (enhanced by the figure of the person without a bicycle who organized and directed the others) does not need an argument to be sustained or justified: it purports to be self-evident and strong. The 1950s were a time of confrontations when different ideas and practices around "the people" constructed this political subject differently. In this configuration Nuriddin's politics of social involvement produced an effective and concrete form of popular mobilization. Predicated on the activism of restricted (and in this sense to a certain degree "secret") groups, it promoted an unlimited publicness articulated through services and things.

The bikers were disciplined people that could be mobilized not only to disrupt demonstrations of the National Front, but also to distribute food, or to organize rituals. Religious discourse interjected these practices without however becoming the totalizing and uniform trajectory "in view."

The pedagogical character of the diagram stages modernity as the difference between "what we are" and "what we should be" and resolves it in utopian fashion by projecting it into an abstract relational machine. The ideology of improvement inscribed in the diagram produces it as a self-contained mechanism that generates its own differential potential in order to fulfill it. This "public sphere" abstracts the struggles of the revolution and harmonizes them in a functional whole regulated by the condition of possibility of *vilayat-i faqih. Vilayat-i faqih* stabilizes the difference between this and other "public spheres" ensuring its self-containment and thus marking its limit. The absolute and restricted character of this principle shades the principled publicness of the diagram, which, from this point of view, appears to be predicated upon a "secret" injunction of conformity to a "non-public" law. The utopian diagram that exhibits the total publicness of its workings is at the same time constructed on the secrecy of its foundation. Religious discourse is on either side of this correlation: it is both the organizing principle through which the public mechanism is regulated and the one that sustains restricted access to the law.

Different instances of the articulation between Islam and the people produced in Iran quite different outcomes that cannot be separated from contingencies. If however one wishes for a moment to congeal conjunctures and open up a discussion about the present, certainly the effects of publicness seem to remain pervasive in today's Iran. Seen through the prism of the quality of publicness and its media, the articulation does seem to have moved from a projected correlation between religious discourse and the people, to a complete identification of the two poles, so that today religious discourse cannot be articulated socially without reference to the people. The effects of publicness have been so pervasive on the articulation that the notion of the people as a sovereign subject seems to be the necessary starting point of any social (and state) intervention, curiously reciprocating the ascribed naturalness of the link as portrayed by Western media. The ubiquity of publicness freezes the articulation of Islam and the people in a set of fixed and prescribed positions that have in many ways dislodged the process of continuous repositioning of the trajectory of religious discourse in the 20th century. The articulation between Islam and the people today seems not only more representationally stable but also less vibrant.

This is however a partial view of the present situation. While in international media circuits the needs of the "people of Iran" are constantly debated, suggestions are put forth, and predictions made, the multitudes of Iran are defying predictions every day and articulating new trajectories whose developments have yet to be made public.

Notes

Research in Shiraz (1997, 2001) was funded by the Italian CNR and several institutions within the University of Michigan. The paper was presented at a workshop run by Amr Hamzawy and Armando Salvatore at the Third Mediterranean Meeting sponsored by the Robert Schuman Center, European University Institute, in Montecatini, March 2002. Portions of it were also presented at the department of Anthropology, Columbia University. I thank audiences in these venues and in particular Partha Chatterjee, Hamid Dabashi, Nicholas Dirks, Josef Glicksberg, Naveeda Khan, Armando Salvatore, and Nader Sohrabi for their helpful comments. I thank the editors of the volume for their careful reading and suggestions. Special thanks to 'Ali Asghar Sayfi. At the editors' request, for reasons of space, references and follow-ups to the different trajectories evoked have been kept to a minimum.

1. I am hinting at discursive formations that would require specific analysis: I do not claim to reconstruct the genealogy of "the people." It should also be clear that I am referring to the ways in which the people were constructed as a subject and object of government, not to any social constituency (though there are links between the two dimensions). For a seminal work in this regard see Asef Bayat (1997).

2. In the semiotic perspective of Charles Saunders Peirce (1998), Publicness is a First, an abstract and absolute category that is sheer possibility and whose limitations and specifications are effected only by its encounter with the here and the now of a Second and the rule and habit of a Third.

3. Particularly significant in this regard appears to be the organization of Baha'i councils that started in the 1880s (Cole 2000: 92–97).

4. *Futuvvat* (see Sarraf 1973) is also relevant here. This construction of sociality around a common purpose could be investigated along the lines of inquiry of the "common good" discussed by LeVine and Salvatore in this volume. In these forms of Iranian male socialization however, the directionality does not amount to the reproduction of a transcendental shared ground through disciplining practices, but rather to an "aesthetics" of social relations, bodily postures, and poetic expression, which, while disciplined, always outdoes the disciplinary mode of conduct and borders on the unruly (also understood in sexual terms). Even in the most ritualized gatherings of this kind, such as communal mourning during Muharram this element is in "full view" and sometimes disturbs members of the religious hierarchies (some of whom however often promote and participate in such meetings). *Anjuman*s instead exhibit a more specific social commitment for the "good," which is however, as I mention, fairly restricted and not completely public.

5. Either directly through the South Persian Rifles or indirectly through "tribal" components; the main concern was the "safety" of trade routes, not the control of land or the well-being of the population.

6. See Public Record Office, F.O. 248/1186.

7. On page 24 of the chronicle there is mention of subsequent issues, however I have no information on whether these were printed or not. I thank Ali Asghar Sayfi for showing the chronicle to me and letting me photocopy it. The original of the chronicle is in his private library. Numbers in brackets at the end of quotations refer to the pages of the report.

8. The word *hujjatulislam* has to be understood here as a synonym of 'ulama. It did not necessarily denote a specific rank among the religious scholars, as it is mostly the case today in Iran.

9. With the notable addition of the agricultural experts and the absence of Qajar princes.

10. Shaykh Murtiza (1867–1930) was a member of the Mahallati family, a family of important religious scholars and leaders, some of whom such as Shaykh Ja'far Mahallati mentioned above were politically involved and participated in anti-British struggles in the south. Shaykh Murtiza was a *mujtahid* who, as a hagiographic short biography states "was very active in the propagation of Islamic values and persecution of sins" (Natiq 1975: 30). His involvement in social activism included the organization of public celebrations on the occasion of religious holidays (especially for the 15th of Sha'ban, the anniversary of the birth of the 12th Imam) that included *çiraqani*, the illumination of a mosque or another building with candles and gas lights and its decoration with carpets, mirrors, and photographs. Similar ceremonies with illumination and exposition of portraits were also used by the shah and governors on specific occasions and were public display of power.

11. Here too the "people" are split between those who are present at the assembly, and have to take action, and the absent needy. The shaykh uses the same term (*mardum*) to refer to one and the other, thus expanding the sense of collectivity, but the two are, at the same time, clearly demarcated.

12. I am referring here to Salvatore's (1998) discussion of "staging virtues," taken here from a different angle.

13. This is contradicted by British sources (Wright 2000). In 1905 a functionary wrote about him "[he] openly practices extortion on a large scale by which means he has accumulated considerable wealth" (ibid.: 107). These judgments as well as Farmanfarma's declarations have to be understood in the context of a colonial situation. What is relevant here is not so much whether the governor is telling the truth or not but the fact that he has to say that he never took any money in order to construct his legitimacy: performing accountability is crucial in the construction of his authority.

14. In the preceding sentence Farmanfarma had quoted *fiqh* and knowledge of trade as other cases of specialized knowledge that he compares to his art of government.

15. The copy of the photograph I discuss appears to be cut in a way that suggests that the original photograph was larger (people on the far right and left of the picture are cut in half).

16. For his biography see Ruknzada-Adamiyat (1959–61: II 267–71) and Imdad (1960: 402–04).

17. It is also possible to argue, with a slight risk of falling into an intentionality trap, that the subjects of a photograph pose in front of a camera for a general public and while posturing they imagine the public viewer's eye in front of them, thus even their posing entails a certain degreee of public quality. The relation between photography and publicness is by no means exclusive and not all photographs produce the same public effects. As elsewhere in the paper, public quality is a matter of degree. Certainly however, photography is a "visible" medium par excellence, even when the subjects photographed are "private."

18. Among these photographs of the late Qajar period, there are several that exhibit a particularly public character such as those of welcome ceremonies for the arrival of a new governor in Shiraz in which the governor is shown standing on the side of a photograph of the Shah with the army and the notables in front of him. Among them is the one depicting the arrival of Farmanfarma (Sana' 1990: 109).
19. Precisely because all the young men wear similar clothes it is possible to draw a significant distinction between those who wear leather shoes and those who wear slippers (*giva*); those who wear a suit and those who wear pants different from the coat, etc.
20. For examples of such diagrams that belong to the Shirazi gnostic tradition see Raz-i Shirazi (1973).
21. The wholeness of the diagram recalls the idea of Unity so dear to Islamic mysticism. This unity is however here projected into a utopian social project that postulates unity as a principle of organization.
22. "Art.2: the Society operates on the basis of Islamic ideology (*iduluji-yi islami*)."
23. These cooperatives were very important during the war with Iraq, when a lot of food was subsidized through a system of "coupons."
24. The booklet does not specify whether the welfare is funded by the *zakat* of the members or otherwise.
25. Khosrokhavar translates it in French as *conscientisation*.
26. Wright calculates that between 1916 and 1918 the governor was given 614,704 *toumans* (£205,000 of the time) some of which were calculated as loans and others as personal payments. Farmanfarma regularly billed the British for the administration of the region. This sum echoes one of the rhetorical questions of Shaykh Murtiza to the governor: "do you have 500,000 *toumans*?"

References

Abedi, Mehdi, and Michael M.J. Fischer. 1993. "Thinking a Public Sphere in Arabic and Persian." *Public Culture* 6: 220–30.

Adle, Chahryar, and Yahya Zoka. 1983. "Notes et Documents sur la Photographie Iranienne et son Histoire." *Studia Iranica* 12: 249–81.

Afary, Janet. 1996. *The Iranian Constitutional Revolution, 1906–1911*. New York: Columbia University Press.

Afshar, Iraj. 1992. *Gangina-yi 'Aksha-yi Iran*. Tehran: Nashr-i Farhang-i Iran.

———. 1983. "Some Remarks on the Early History of Photography in Iran." In *Qajar Iran: Political, Social and Cultural Change 1800–1925*, ed. Charles Edmund Bosworth, Edinburgh: Hillenbrand.

Anderson, Benedict. 1991. *Imagined Communities*. London: Verso.

Asad, Talal. 1986. *The Idea of an Anthropology of Islam*. Washington D.C.: Georgetown University Center for Contemporary Arab Studies.

Barthes, Roland. 1980. *La Chambre Claire. Note sur la photographie*. Paris: Cahiers du Cínema.

Bayat, Asef. 1997. *Street Politics: Poor People's Movements in Iran*. New York: Columbia University Press.

Bayat, Kava. 1990. *Iran va Jang-i Jahani-yi Avval*. Tehran: Saziman-i Asnad-i Milli.

Bayat, Mangol. 1991. *Iran's First Revolution: Shi'ism and the Constitutional Revolution of 1905–1909*. New York and Oxford: Oxford University Press.

Beck, Lois. 1990. "Tribes and the State in Nineteenth and Twentieth-Century Iran." In *Tribes and State Formation on the Middle East*, ed. P. S. Khoury and J. Kostiner, Berkeley: University of California Press.

Benjamin, Walter. 1968. "The Work of Art in the Age of Mechanical Reproduction." In *Illuminations*, ed. and with an introduction by Hannah Arendt, trans. Harry Zohn, New York: Schocken Books.

Browne, Edward. 1914. *The Press and Poetry of Modern Persia*. Cambridge: Cambridge University Press.

Cole, Juan. 2000. *Modernity and the Millennium: The Genesis of the Baha'i Faith in the Nineteenth-Century Middle East*. New York: Columbia University Press.

Geertz, Clifford. 1973. *The Interpretation of Cultures*. New York: Basic Books.

Habermas, Jürgen. 1989 [1962] *The Structural Transformation of the Public Sphere*, trans. Thomas Burger, Cambridge, MA: MIT Press.

Imdad, Hasan. 1960. *Shiraz dar Guzashta va Hal*. Shiraz: Musavi.

Iraji, Nasir. 1999. *Il-i Qashqayi dar Jang-i Jahani-yi Avval*. Tehran: Shiraza.

Kashani-Sabet, Firoozeh. 1999. *Frontier Fictions: Shaping the Iranian Nation, 1804–1946*. Princeton: Princeton University Press.

Khosrokhavar, Farhad. 1997. *Anthropologie de la révolution iranienne*. Paris: L' Harmattan.

Najmabadi, Afsaneh. 1997. "The Erotic Vatan [homeland] as Beloved and Mother; To Love, To Possess and To Protect." *Comparative Studies in Society and History* 39, 3: 442–67.

———. 1998. *The Story of the Daughters of Quchan: Gender and National Memory in Iranian History*. Syracuse, NY: Syracuse University Press.

Natiq-iShirazi. 1975. *Ayatullah Mahallati va khandan-i Sisad sala ruhaniyat va fiqahat*. Shiraz: no publisher.

Oberling, Pierre. 1974. *The Qashqa'i Nomads of Fars*. The Hague: Mouton.

Peirce, Charles Sanders. 1998. *The Essential Peirce: Selected Philosophical Writings*, ed. P. E. Project, vol. 2, Bloomington and Indianapolis: Indiana University Press.

Raz-i Shirazi. 1973 [1352]. *Tabashir al-Hukima*. Shiraz: Khaneqah-e Ahmadi.

Royce, William R. 1981. The Shirazi Provincial Elite: Status Maintenance and Change. In *Continuity and Change in Modern Iran*, ed. M. Bonine and N. R. Keddie, Albany, NY: State University of New York Press.

Ruknzada-Adamiyat, and Muhammad Husayn. 1959–1961 [1338–1340]. *Danishmandan va Sukhanvaran-i Fars*. 4 vols. Tehran: Khayyam.

Ruknzada-Adamiyat, Muhammad Husayn. 1991 [1370]. *Fars va Jang-i Bayn al-Milal Avval*. Tehran: Iqbal.

Salvatore, Armando. 1998. "The Disembodiment of Self-correctness and the Making of Islam as Public Norm." In *Islam—Motor or Challenge of Modernity*, vol. 2 of *Yearbook of the Sociology of Islam*, ed. Georg Stauth, 87–120.

Sana', Mansur. 1990. *Paydayash-i 'akkasi dar Shiraz*. Tehran: Surush.

Sarraf, Morteza. 1973. *Traités des compagnons-chevaliers*. Tehran: Institut Français d'Iranologie de Téhéran.

Sohrabi, Nader. 1999. "Revolution and State Culture: The Circle of Justice and the Constitutionalism in 1906 Iran." In *State/Culture: State-Formation after the Cultural Turn*, ed. George Steinmetz, Ithaca, NY, and London: Cornell University Press.

Tavakoli-Targhi, Mohamad. 2001. *Refashioning Iran: Orientalism, Occidentalism and Historiography*. Hampshire, UK, and New York: Palgrave Macmillan.

Wright, Dennis. 2000. "Prince 'Abd ul-Husayn Mirza Farmanfarma. Notes from British Sources." *Iran* 38: 107–14.

CHAPTER 3

"DOING GOOD, LIKE SAYYIDA ZAYNAB": LEBANESE SHI'I WOMEN'S PARTICIPATION IN THE PUBLIC SPHERE

Lara Deeb

Over the past two decades, women's participation in public welfare has increased substantially in the southern *al-dahiyya al-janubiyya* suburbs of Beirut (henceforth al-Dahiyya).[1] The visibility of women in public activities has accompanied the establishment or growth of numerous Islamic community welfare and/or charitable associations, known as *jam'iyyat khayriyya*. Both phenomena reflect a strong commitment to public welfare and community service in the area; a commitment linked to the religious and political groundings of the Shi'i Islamic movement in Lebanon, most prominently represented today by Hizbullah. Particularly for women in this area of Beirut, commitment to community service, *al-iltizam bi-l-'amal al-ijtima'i*, is manifest on a personal level as well as a public one. Moreover, it extends well beyond paying one's *khums* (a Shi'i religious tax) or seeking employment in the administrative offices of *jam'iyyat* to volunteering long hours in face-to-face work assisting the poor.

In this chapter, based upon 22 months of ethnographic field research in four neighborhoods in al-Dahiyya, I use the empirical case of the emergence of volunteering as a "new" social norm for pious Shi'i women in order to examine what happens to notions of the public sphere when Islamist women's activities are written into it. After touching upon volunteers' motivations, as they confront a community history of poverty and occupation, I move to a consideration of the narrative reference that frames much of their discourse about community participation: the 'Ashura story. Parallel with increasing community service, 'Ashura—the commemoration of the martyrdom of Imam Husayn—has undergone a transformation from "traditional" practices and meanings to newly "authenticated" ones. The reconfigured version of 'Ashura has emerged prominently into public spaces and discourses. In particular, the reinterpretation of the behavior of the Imam's sister Zaynab has provided a salient role model for women volunteers.

I argue that, in part through the impact of these discourses, volunteering has been institutionalized as a social norm and incorporated into a normative moral system for women in al-Dahiyya. Moreover, I explore the implications of locating women's community work within the public sphere, offering a critique of the assumption by the majority of scholars that the voluntary associations that constitute civil society and the public sphere are largely male preserves, and arguing that women's community service is clearly public in terms of the spaces where it occurs, the responsibility for social welfare it entails, the public marker of morality it carries, and the moral and revolutionary discourses with which volunteers are reciprocally engaged.

Confronting a Community History of Oppression with *Takaful Ijtima'i*

While some women in al-Dahiyya volunteer sporadically, or exclusively during Ramadan, for countless others volunteering is a responsibility taken as seriously, and often more seriously, than employment. Particularly for women, volunteer work is undertaken in addition to household and family work, and sometimes in addition to employment as well. Women volunteers are choosing to take on a double or triple shift in order to contribute to their community through unpaid labor in *jam'iyyat*.

In discussing their reasons for adding volunteering to their already full lives, women often drew upon the notion of *takaful ijtima'i*, a phrase meaning "mutual social responsibility or solidarity" that is consistently used by volunteers to convey the crux of their inspiration.[2] *Takaful* stems from the root *kafala*, meaning to support or sponsor. In Islamic jurisprudence, *kafala* refers to guardianship and maintenance, primarily a means of ensuring economic support and moral upbringing for orphaned children. In al-Dahiyya, *takaful* maintains this meaning as well, as the offices and programs through which orphans are supported are called *maktab al-takaful*.

For volunteers, *takaful ijtima'i* expresses acceptance of a God-given responsibility for the social welfare of the world—in the often cited Quranic phrasing, a human being is "God's deputy on earth," *khalifat allah fi-l-'ard*. As a local sayyid explained to me, "This means that each person is a representative of God, who should carry out the duties of the world, uphold the general (Godly) principles, and behave with full responsibility." *Takaful ijtima'i* is here a quintessential example of a reformulated "discourse of the common good" as discussed by the editors and other contributors to this and other recent volumes on the public sphere in Muslim contexts (LeVine and Salvatore, chapter 1 in this volume; Eickelman and Salvatore 2004 [2002]; Höfert and Salvatore 2000).

By citing *takaful ijtima'i* as one of their primary motivations for community participation, most volunteers indicated the inseparability of humanitarian sentiment and religious faith, or rather, the inevitability of the former stemming from the latter. There were, however, a few who consciously separated the two. At the extremes of this spectrum were Hajjeh Fatima,[3] who singularly refrained from referring to religion in any way when explaining why she volunteered, and Hajjeh Khadija, from the same *jam'iyya*, who observed that her sole motivation for volunteering was the knowledge that she would be paid in *'ajr* (divine recompense). Both these views, however, were exceptional, as most women expressed the belief that true faith necessarily incorporated a deep-felt humanitarianism, though they conceded that it was possible for a nonbeliever to feel some level (though inadequate) of humanitarian sentiment. Maliha elegantly noted the lack of distinction between the two:

> They are the same thing, perhaps because as soon as a person becomes aware, intellectually and of his principles, and also becomes more involved in Islam, he begins to understand that our religion strongly tells us to help others, that this is important.

The impetus to *takaful ijtima'i* was viewed as particularly crucial in the context of al-Dahiyya, due to the volunteers' perceptions about the disproportionate extent of poverty in the area as well as the political and economic marginalization of the Shi'a as a confessional group in Lebanon and the ravages of the civil war. In a nation-state where sectarian political-economic power translated to selective access to modernization for particular areas of the country, the Shi'a resided primarily in the least developed regions, without access to infrastructural and institutional developments occurring in the rest of Lebanon. The institutionalization of sectarianism in the Lebanese political system led to the establishment of sectarian institutions (e.g., schools, hospitals) rather than public secular ones (Joseph 1975). Because sect was a means of accessing resources, Shi'i underrepresentation in the government led to poverty. Differential population growth added to their underrepresentation so that by the late 1960s class differentiation in Lebanon fell largely along sectarian lines (Cobban 1985; Richani 1998). The first inclusive mobilization of the Shi'a did not occur until 1974 when Sayyid Musa al-Sadr founded the "Movement of the Deprived" (*harakat al-mahrumin*); the legacy of which continues on through the political parties Harakat Amal and Hizbullah.[4]

Within al-Dahiyya, a sense of collective Shi'i deprivation is fueled by the sheer visibility of poverty. There is little economic segregation; poor and wealthy families reside in the same buildings and come from the same extended families. With the exception of the Palestinian refugee camps the area is the most densely populated in Lebanon; its population made up primarily of Shi'i Lebanese displaced from the south and the Bekaa during the Lebanese civil war and the Israeli occupation. To nonresidents, mention of al-Dahiyya often elicits responses of discomfort, ranging from caution mingled with curiosity to outright trepidation. Such responses are built on stereotypical associations of al-Dahiyya with poverty, illegal construction, refugees, armed Hizbullah guards, and "the Shi'i ghetto." As Mona Harb el-Kak (2000) has also noted, such stereotypes obscure the complexity and diversity within al-Dahiyya, which includes non-Hizbullah areas, older residential districts, some lingering Christian residents, and an emerging Shi'i "middle-class."

This history of marginalization relative to other groups in Lebanon, as well as assumptions about disproportionately high levels of poverty in al-Dahiyya are often noted by volunteers as they emphasize the importance of their work in a context of perpetual "catching-up" with other confessional groups. Their sense of being "behind" the rest of the country was exacerbated by the general lack of government services in Lebanon resulting from the prolonged civil war. Even when government services were reestablished or subcontracted to private corporations, residents of al-Dahiyya were hesitant to trust that the services actually functioned properly in their neighborhoods although willing to believe that they worked for "other areas of Lebanon." The *jam'iyyat* are conscious that they are working to fill governmental lacunae, and volunteers and administrators alike frequently complained that "if there were only a government" much of the poverty and systemic and infrastructural disrepair would be alleviated.

Furthermore, while the Lebanese civil war[5] (1976–1990) exacerbated poverty and the lack of government services throughout Lebanon, it was the predominantly Shi'i regions of the south and the Bekaa that bore the brunt of two Israeli invasions (1978 and 1982) and the Israeli occupation that continued until May 2000. Additionally, most of the participants (and martyrs) in the military resistance to occupation were Shi'a, organized primarily through Hizbullah's Islamic Resistance, and also through Harakat Amal. In effect, war did not end for this community in 1990 as it did for much of Lebanon, but continued until May 2000.[6]

The juxtaposition of this shared sense of suffering during the war and occupation with the duty of *takaful ijtima'i* reminds of the necessity to acknowledge the consciousness of many volunteers that their community work had two related political flavors: it represented both a means of participation in the resistance to Israeli occupation and a way to constitute a Shi'i political community in Lebanon via social welfare provision in the absence of the state.[7] Yet again, these political tones were not seen as separate from volunteers' socio-religious consciousness, but as intrinsic aspects of it. The inseparability of these elements can be seen most clearly in the religio-historical figures emulated by most volunteers. As they confronted poverty (including state neglect), war, and oppression through embracing their duty in *takaful ijtima'i*, most volunteers sought role models for their work in religion and history. Specifically, they looked to 'Ashura, the commemoration of the martyrdom of Imam Husayn, grandson of the Prophet Muhammad.

In A.D. 680 Husayn was killed in a battle at Karbala by an army sent by the Caliph Yazid. This was among the most important of the conflicts over succession to the leadership of the Islamic community that eventually split Shi'i from Sunni Muslims. During the battle, which took place on the 10th of Muharram, all the men with Husayn were killed except one of his sons, and the women and children were taken captive. Among them was Husayn's sister Zaynab, who led the community in captivity, a point to which I return below.[8]

The martyrdom of Husayn and his companions and the subsequent trials of the women who were with him at Karbala represent a pivotal point in the historical foundation of Shi'ism. Today, an "authenticated" version of the 'Ashura story provides historical links to the present and an essential narrative framework for much of the volunteer work occurring in al-Dahiyya. In order to explore how volunteers draw upon these authenticated 'Ashura discourses in explaining their own commitment to their community, it is first necessary to consider the transformation from "traditional" to "authenticated" 'Ashura itself.

Obviously there are a wide range of 'Ashura meanings and practices—a continuum of forms—that are not reducible into two static and absolute categories, but I have found it useful to follow the contrast set up by my interlocutors as a heuristic tool by which to trace these recent changes. Participants in both types of commemorations labeled 'Ashura as it was commemorated for much of the 20th century (and continues in some areas) as traditional (*taqlidi*). In contrast, those who advocated for what I call "authenticated" 'Ashura often opposed their commemorations to these traditional ones, utilizing temporal and modernization oppositions (e.g., "now" versus "before" and "developed" or "cultured" versus "backward") in order to reify a distinction between forms. Advocates of authenticated 'Ashura used the adjective *haqiqi* to describe their commemorations and interpretations, a term for which the range of meanings includes "true," "real," "genuine," and "authentic." I have consciously drawn upon the latter translation in using the term "authenticated" to describe this local category of "new" or "now" forms of 'Ashura commemoration because it captures both the claims to truth and authority being made *and* the processes of historical method and assumptions about the accuracy and authority of that method that are inherent in those claims.[9]

Ritual Reconfiguration: From Traditional to Authenticated 'Ashura

In Lebanon, 'Ashura is generally commemorated during the first ten days of Muharram, and includes *majalis*, or mourning gatherings, where the history of the martyrdom is retold, and 10th-day lamentation processions, where men perform *latam*, a ritualized self-flagellation. Both the structure and the meaning of 'Ashura and these lamentation events have always been historically fluid, incorporating different elements in different locales and reflecting the changing political and social status of the Shi'a. However, a particularly dramatic transformation has been taking place in Lebanon over the past decade and a half, mirroring the growing popularity of Hizbullah and accompanying the unprecedented commitment to community service in al-Dahiyya. This can be seen as a shift from a traditional 'Ashura toward an authenticated one.

'Ashura commemorations similar to the contemporary commemorations that my interlocutors labeled "traditional" have occurred in rural Lebanon and in what is today al-Dahiyya since the beginning of the century.[10] However, the urban visibility of 'Ashura grew in tandem with the urbanizing Shi'i population in the 1960s. The commemorations were and are viewed by many nonparticipants as a frightening display of "backward" (*mutakhallif*) Shi'i practices, and were cited as a point of difference marking the Shi'a as less modern and developed than other Lebanese communities. Many of my interlocutors, as well as non-Shi'i Lebanese colleagues, characterized the traditional form of self-flagellation as "barbaric." Yet aside from this stigma, it was not until the mid-1980s that strong popular opposition to traditional 'Ashura forms appeared among Lebanese Shi'a. The factors leading to this opposition included the Islamic Revolution in Iran, the Lebanese civil war, the Israeli invasions, and the formation of Hizbullah. Iran in particular provided a model for opposition, as Iranian reformist and Islamic intellectuals had cultivated a new 'Ashura discourse that linked it to a revolutionary Shi'ism, in contrast to a politically quietist one (Fischer 1980; Hegland 1983, 1987; Momen 1985).

The shift from traditional to authenticated 'Ashura is especially apparent in three areas: the *majalis*, the processions, and most crucially, the meaning of the events of Muharram. *Majalis* are held during the first 10 days of Muharram, and continue with less regularity for the next 40 days. During a *majlis*, someone versed in the 'Ashura story narrates a part of the battle's history in a lamentation style reminiscent of a liturgy, detailing graphically the suffering and martyrdom of Husayn and his companions. Some recitors include a sermon that explains lessons to be learned from Karbala and the meanings of the events. The affect of the audience parallels these shifts in the speaker's tone, with the lamentation liturgy evoking intense crying that quiets to a pensive concentration during the sermon sections.

While all *majalis* include the lamentative narration of the events of Karbala, traditional reciters include as much detail of suffering as possible in this narration, in order to elicit maximum levels of emotion from the audience. Many add poetic embellishment and dialogue among Husayn, Zaynab, and others who were with them. Zaynab in particular is often portrayed as buried in grief, pulling at her hair and shedding copious tears over the dead and dying. The ultimate goal for a traditional style reciter is to move people to cry as much as possible for the martyred Imam and his family and companions. As one shaykh put it, "There are some (reciters) who are very traditional and backward and others who are cultured. The backward ones read only to make people cry, but the cultured ones teach lessons in their recitations."

As alluded to by the shaykh, authenticated *majalis* are characterized by longer sermons and a more restrained narration. Eliciting an emotional response is still a goal, but a secondary one. These *majalis* are intended to teach religious, social, and political lessons, to instruct the audience about the "true" meanings of Karbala and to link the past to the present. Those who recite *majalis* and strive for authenticity are concerned with the historical accuracy of their narrations and avoid including unfounded exaggerations that they see as being merely to heighten emotions and make people cry. Both reciters and those who have attended *majalis* over the past three decades articulate this shift, often noting that "today" people attend *majalis* in order to learn lessons "from the school of Imam Husayn" and not "just" to cry. Emotion remains a crucial element for both reciters and audience, yet emotion is given purpose in its revision from an end to a means.

Following the *majlis* on the 10th of Muharram lamentation processions take place around Lebanon. During processions characterized as "traditional,"[11] men play the prominent role, performing a style of *latam* that involves shedding their own blood, while women line the streets and lean over balconies and from nearby rooftops to watch. In contrast, no blood is shed during men's *latam* in authenticated processions,[12] and—more importantly, due to its implications for gender roles in the community—women are no longer relegated to an observational role. The Hizbullah processions include women and girls, dressed in full *'abaya* (the post-Revolution Iranian-style cloak that covers everything but the face and hands),[13] and organized by age in ordered groups. These groups form the latter part of the procession, and, while they do not perform *latam*, each group is led in chants or *nadbat* (lamentation songs) by a leader.

In typical fashion,[14] the mobilizing Lebanese Shi'i movement called upon women to participate publicly in 'Ashura commemorations, as well as in the community more generally. Women's active participation in the processions is viewed by many Lebanese Shi'a as both "more developed" (*mutatawwar*) and more authentic historically—perhaps a response to the stereotyping of traditional 'Ashura as backward.

As can be inferred from these descriptions, the traditional meanings surrounding 'Ashura center on both grief and regret. Tears shed for the martyrs of Karbala are *mustahabb*, or religiously commendable. Traditional belief holds that both evoking these tears and shedding them are acts that may increase one's chances of entering heaven. Blood spilled in memory of the events of Karbala is similarly an embodiment of grief and an empathetic expression of solidarity with the Imam's pain and sorrow. Yet it can also be an expression of remorse at not being at Karbala with the Imam. In pre–civil war Lebanon, when the Shi'a were the least politically organized group in the country, all of these meanings can be seen as stemming from a Shi'ism that was politically quietist. The emphasis during 'Ashura was on individual religious experiences of mourning and regret, embodied through tears and blood. While at first glance the association of blood and quietism may seem contradictory, in this instance, harm is directed at the self, rather than outward, implying a personal expression of grief and regret and the potential for salvation, rather than collective political or social action.[15] It is less clear whether traditional commemorations since the Shi'i Islamic mobilization carry the same connotations of quietism—certainly for some participants they do, while for others tears and blood demonstrate their readiness for self-sacrifice for the community.

From the perspective of the emergent alternative Shi'ism that espoused authenticated 'Ashura, the blood and tears of traditional commemorations are both un-Islamic and passive. Instead, advocates of authentication note that "Emotions are necessary, but they should be understood as a way of arriving at learning the lesson of Husayn. The heart should be used to reach the head, not as an endpoint in and of itself."

Accompanying the discouragement of traditional *latam* and the historical authentication of the *majalis* was a redirection of the message of 'Ashura outward, shifting the meaning from one of personal mourning and regret to a revolutionary lesson.[16] In the context of war and poverty, where the Shi'i Islamic community needed to mobilize militarily *and* socially, the message of revolution in the events of Muharram was highlighted. This was done by emphasizing historical accuracy, in order to unearth the authentic and liberatory historical record—one that demonstrated that the battle occurred in a revolutionary context.

Authenticated 'Ashura in Public Spaces and Discourses

Concomitant with the new emphasis on historical accuracy, emotional restraint, and the revolutionary message is a transformation of the relationship between 'Ashura commemorations and public space. This is especially apparent with regard to *majalis*. While privately held *majalis* continue to be held in homes, loudspeakers and microphones guarantee that they will be heard throughout buildings and neighborhoods. It often seems as though at any moment walking down a street in al-Dahiyya during 'Ashura, at least one *majlis* can be heard. Additionally, there are numerous public *majalis* held in mosques and Husayniyyat (Shi'i ritual gathering halls), and more recently, in the gathering spaces of *jam'iyyat*. Since the mid-1990s *majalis* have also been held in tents constructed by Hizbullah and Harakat Amal in parking lots and other empty spaces around Beirut. In 2001, according to Hizbullah's weekly newspaper, no less than fifty-one official Hizbullah-sponsored *majalis* were held in Beirut alone.[17] Most prominent among them is the main Hizbullah "tent" from which evening *majalis* have been broadcast over the party's television station since 1995, and where on alternate nights Secretary General of Hizbullah Sayyid Hasan Nasrallah speaks to a crowd of approximately ten thousand attendees.

Public *majalis* are not new; in the southern town of Nabatiyye, a passion-play/recitation has been held each year on the 10th day of Muharram since sometime in the early 1900s. Even during the Ottoman Empire, when Lebanese Shiʻi often practiced *taqiyya*—concealing their religious beliefs to protect themselves in the majority Sunni empire—public *majalis* were carefully held in the al-Khansaʼ familyʼs Husayniyya in al-Dahiyya. Yet the number and levels of attendance of both private and public *majalis* have increased dramatically over the past decade.

The spread and growth of ʻAshura commemorations indicate broader public exposure to and participation in the articulation and use of authenticated ʻAshura discourses—namely, discourses that embrace the revolutionary and liberatory meanings of ʻAshura—as well as in the production of authenticity itself. One aspect of this involves new religious and political media, including Hizbullahʼs weekly newspaper al-ʻAhed, radio station al-Nur, and television station al-Manar, as well as al-Bashaʼir, the radio station affiliated with Sayyid Muhammad Hussein Fadlullah. While these media provide wider access to the officially produced discourses of sayyids and shaykhs, they also afford greater participation in the production of ʻAshura discourses, through a plethora of call-in radio shows for both adults and children and television ranging from Karbala-inspired serials to specials about ʻAshura poetry.[18]

Another crucial component of the articulation of authenticated ʻAshura discourses involves informal conversations—daily talk among volunteers and their relatives and neighbors. Some of these conversations, especially during and immediately after ʻAshura, contributed to the authentication of particular ʻAshura narratives. Whether over coffee in a neighborʼs kitchen, or en route to or from a *majlis* with a cousin or "sister" from the *jamʻiyya*, women often debated the accuracy of details of the events of Karbala.[19] For example, sitting on the balcony one afternoon, ʻAziza and her neighbor discussed at length whether it could be corroborated that—as the reciter of a *majlis* the day before had depicted—Husayn had indeed given his young daughter Ruqayya a cup before his death, telling her that it would turn black inside if he were killed. Some of these conversations were sparked by a listenerʼs skepticism toward a specific reciter, others triggered by discord between the version of an episode heard in a *majlis* and the version broadcast over the radio in the car on the way home.

Other instances of daily talk explicitly or implicitly linked ʻAshura to current events and to the struggles of Shiʻi Lebanese. Perhaps the most obvious illustration of these links can be seen in Hizbullahʼs employment of the example of Husayn to mobilize participants in and supporters of the Islamic Resistance. Here ʻAshura provides a significant narrative not only for potential martyrs but for the mothers of martyrs as well, as expressed by an administrative employee at the Martyrʼs Association:

> You must remember that not only was Husayn a martyr, but he was martyr
> with a family. His importance is that in order to fight against oppression he
> sacrificed himself *and* his family. In our society, when someone is martyred,
> his mother says, "I gave nothing in comparison to what Fatima al-Zahraʼ

gave." 'Ashura gives our community the motivation to face oppression and to give sacrifices.

However, despite the public prominence of the relationship between Karbala and the Islamic Resistance, authenticated 'Ashura discourses also provide a crucial narrative reference for women that extends beyond both gendered limitations of direct military action and gendered expectations of motherhood.[20] While discussing the importance of community service—whether explaining their reasons for participating, encouraging new recruits, or bemoaning the insufficiency of volunteerism—women drew upon 'Ashura's revolutionary lesson, and especially on the example set by Zaynab at Karbala. In doing so, they posited themselves as active and necessary participants in the public welfare of the community.

Sayyida Zaynab: "Heroine of the Heroes"

For many women, the most essential aspect of the revolutionary lesson in the shift from traditional to authenticated 'Ashura lies in the reinterpretation of Zaynab's behavior at Karbala. Representations that had depicted her as a plaintive mourner were transformed to renderings that accentuated her courage, strength, and resilience.[21] Reciters of authenticated *majalis* along with their audiences criticized traditional portrayals of Zaynab for their exaggerated emphasis on her tears:

> Some readers will add talk for Sayyida Zaynab, things she would not have said, I do not like it when they portray her as crying. Sayyida Zaynab was strong, she stood up in the face of the oppressor, she was not weak, she told him that she was the victor, she considered herself the victor by the blood of Imam Husayn. She is the victor in meaning.

In particular, three new characteristics emerge in Zaynab's reformulation: her strength of mind, her compassion and dedication to others, and her courage to speak. Consistent with their expected role as mothers of martyrs, women frequently pointed to Zaynab's strength of mind and ability to endure the loss of all the men in her family. Numerous mothers who had lost their sons in the resistance and sisters who had lost their brothers explained that they coped with their grief by emulating Zaynab's equanimity as she watched her male relatives die. They compared their losses to hers, and in so doing, expressed feeling that they had lost little in comparison: "We didn't lose everyone, like Sayyida Zaynab did. We have to say, if she could go on, why can't we? And we at least have role models; there is acknowledgment in society for the mothers of martyrs, the Sayyida had none of that."

The other two ideal qualities seen in Zaynab's example highlight her ability to act despite her grief and the turmoil of her surroundings.

Volunteers compared their contributions to society with hers, observing that they had given relatively little, and citing her as one of the most salient models for their dedication to the public welfare of their community. In the context of al-Dahiyya, this plays a role in inspiring hundreds of women to volunteer their time and energy to work in *jam'iyyat*. One volunteer explained it thus:

> Sayyida Zaynab, after the martyrdom of Imam Husayn, she brought up his children, all the orphans . . . she stood by their side, and lessened their pain, even though Imam Husayn was her brother, when he was martyred, that was her brother who died, and the children of her brothers were martyred, and *her* children were martyred . . . She was able to handle all the suffering that she experienced, and all the problems and pain, and at the same time she could help others. She has taught us that no matter what we experience . . . it will never be as much as what she dealt with. Because of this she is the model for our community work.

Yet it is not only Zaynab's emotional strength and her maternal caretaker role that are esteemed by volunteers. Women also underscore her outspokenness regarding her brother's message, noting that she confronted Yazid during her imprisonment and spoke eloquently to challenge him, and that she played an indispensable role in spreading the revolutionary message of Karbala after the Imam's martyrdom.

> What would have happened if the Imam Husayn went to Karbala and was martyred and Sayyida Zaynab wasn't there? Because the story always begins after the martyrdom. So Zaynab, she went and witnessed, and she was the one who carried the truth of Karbala with her. She stood before Yazid and spoke to him, and she showed the world the events that occurred when the Imam Husayn was martyred. So it was she who carried the message of revolution to others. It was she who made possible 'Ashura. This is the role of women. (Salwa, volunteer)

More than either of her other ideal attributes, Zaynab's courage to speak positioned her as "the heroine of the heroes" for many volunteers. In this regard, as discussed further below, the shift to an authenticated understanding of 'Ashura undermines common associations of women with the private domain; a challenge evoked symbolically in the organized and public participation of women in authenticated 'Ashura processions.

Courage to speak out against oppression, emotional strength, and above all, dedication to others are qualities valued by women in al-Dahiyya; qualities they cultivate in themselves and in those around them. The reformulation of Zaynab as embodying these qualities is an aspect of authenticated 'Ashura directed specifically at women, to such an extent, that it has contributed to the emergence of active participation in community work as a "new" social norm for women in al-Dahiyya.

Volunteering as a "New" Social Norm
for Women

In many ways, authenticated discourses about Zaynab set a standard of behavior to which many pious Lebanese Shi'i women aspire. Whether confronting the general state of hardship or minute and specifiable daily difficulties, volunteers frequently compared their responses to what they imagine Zaynab would have done in their place. Hajjeh Widad articulated this clearly:

> Now, whenever I am faced with some problem, I ask myself, am I going to act like Zaynab or not? If someone knocks at my door am I going to help him or not? Am I going to feel with others or not, am I going to give even more of myself or not, am I going to have the courage to face oppression or not?

Not only does this chronic comparison lead to idealized self-expectations, but it fosters pressure on others to hold themselves to the same standard. In more than one meeting at various *jam'iyyat*, a senior volunteer reminded others to think about "what Zaynab would have done"—both in situations where volunteers seemed disheartened by the never-ending nature of their work and when cooperation within the group seemed to be faltering.

Those who contribute to the welfare of the community are seen to embody the very qualities in Zaynab that are emulated—emotional strength, outspokenness, and dedication to others. Although volunteering in a *jam'iyya* is only one possible way of "doing good, like Sayyida Zaynab," it has become the most commonly accepted and expected way. Taking this to an extreme, some volunteers have internalized these social expectations into an unorthodox conviction that community service is a religious "duty" on a par with prayer, "For us it's not that it's a good thing for us to do this work, no, for us it's become an obligation, like prayer and fasting."

Another highly active volunteer who balances her duties at her *jam'iyya* with raising three children stated:

> It's not possible for all this to happen around me and for me to remain on the margins. Perhaps before this was allowable and there wasn't this responsibility, but now if I were a person on the margins, I would be depriving society of the energy that I am able to contribute. We are responsible for our time, before God and before ourselves, and me, I can't live traditionally, with only *subhiyyat* (morning visits) and housework.

In the statement above, Hajjeh Ruba emphasizes her sense of responsibility to society, and the importance of fulfilling that responsibility before herself and God. Yet demonstrating social responsibility is no longer critical before self and God alone. Today in al-Dahiyya in order to be seen as a "good" middle-class Muslim woman—barring exempting circumstances (e.g., being a full-time student or employee, having several young children)— a woman is expected to participate in at least some of the activities of at least one *jam'iyya*. Community service has become a "new" social norm for pious Shi'i women in al-Dahiyya.

This expectation is conveyed by volunteers to their relatives, friends, and neighbors in conversations about *jam'iyya* activities as well as outright attempts at recruitment. Once a *jam'iyya* network identifies a potential participant who is judged to be of good moral character—or occasionally when an interested woman herself initiates contact with a *jam'iyya*—she will receive a steady stream of telephone calls and invitations to attend fundraisers and other events. Gradually, unless her interest wanes significantly, she will be drawn into working with the *jam'iyya* more regularly.

It is necessary here to interrogate what exactly it is that is "new" about Shi'i women's volunteerism. As we saw above, in explaining why they volunteer, women frequently draw upon concepts like *takaful ijtima'i*, which builds upon Islamic notions of *kafala*. In doing so, they locate the roots of women's community service in a long-standing Islamic moral discourse. Similarly, women's emulation of Zaynab connects their contemporary activities to the historical and religious past of the community. Yet for women in al-Dahiyya today, volunteerism has been institutionalized into a broader public sphere in ways that are new. Furthermore, it is within that same public sphere that the linking of community service to morality is taking place via new forms of media and discourse.

The vast presence of *jam'iyyat* in al-Dahiyya stems from the institutionalization of the Shi'i Islamic movement in Lebanon and ranges from small women-founded and run organizations to family-based organizations to larger umbrella organizations that maintain multiple institutions (e.g., schools, orphanages, etc.) and that usually have specific political or religious affiliations. Prior to this, pious individuals remembered the poor during Ramadan, and often gave food and goods, in addition to paying their *khums* and *zakat*. Yet these acts of piety, of *takaful ijtima'i*, were not necessarily visible. There were those in the community who were known for their pious generosity, but the possibility of censure of those who did *not* demonstrate such generosity did not exist in the same way. The institutionalization of *takaful ijtima'i* in the *jam'iyyat* made giving time, as well as money, an explicitly public act.

As a new social norm for women, community service in a *jam'iyya* provides an externally visible marker of a woman's morality. While not volunteering does not necessarily damage a woman's status or reputation—unless she is assumed to spend her time frivolously—participating in the activities of a *jam'iyya* may add significantly to public perceptions of her moral character. Like the *hijab* (headscarf), also an external marker of women's morality, community service has been incorporated into a normative moral system for women in al-Dahiyya.[22] Yet just as the *hijab* does not always represent piety, active participation in *jam'iyya* activities does not necessarily follow from religious conviction. There were also women who viewed volunteering as a socially acceptable way to "get out of the house," those who attended *jam'iyya* functions primarily to escape (albeit temporarily) social pressures to do so, and those who valued the *jam'iyya* above all as a social venue. Over-assuming the prevalence of the latter phenomenon, one male administrator grumbled that all-women *jam'iyyat* promoted "the *subhiyya* model" of community work, a reference to the morning coffee visits associated with "idle" middle- and upper-class women in Lebanon.

Despite the variation in women's actual motivations for volunteering, for the many who argue that all "good" Muslim women who are able to should participate in some form of community service, volunteering is seen as the obvious "rational" choice to be made if a woman uses *al-'aql* (mind or reason).[23] This is most commonly heard from women who look to Fadlullah as their *marja' al-taqlid* (highest authority on juridical matters), as he places particular emphasis on *al-'aql* in his teachings. For example, in his lecture at the annual women's Ramadan fundraiser for the al-Mabarrat Association sponsoring war orphans, to resounding applause he called upon women to use *al-'aql*, stressing that women are as rational as men and that therefore God gave women just as much responsibility for *takaful ijtima'i* as he gave men. Yet if women and men share mutual responsibility for the social welfare of the community, why is it primarily women who are engaging in community work?

Why Women?

Why is it that community service has become a social norm particularly for women in al-Dahiyya? The answer lies in the felicitous convergence of beliefs about the natural dispositions and proclivities of the sexes with the structure and method of community work itself and the economic situation in Lebanon.

Authenticated 'Ashura discourses and the Lebanese Shi'i Islamic movement call upon both women and men to actively resist structural poverty and occupation,[24] yet the participation of women is bounded, in keeping with beliefs about the essential nature of women as nurturing and a fundamental incongruity between women and the battlefield. When clarifying the different natures of the sexes, however, women always emphasized that different did not mean differently valued. They actively espoused gender equity (*'adala*) as opposed to gender equality (*masawa*), with the former term embracing difference and the latter entailing "sameness."[25] Some volunteers compared their community service activities with the role of male resistance fighters, noting that both are uniformly valued, and expressing their gratitude that God has provided women with a means of *jihad*—of exerting themselves toward the furthering of Islam and their community.

Women are relegated to the realm of community service not only because they are believed to be innately unsuited to military service (unless they are forced to defend their selves, children, or property), but also because they are believed to be inherently suitable for community work. This does not mean that community service is women's role in society, but rather that while women *and* men alike should do good work on earth, women's proclivities make them better volunteers.

To a certain extent, this perceived compatibility obtains from the structure and method of the work itself. In many *jam'iyyat*, volunteers are assigned specific families that then become their responsibility. In essence, they function as liaisons between these families and the resources managed and distributed by the *jam'iyya*. Frequent visits to the families' homes are a crucial component of this process. In a community where a woman's—and her family's—reputation would be severely compromised if she were to receive unaccompanied male visitors in her home, household visits would be nearly impossible for male volunteers. Within the *jam'iyyat* as well, female volunteers field questions and requests from aid recipients, because the family member seeking assistance is usually a woman.

Through continual contact, volunteers build intense personal relationships with the assisted families. Here the view that women are better suited to community service because they have greater empathetic capacities comes into play. As volunteers begin to enter households "as though it is her home" and come to feel that they are a part of the families they assist, the emotional distance between them shrinks, to the extent that volunteers often begin to cry when describing the situation of one of "their" families or while negotiating extra *jam'iyya* resources for a particular case.

The cultivation of these personal relationships between volunteers and aid recipients is encouraged by many of the *jam'iyyat*, as they struggle to maintain what one administrator called "a more human and Islamic" approach to community welfare in the face of burgeoning bureaucracy. Larger *jam'iyyat* in particular are constantly confronted with the necessity of negotiating the tension between a face-to-face public and an anonymous one. Providing assistance through personal relationships allows *jam'iyyat* to nurture historical links to notions of social welfare rooted in Islamic tradition, even as their larger bureaucratic structures and funding concerns reflect their positions in the professionalizing world of international NGOs.[26]

With the obvious exception of all-women *jam'iyyat*, the tensions between face-to-face relationships and the bureaucracy associated with an anonymous public arena is reflected in the gendered division of labor in *jam'iyyat* with predominately female volunteers and male employees. This division of labor is amplified by the crumbling Lebanese economy and high levels of unemployment. Because in this community it is primarily men who are responsible for financially supporting their families, a slow economy makes it doubly difficult for women to find employment. The current Lebanese economy, along with the correspondences between beliefs about women's nature and the structure of community work, helps to ensure that the actual daily provision of assistance is women's work—a gender-specific form of active participation in the community.

Conclusion: Locating Women's Community Service in the Public Sphere

Generally, researchers and theorists locate the voluntary associations that constitute civil society in the public sphere and, because they largely assume a gendered public/private divide, particularly in studies of the Middle East/North Africa, associate them with men (Joseph 1997b). Yet women's community service is clearly public, with regard to the spaces where it occurs, the responsibility for social welfare it entails, the public marker of morality it carries, and the moral and revolutionary discourses with which volunteers are reciprocally engaged. Building on numerous critiques of the rigidity, ahistoricity, and gendering of the "public/private" distinction (Reiter 1975; Joseph 1983 and 1997a; Ayubi 1995; Singerman 1995; Hale 1996; Abu-Lughod 1998), I want to instead emphasize that a public/private distinction does not make sense in this context. Locating women's community service and its accompanying discourses—ranging from authenticated 'Ashura discourses to those incorporating volunteering into a moral system—firmly in the public sphere raises several key issues.

The first of these is the exclusionary nature of the public sphere as it is sometimes conceptualized and manifested. As Armando Salvatore argues, real public spheres consist primarily of "norms, disciplines, and procedures of communication" and are shaped by social norms and "specific, socially and historically contingent, rationalities" (2000: 93). These social norms and contingent rationalities include gender-specific limitations and expectations.

One way these limitations are manifest is through masculine discursive protocols (Fraser 1999). My interlocutors voiced awareness of gendered exclusions through the definition and valuation of "appropriate" discursive strategies as masculine. Expounding on the importance of women's *jam'iyyat*, Hajjeh Nawal observed, "men think that women can't have a *jam'iyya* that works, because they think that when women gather we just gossip or fight." She went on to assert her hopes that her *jam'iyya* would provide "an example of how women's *jam'iyyat* work *democratically and rationally*, with elections and a strong organizational structure." By consciously embracing ideals of democracy and rationality, she troubled the definition of those ideals as masculine in order to assert that women are crucial participants in the public arena.

Another manifestation of gendered limitations emerges from the assumption of a gendered boundary between "domestic" and "public" activity. As Schirin Amir-Moazami notes with regard to the headscarf, the headscarf moves religion out of domestic spaces and into public spaces, yet retains a reminder of women's domestic roles (2001). Yet if we consciously locate women's volunteerism in the public arena, rather than moving out of the domestic realm, women's activities can be understood as redefining what is included in the public. Rather than challenging the notion of essentialized gender roles, this challenges external assumptions that map those roles onto a public/private division. Domestic-type activities become one part of the public sphere, particularly as they intersect with social welfare.

Second, it is clear that women, and especially volunteers, are participating in the production of public discourses in al-Dahiyya. Through these discourses they are contributing to the authentication of 'Ashura, the construction of community service as a social norm, and the proliferation of a broader normative moral system, as well as ongoing discussions about gender roles, natures, relations, and equity. In essence, women are participating in defining the public, not merely through their visibility and presence, but through their active engagement in public debate on these issues as well. However, it is unclear to what degree these women's discourses and debates are heard and by whom they are heard.

This is due in part to the existence of gendered spaces, like women's *jam'iyyat* and *majalis*. It is also due to the inescapably embodied quality of communicative practices that marks women's discourses as *women's* discourses. Women in al-Dahiyya today have achieved higher levels of education than ever before, and have begun to play a vocal and visible role in spaces that have been historically marked as male (e.g., as doctors, theologians, engineers, etc.). Yet when they speak and act, their words and actions are still gendered. Even as participants in the public, to a certain extent, women are inhabiting a separate sphere.

One response to this situation is to suggest that women's discourses comprise one of several possible coexisting publics. The question then remains of how and where these publics intersect; with regard to both who produced public discourses and who are engaged in their reception. Yet rather than assume a situation of multiple separate publics, it might be useful to imagine a "trans-gendered space"; a space of overlap and fluidity between male and female public spheres, and a space that is in critical ways determinant of those spheres.[27] A transgendered space includes women's discourses as a constituent part of the public sphere without erasing the hierarchies and structural limitations women face in their participation.

In conclusion, let us consider some of the real effects of limitations and expectations women face with regard to public participation. Even where physical or formal exclusions do not exist, "social inequalities can infect deliberation" through both subtle techniques of control and blatant structural limitations (Fraser 1999: 119). The effect that the convergence between beliefs about women's natural proclivities and the structure of community work has on the division of labor in *jam'iyyat* is a case in point. This extends beyond the *jam'iyyat* to political and other leadership more generally.[28] Politics in Lebanon meets stereotypical expectations of corruption, and elections generally involve economic and family interests. As such, politics, especially at the state level, is one of the arenas in which women's voices are least audible. Those few women who are elected to Parliament generally attain office based upon their relation to prominent male relatives (e.g., the sister of the prime minister).

Some Hizbullah women view the state as an arena where women should make their voices heard, often citing the Iranian Parliament as an example. At one discussion of the party's women's committee, the question of how to include a woman on the list of candidates for the next parliamentary elections provoked heated discussion. Those present drew upon religious texts about the importance of women's public responsibilities, asserting the need to facilitate women's participation in government. It was generally bemoaned that the time was not right, for two reasons, both revolving around religiously inflected education.

The first involved the necessity of educating men about the proper interpretations of Islam, so that they would support the participation of women in the public sphere.[29] The second reason concerned the need to educate women, due to a perceived dearth of women qualified for political office. The Hizbullah women at the meeting exemplified the statement of a leading shaykh who follows Fadlullah: "Women have to master theology and Shi'i law and interpret it independently . . . they can make Islamic theology from women for women" (quoted in Böttcher 2001: 5). This should not imply, however, that public discourses produced by women do not contribute to the limitations of the public sphere. An apt example is when volunteers use the notion that women have the same capacity for *al-'aql* as men to argue that community service should be the "rational" choice for "good Muslim" women in al-Dahiyya—the logical extension of a God-given moral responsibility and the ideal way to emulate Sayyida Zaynab's revolutionary example. While this argument draws upon notions of gender equity, it also contributes to the construction of a social norm that carries moral implications for women with regard to status and reputation. Such gender-specific expectations affect participation in the public sphere just as gender-specific limitations do.

The fact that Hizbullah women at the meeting were interested in women's state-level political participation—this despite the palpable absence of the Lebanese state in al-Dahiyya—reflects the ambivalence of the party and Islamist Shi'i Lebanese in general toward the state lacunae filled by their social welfare services.[30] On the one hand, those lacunae have provided impetus to social solidarity that extends to political solidarity around elections and in support of the Islamic Resistance. It also allows for local level prioritization of Islamic ideals of *takaful ijtima'i* over other notions of welfare. On the other hand, since its participation in the 1992 Lebanese elections, Hizbullah has explicitly not sought to establish an Islamic state in Lebanon, instead emphasizing coexistence in a multi-confessional state. In this regard, the absence of the state is viewed as a burden that prevents the community from "catching-up" to other groups in the country.

Notes

The field research in Beirut on which this essay is based took place from October 1999 through July 2001, and was made possible by a Social Science Research

Council International Dissertation Research Fellowship, a National Science Foundation Dissertation Research Fellowship, a grant from Emory University's Internationalization Fund, and a PEO International Scholar Award. The Center for Behavioral Research directed by Dr. Samir Khalaf provided an academic home in Beirut. Portions of this paper were presented at the 2001 Annual Meeting of the American Anthropological Association, the 2002 Annual Meeting of the Middle East Studies Association, and the Vernacular Modernities seminar at Emory University. I am grateful to those panels and audiences as well as to Donald Donham, Sondra Hale, Suad Joseph, Bruce Knauft, Corinne Kratz, Donna Murdock, and Armando Salvatore for their valuable feedback. My greatest gratitude is reserved for the Lebanese women and men who shared this part of their lives with me and who continue to do so.

1. "al-Dahiyya" means "the suburb." While the southern suburb is not Beirut's only suburb, popular usage has designated it "the suburb," while others are referred to by name.
2. *Takaful ijtima'i*—in its meaning of mutual social responsibility—was also used by Sunni Islamist scholars, including Sayyid Qutb (Beinin 2001).
3. With the exceptions of prominent political or religious figures (e.g., Sayyid Muhammad Hussein Fadlullah), all names have been altered.
4. After Musa al-Sadr's disappearance, his legacy was taken up in different forms by these political parties, as well as by his sister Sayyida Rabab al-Sadr and Sayyid Fadlullah, among others. Hizbullah was founded in October 1982 by a group that broke away from Harakat Amal, citing their overly secular nature and their ineffective efforts at resisting Israeli occupation. For more on this, see Hudson (1968), Ajami (1986), Norton (1987), and Halawi (1992).
5. For a comprehensive journalist's overview of the war, see Fisk (1990).
6. Though the border is still disputed and Israeli planes continue to fly over Lebanon, active violence has subsided significantly since Israeli withdrawal.
7. See Manoukian's discussion (chapter 2 in this volume) of Nûr id-dîn's welfare activities as constituting a political movement.
8. For more on Shi'i Islam and 'Ashura see Momen (1985), Richard (1995 [1991]) and Pinault (1992).
9. Advocates of authenticated 'Ashura pointed to scholarly attempts to ascertain the most accurate history of the battle in order to combat what they viewed as its unfortunate mythologization.
10. While *majalis* were probably held throughout Shi'i history in what is now Lebanon, the practice of self-flagellation was brought to Lebanon from Iran early in the 20th century (Ende 1978).
11. Today these occur mainly in the southern Lebanese town of Nabatieh (see also Norton and Safa 2000).
12. Following the lead of Iran, Lebanese Shi'i clerics have issued fatwas condemning the practice, and Hizbullah banned it outright in the mid-1990s. See Deeb (2003).
13. Specifically, *'abaya* is the colloquial Arabic word for the Iranian-style long loose black cloak women wear over their hair and clothing, leaving only face and hands visible. In Lebanon, wearing an *'abaya* often signifies either membership in Hizbullah or relation to a prominent religious figure. Other Islamist Shi'i women wear the more common *"shar'i* dress," a long coat-dress worn with a scarf (*hijab*) carefully pinned to show only the face. It is rare to see a Lebanese Shi'i woman wearing a face veil (*fish*).

14. The classic examples of women's mobilization as part of larger national or religious revolutionary or resistance movements are Iran and Algeria. See also Peteet (1991) on the Palestinian national resistance, and Hegland (1998) on the Pakistani Shi'i Islamist movement.
15. Contrast Hegland's (1987) observation that at her Iranian research site practices of self-injurious flagellation using chains were revived during the revolution as a form of political resistance.
16. Donham reminds us that the concept of revolution as "an attempt rationally to design a new political order" did not emerge until after 1789 (1999: 1). No doubt the linking of Shi'ism and revolution—originally in Iran—owes much to Shari'ati and others who were influenced by Marxism and the political left. In Lebanon 'Ashura's reinterpretation as revolutionary was fueled by Iran's Islamic Revolution that Hegland (1983) calls the " 'Imam Husain as Example' framework." The political meanings of what Fischer (1980) calls "the Karbala paradigm" have also been discussed by Peters (1956), Thaiss (1972), Fischer (1980), Hegland (1983), Mottahedeh (1985), Good and Good (1988), Keddie (1995), and Aghaie (2001).
17. *Majalis aza' fi beirut wa al-junub wa-l-Bekaa*, March 30, 2001, 10.
18. As discussed by Eickelman and Anderson, these media become more participatory as the asymmetries between producers and consumers are reduced, and "the boundaries between public and private communication that once seemed clear become blurred" (1999: 4). Blurring here occurs as radio call-in shows bring conversations that were once privately held into the public arena.
19. While some of these conversations no doubt were prompted by my presence, heated conversations during which I was not present were frequently related to me after they ended, and I entered into several discussions of *majalis* details already in progress.
20. For discussions of how investing reproductive activities with political meaning both transforms and reproduces gendered divisions of labor and structures of domination, see Peteet (1991) on Palestinian women, Hale (1996) on Sudan, and Kamalkhani (1998) on Iran.
21. Another parallel shift is that Zaynab is emphasized more by volunteers (not the religious leadership) than Fatima, often considered the paramount female model in Shi'ism. See Friedl (1997) for a comparison of these models.
22. This parallels, or perhaps follows as a later component of, the reformulation of the *shari'a* as a normative system (Salvatore 1997: 48, 2000), and is an element of the discourse Salvatore discusses as "able to convert a more encompassing transcendent order into a set of socially immanent norms" (1997: 49).
23. I use the term the way that my interlocutors did, to refer not only to reasoning with regard to Islamic jurisprudence, but also to an individual's capacity for reasoning in daily life.
24. Despite Israeli withdrawal, the emphasis on participation in the resistance community had not subsided by July 2001. Reasons for this include the continuing border dispute, ongoing Israeli bombardments and Israeli occupation of Palestine, in addition to the inspiration provided by the victory of the resistance.
25. Activist women in this community generally criticized Western feminism for equating men and women as essentially the same, and linked that "sameness" to *masawa*. Along with advocating *'adala* (equity, justice), they promoted feminist interpretations of Islam that emphasized what Leila Ahmad (1992) calls

the "ethical egalitarianism" of Islam (cf. Böttcher 2001). For more on Shi'i Islam and feminism see Afshar (1998), Mir-Hosseini (1999), Moghissi (1999) and Böttcher (2001).

26. While for obvious political reasons these *jam'iyyat* do not have any direct financial links to the U.S.-dominated INGO funding system, they maintain multiple transnational ties to resources, both within and outside the Muslim world.

27. Here I draw on Höfert and Salvatore's notion of a "transcultural space" (2000).

28. This is not to say that there are no women in leadership positions in the community, just that they are few and far between. For example, the director of one of the al-Mabarrat Association's schools is a woman, as is the chief of staff of the hospital run by the Martyr's Association.

29. The women in this meeting suggested that men's education should include the necessity of assisting their wives with housework and childcare, to facilitate their obligations with regard to the social welfare of society.

30. Indeed, this dynamic can be contrasted with Manoukian's discussion (chapter 2 in this volume) of the way that social welfare has been institutionalized as part of the state in postrevolutionary Iran.

References

Abu-Lughod, Lila. 1998. *Remaking Women: Feminism and Modernity in the Middle East*. Princeton: Princeton University Press.

Aghaie, Kamran. 2001. "The Karbala Narrative: Shi'i Political Discourse in Modern Iran in the 1960s and 1970s." *Journal of Islamic Studies* 12, 2: 151–76.

Afshar, Haleh. 1998. *Islam and Feminisms: An Iranian Case Study*. New York: St. Martin's Press.

Ahmed, Leila. 1992. *Women and Gender in Islam: Historical Roots of a Modern Debate*. New Haven: Yale University Press.

Ajami, Fouad. 1986. *The Vanished Imam: Musa al-Sadr and the Shi'a of Lebanon*. Ithaca: Cornell University Press.

Amir-Moazami, Schirin. 2001. "Hybridity and Anti-Hybridity: The Islamic Headscarf and its Opponents in the French Public Sphere." In *Muslim Traditions and Modern Techniques of Power*, vol. 3 of *Yearbook of the Sociology of Islam*, ed. Armando Salvatore, Hamburg: Lit; New Brunswick, NJ: Transaction, 309–29.

Antoun, Richard, and Marie Elaine Hegland, eds. 1987. *Religious Resurgence: Contemporary Cases in Islam, Christianity, and Judaism*. Syracuse: Syracuse University Press.

Ayubi, Nazih. 1995. "Radical Islamism and Civil Society in the Middle East." *Contention* 4, 3: 79–105.

Beinin, Joel. 2001. "Late Capitalist Crisis, Middle East Oil, and Political Islam." *Between the Lines*, April.

Beinin, Joel, and Joe Stork, eds. 1997. *Political Islam: Essays from Middle East Report*. Berkeley: University of California Press.

Böttcher, Annabelle. 2001. "Im Schatten des Ayatollahs: Schiitische Feministische Theologie in Libanon am Anfang." *Neue Zürcher Zeitung*, March 7: 5.

Calhoun, Craig. 1999. "Introduction: Habermas and the Public Sphere." In *Habermas and the Public Sphere*, ed. Craig Calhoun, Cambridge, MA: The MIT Press, 1–50.

Cobban, Helena. 1985. *The Making of Modern Lebanon*. London: Hutchinson.

Deeb, Lara. 2003. *An Enchanted Modern: Gender and Public Piety Among Islamist Shi'i Muslims in Beirut*. Ph.D. dissertation, Emory University.

Eickelman, Dale F., and Jon W. Anderson. 1999. "Redefining Muslim Publics." In *New Media in the Muslim World*, ed. Dale Eickelman and Jon Anderson, Bloomington: Indiana University Press, 1–18.

Eickelman, Dale F., and Armando Salvatore. 2004 [2002]. "Muslim Publics." In *Public Islam and Common Good*, ed. Armando Salvatore and Dale F. Eickelman, Leiden and Boston: Brill, 3–27.

Ende, Werner. 1978. "The Flagellations of Muharram and the Shi'ite 'Ulama'." *Der Islam* 55: 19–36.

Fischer, Michael. 1980. *Iran: From Religious Dispute to Revolution*. Cambridge, MA: Harvard University Press.

Fisk, Robert. 1990. *Pity the Nation: The Abduction of Lebanon*. New York: Simon and Schuster.

Fraser, Nancy. 1999. "Rethinking the Public Sphere: A Contribution to the Critique of Actually Existing Democracy." In *Habermas and the Public Sphere*, ed. Craig Calhoun, Cambridge, MA: The MIT Press, 109–42.

Friedl, Erika. 1997. "Ideal Womanhood in Postrevolutionary Iran." In *Mixed Blessings: Gender and Religious Fundamentalism Cross-Culturally*, ed. Judy Brink and Joan Mencher, New York: Routledge, 144–55.

Good, Mary-Jo DelVecchio, and Byron J. Good. 1988. "Ritual, the State, and the Transformation of Emotional Discourse in Iranian Society." *Culture, Medicine and Psychiatry* 12: 43–63.

Habermas, Jürgen. 1989 [1962]. *The Structural Transformation of the Public Sphere*, trans. Thomas Burger, Cambridge, MA: MIT Press.

Harb el-Kak, Mona. 2000. "Post-War Beirut: Resources, Negotiations, and Contestations in the Elyssar Project." *The Arab World Geographer* 3, 4: 272–89.

Halawi, Majed. 1992. *A Lebanon Defied: Musa al-Sadr and the Shi'a Community*. Boulder, CO: Westview Press.

Hale, Sondra. 1996. *Gender Politics in Sudan: Islamism, Socialism, and the State*. Boulder, CO: Westview Press.

Hegland, Mary Elaine. 1983. "Two Images of Husain: Accommodation and Revolution in a Iranian Village." In *Religion and Politics in Iran: Shi'ism from Quietism to Revolution*, ed. Nikkie R. Keddie, New Haven, NJ: Yale University Press, 218–35.

———. 1987. "Islamic Revival or Political and Cultural Revolution? An Iranian Case Study." In *Religious Resurgence: Contemporary Cases in Islam, Christianity, and Judaism*, ed. R. Antoun and M. E. Hegland, Syracuse: Syracuse University Press, 194–219.

———. 1998. "The Power Paradox in Muslim Women's *Majales*: North-West Pakistani Mourning Rituals as Sites of Contestation over Religious Politics, Ethnicity, and Gender." *Signs* 23: 392–428.

Höfert, Almut, and Armando Salvatore. 2000. "Introduction: Beyond the Clash of Civilizations: Transcultural Politics between Europe and Islam." In *Between Europe and Islam: Shaping Modernity in a Transcultural Space*. Brussels: P.I.E.-Peter Lang, 13–35.

Hudson, Michael. 1968. *The Precarious Republic: Political Modernization in Lebanon*. New York: Random House.

Joseph, Suad. 1975. *The Politicization of Religious Sects in Borj Hammoud, Lebanon*. Ph.D. dissertation, Columbia University.

————. 1983. "Working Class Women's Networks in a Sectarian State: A Political Paradox." *American Ethnologist* 10, 1: 1–22.

————. 1997a. "The Public/Private—The Imagined Boundary in the Imagined Nation/State/Community: The Lebanese Case." *Feminist Review* 57: 73–92.

————. 1997b. "Gender and Civil Society" (Interview with Joe Stork). In *Political Islam: Essays from Middle East Report*, ed. Joel Beinin and Joe Stork, Berkeley: University of California Press, 64–70.

Kamalkhani, Zahra. 1998. *Women's Islam: Religious Practice Among Women in Today's Iran*. London: Kegan Paul International.

Keddie, Nikki R., ed. 1983. *Religion and Politics in Iran: Shi'ism from Quietism to Revolution*. New Haven: Yale University Press.

————. 1995. *Iran and the Muslim World: Resistance and Revolution*. New York: New York University Press.

Mir-Hosseini, Ziba. 1999. *Islam and Gender: The Religious Debate in Contemporary Iran*. Princeton: Princeton University Press.

Moghissi, Haideh. 1999. *Feminism and Islamic Fundamentalism: The Limits of Postmodern Analysis*. New York: Zed Books.

Momen, Moojan. 1985. *An Introduction to Shi'i Islam: The History and Doctrines of Twelver Shī'ism*. New Haven: Yale University Press.

Mottahedeh, Roy. 1985. *The Mantle of the Prophet*. New York: Simon and Schuster.

Norton, Augustus Richard. 1987. *Amal and the Shi'a: Struggle for the Soul of Lebanon*. Austin: University of Texas Press.

Norton, Augustus Richard, and Ali Safa. 2000. " 'Ashura in Nabatiyye." *Middle East Insight* 25, 3: 21–28.

Peteet, Julie. 1991. *Gender in Crisis: Women and the Palestinian Resistance Movement*. New York: Columbia University Press.

Peters, Emrys Lloyd. 1956. "A Muslim Passion Play: Key to a Lebanese Village." *Atlantic Monthly* 198: 176–80.

Pinault, David. 1992. *The Shiites: Ritual and Popular Piety in a Muslim Community*. New York: St. Martin's Press.

Reiter, Rayna. 1975. "Men and Women in the South of France: Public and Private Domains." In *Toward an Anthropology of Women*, ed. Rayna Reiter, New York: Monthly Review Press.

Richani, Nazih. 1998. *Dilemmas of Democracy and Political Parties in Sectarian Societies: The Case of the Progressive Socialist Party of Lebanon 1949–1996*. New York: St. Martin's Press.

Richard, Yann. 1995 [1991]. *Shī'ite Islam: Polity, Ideology, and Creed*, trans. Antonia Nevill, Oxford: Blackwell.

Salvatore, Armando. 1997. *Islam and the Political Discourse of Modernity*. Reading, UK: Ithaca Press.

————. 2000. "The Islamic Reform Project in the Emerging Public Sphere: The (Meta-)Normative Redefinition of *Shari'a*." In *Between Europe and Islam: Shaping Modernity in a Transcultural Space*, ed. Almut Höfert and Armando Salvatore, Brussels: P.I.E.-Peter Lang, 89–108.

Singerman, Diane. 1995. *Avenues of Participation: Family, Politics, and Networks in Urban Quarters of Cairo*. Princeton: Princeton University Press.

Thaiss, Gustav. 1972. "Religious Symbolism and Social Change: The Drama of Husain." In *Scholars, Saints, and Sufis in Muslim Religious Institutions in the Middle East Since 1500*, ed. Nikki R. Keddie, Berkeley: University of California Press, 349–66.

CHAPTER 4

"BUILDING THE WORLD" IN A GLOBAL AGE

Raymond William Baker

I slam has become the emblem of many resurgent nationalisms and violent "fundamentalisms" that have emerged in the Middle East in reaction to globalization. But this version of Islam does not stand alone; there are indeed multiple Islams, and for all the attention to the extremism and violence symbolized by the 9/11, 2001 terrorist attacks reluctant awareness has begun to seep in of a far more important, diverse, and vital transnational Islamic mainstream. Known in Arabic as the *wasatiya*, the Islamic mainstream claims hundreds of millions of adherents and is growing steadily.

Indeed, the overwhelming majority of the world's billion Muslims find in the Islamic mainstream the best expression of their own understanding of Islam. In their theoretical and activist work, a worldwide network of centrist intellectuals is elaborating for a global age a mainstream under-standing of the meaning of *istikhlaf*, that is, God's charge to humankind to complete His work on earth by "building the world" (Abu-l-Majd 1992: 8). Yet their constructive work, and the promise it carries of an opening for dialogue and constructive cooperation between cultures, has yet to be appreciated adequately in the West.[1]

This essay explores what can be understood as a politics of hope that is embodied in the discourse of the *wasatiya*. What adaptations of the Islamic legacy has the mainstream made and in what ways do these centrist interpretations meet the needs of a global age? How does the *wasatiya* understand the *maslaha 'amma* (the common good) in a globalized world and with what implications for the development of public spheres can that good be pursued? Why have the advancements of the Islamic main-stream received so little attention in the West? These are all the questions I address in the following pages.

It is not difficult to discern the Islamic rationalization of the kind of terrorism that brought the World Trade Center down. Criminal political acts were first thought out in an Islamic vocabulary of *jihad* (struggle for the faith) and *jahiliya* (condemnation as un-Islamic, atheist, or pagan), traceable to extremist Islamist thinkers Abul A 'la Mawdudi and, even more emphatically, Sayyid Qutb. For all the power of this linkage, it is nevertheless important to acknowledge the quite distinctive character of these readings of Islam's sacred texts. These extremist interpretations originate from prison "think tanks." They are written in blood drawn by torturers, a disciplining of the body by highly repressive regimes that engenders a refusal among militant Muslims of all efforts to build a nonviolent middle space, or an alternative to resisting colonialism—and today globalization. Rather, only counterviolence can salve their wounds; existing regimes are not only repressive but are also subservient to the interests of hegemonic Western powers. And so some militants from throughout the Islamic world join forces to advocate violence as their response to the rapacious "clash of civilizations" precipitated by the West and known as colonialism, rewritten and updated by the dismal record of exploitation and oppression once labeled "neo-colonialism."

Militant Islamists remind us that violence on a wide scale was the price for the success of what Theodor von Laue terms "the world revolution of Westernization."[2] The extremist networks argue to very receptive audiences that the continuing violence of the West and of the regimes it supports must be met by armed counterattack. They point out, accurately, that existing political systems in the Arab Islamic world and the public arenas they just barely tolerate have a conception of the *maslaha 'amma* that in fact goes no further than the sons, literally, waiting in the wings, for their turn to appropriate the resources of the nation while serving the interests of the dominant West.

Meanwhile, economic globalization promises a better world but only widens the gap everywhere between the privileged and the poor. The provocative wealth of the new strata of highly mobile "globals" exacerbates the anger of the militants and increases the audience for their message among the stranded "locals." The extremists address their call for vengeance to a growing army of "vagabonds," dispossessed and left behind by a world moving at the speed of light flashes on computer screens that track capital flows around the world (Bauman 1998: 77–102). What the phenomenon of militant Islam teaches us is that people who find neither hope nor even a place to stand in a world set in motion by others will adopt any means at their disposal to slow it down. Thus they take refuge in simplistic understandings of an imagined faith of unchanging institutions and fixed formulas. The slogans of the *amir*s (leaders of militant groups) promise to take hold of a world spinning out of control, and so, "Islam is the solution."

Yet Islam has maintained the capacity to inspire hope for peaceful social change in the face of all this violence. For the purposes of this study, the Islamic mainstream or *wasatiya* is defined as the broad, centrist current that is driving the contemporary, transnational Islamic revival that began in the 1970s and continues to this day. This definition of the mainstream derives from the self-understanding of major centrist figures, groups, and movements that regularly assign their origins to the reformist trend that originates in the pioneering work of the Iranian Jamal-al-Din al-Afghani (1838–1897) and his most influential disciple, the Egyptian Muhammad 'Abduh (1849–1905). 'Abduh's reforms aimed, through reasoned interpretation, to restore Islam to its leading role as a civilization with a universal message of peace and progress for humankind.

The contemporary mainstream thus originated with 'Abduh in Egypt in the late 19th century. It transformed itself from an elite to a mass phenomenon by the mid-20th century and enjoyed a worldwide resurgence in the decades from the 1970s to the present. The mainstream today consists of a complex network of centrist Islamist scholars, groups, and movements that share a common orientation of resistance, peaceful if possible, to Western intrusions into the Islamic world and openness to accommodation with superior Western power on the global level. At the same time, the mainstream pushes relentlessly for reforms of the inherited Islamic tradition in line with the needs of the new age (al-Qaradawi 2002 [2000]).

It is important to note that once the Islamic mainstream is brought into view, it becomes clear that the distorted and criminalized Islam of the networks of violent groups, with its deadly appeal to terrorist minorities around the world, is not the Islam most important nor most worthy of sustained attention and analysis by scholars. Remarkably, alongside the violent militants, the Muslim world has produced "radicals of the center" who by and large renounce offensive violence (with Palestine and Iraq being exceptions, as Dyalah Hamzah explores in chapter 7) and look for profound but peaceful social transformation, reform, and revitalization of inherited traditions. Islam is fully implicated in their dreams as well. They, too, are building global networks for the exchange of ideas and joint actions. However, their aim is to create or identify new spaces of opportunity for reform and modes of resistance consistent with their pacific ends. They work to strengthen existing public arenas, even as they critique their inadequacies for democratic transformations. These centrists move with particular deftness through the new public spheres of our electronic age, to join other prophets of reconstruction and reconciliation around the globe. However, the wellsprings of their strength and implications of utilizing it are little understood. Strangely, they have been barely noticed in the West.

The Islamic mainstream draws most effectively of all Islamic groupings on the inherent sources of absorption and adaptation of the Islamic civilizational heritage (Waines 2000 [1995]: 33–59). Mainstream centrist intellectuals reassert the necessity of a creative and collective *ijtihad* (interpretation) in the interest of the *maslaha 'amma*. They act consciously and deliberately to recover and rejuvenate the roots in the faith for such an interpretative project. In doing so, they create the flexible foundations for an Islamist project of peaceful resistance, intellectual reform, and gradual social transformation in the unprecedented conditions of a globalized world. They explain patiently that in contemporary conditions the realization of the *maslaha 'amma* is tied not so much to particular arenas of civic and political action but rather to the strengthening of an Islamic civilizational identity without which neither effective resistance nor self-directed reform is possible. In this precise sense their project evokes the power of an Islamic identity attuned to our global age. They show how Islam, in the face of the cultural destructiveness of the forces of globalization, can adapt to new conditions without sacrificing the most fundamental elements of Islamic civilizational identity, notably the commitment to *istikhlaf*.

The accomplishments of the "Islamic awakening" since the 1970s have hardly been registered in the West. Western analysts of this awakening have for the most part failed to understand the surprising congruence between a revived Islamic civilizational heritage and the new conditions of globalism. They have not grasped the ways in which the Islamic mainstream draws on the inherent flexibility of the Islamic civilizational heritage to create networked structures well adapted to the new conditions of our global age.

This chapter draws on complexity theory for a new and particularly promising angle of vision from which to address the enigma of the surprising success of the worldwide Islamic revival in the new conditions of globalism. Although complexity theory originated in the natural sciences, particularly biology and physics, it is also useful for the study of theories of cultural traditions. The notion of a "complex adaptive system" and the distinctive logic required to understand such a system existing in the conditions of what Manuel Castells has termed a "network society" opens new interpretive possibilities for scholars. More specifically, the principal substantive argument here, cast in the language of complexity theory, is that mainstream Islam, elaborated as a civilizational project since the 1970s in transnational networks of Islamic centrists, has taken on the character of a complex adaptive system (Baker 2005).

The *wasatiya* is the most important experience of Islam in this context, and is best understood in terms of the codes and logic of complex adaptive systems as they are brought into view by complexity theory. The core concepts of complexity theory serve to clarify the ways in which such systems, including theories and cultural traditions like Islam, adapt to a rapidly changing environment. If we focus on how these systems emerge we can use complexity theory to explore how complex systems first take shape and often assume forms difficult to recognize as wholes. We can then use the concept of "evolution" within complexity theory to explain how these "difficult wholes" develop as self-organizing systems, exploring along the way how they use processes of "screening" to help stabilize the fluid identities that these new systems project (Castells 1996a, 1996b; Taylor 2001).

There is, of course, more than one way of bringing groups like the New Islamists of the *wasatiya* into view. Some of the more interesting Western work approaches Islamist groups by using the theoretical lens of civil society in creative tension with the nation-state. Other scholars seek to understand the development of the mainstream by placing it in the context of the inherited, classic notions of *islah* (reform) and *tajdid* (renewal). Such approaches are valuable because they offset the devil theories of Islam that represent little more than a demonization, rationalized by a single-minded and distorting focus on the extremists. These civil society and Islamic reform approaches also serve comparative ends, more often than not setting developments in the Islamic world against the historical experience of the West. From this comparative perspective, questions that have both theoretical and practical relevance are raised: Is Islam creating forms and institutions that approximate the modern polity? Should Western-supported regimes, like the one in Egypt, allow Islamists to compete freely in democratic elections? Are Islamists capable of generating democratic politics with the active public spheres that enable citizens to control their own destinies? More generally, should Islamists be accommodated or confronted by the West?

By utilizing complexity theory, this chapter can explore possible Muslim futures without reference solely to the Western past, situating them within the context of a truly worldwide globalization. As Marx foresaw, in an age marked by the worldwide triumph of capitalism, all fixed forms and structures of public life dissolve into thin air. Complexity theory explores how, under these conditions of chaos, new patterns of meaning and social action develop in public spheres defined above all by the electronic technologies that bind a singular global order. In particular, complexity theory provides a useful angle of vision from which to take note of the fate of Islam in these unprecedented conditions and as yet not fully understood social spaces. Complexity theory provides insight into how to best track the emergence and evolution of adaptable meanings and mutable patterns of action in the new public spheres of an age of global capitalism.

The argument for the suitability of complexity theory is premised on the historical judgment, still controversial of course, that the world is experiencing epochal change and entering a new age, that is, the global age (Castells 1996a). The technological innovations of the Information Revolution are everywhere triggering revolutionary changes in the nature of economy, society, and culture. Among their most far-reaching effects is the ostensible weakening of the nation-state and the national civil societies it makes possible. These forces of fundamental transformation arise from the most developed societies, but no human community can now escape their effects. They first took hold in the 1970s in the most developed industrial states and are today registering their effects worldwide. Everywhere these new economic, social, and cultural forms are challenging the autonomy and power of states and civil societies.

Consequently, ways of interpreting the changes brought about by globalization and their human consequences can no longer be centered exclusively on the state and the public spheres it defines. Nor can those who study Islam afford to focus exclusively on the unfolding of tradition or even its reform and renewal without attention to the powerful new forces that are changing the global realities within which all such developments will take place. The perspective here raises different questions: What are Islam's prospects in a global age? More specifically, can the broad and inclusive Islamic civilizational identity that the New Islamists cultivate meet the challenges of the new age? What can be learned from their experiments in adapting an inherited tradition to a transformative identity project of pacific social change in the face of the assertive forces of global-ization? In what ways does the character of the New Islamist School itself mirror the new network logic operative in the transformed social terrain that is opening up everywhere around us? What does the work of the New Islamists tell us about the new network structures that complex adaptive systems are now generating?

Given the contemporary crisis of the nation-state and civil society, issues of identity have moved center stage in social and political theory. The power of identity in the global age is widely appreciated, with impor-tant distinctions registered between the restrictive politics of narrow, exclusive identities and the more expansive political possibilities of more inclusive project identities (Castells 1996a, 1996b). Complexity theory provides new and useful ways of looking at groups that inherit a sacred tra-dition and attempt to "read" it in ways that provide the intellectual and cultural resources to move from narrow resistance to broad project identi-ties. This development of new and more open and inclusive identities is linked to engagement in public spheres with broad issues of the public good like development and democracy. It finds tangible expression in con-crete projects that take shape as part of efforts to rebuild societies in a self-directed way despite extreme pressure from intrusive external forces. To give sharper focus and precision to the analysis that follows, the Egyptian New Islamist School will stand for the larger universe of moderate and independent Islamists who now have a presence that reaches throughout the Arab Islamic arena and the larger world beyond.

The Egyptian New Islamist School

The New Islamists coalesced as a group in the late 1970s and early 1980s. They aimed to establish an independent public presence to guide the Islamic Awakening without inviting repression. To this end, they constituted themselves loosely as a "school" of Islamist thinkers rather than a mass movement or a political party. The core group of diverse Islamist intellec-tuals, including both lay and religious figures, in 1981 wrote the manifesto for the group. They initially circulated their statement informally among "approximately one hundred and fifty intellectuals," not publishing the document until a full decade later (Abu-l-Majd 1992 [1991]: 23, 34). From the outset, the school has had the horizontal structure of a flexible network rather than a rigid hierarchy.

Relying on overlapping personal contacts, the boundaries of the net-work are never clearly demarcated, giving the school a permeable and open character. Moreover, as "a statement of principles, rather than a precise working program" tied to a specific time and place, the group's manifesto invites like-minded centrists to recreate the school, adapting to their own special circumstances (ibid.: 33). This approach creates a capacity for self-organization and reorganization. The coherence of the principles, coupled with the flexibility of the forms in which they can be instantiated, gives the emerging networks an infinitely adaptable character while still remaining recognizable. A guiding intelligence for the school emerges through spontaneous intellectual exchange, dialogue, and debate, rather than a fixed leadership in any formal sense. This approach avoids the common pitfall of singular leadership figures vulnerable to repression. In this way, the school works through informal and spontaneous cooperative efforts that mimic the "parallel processing" of computer networks.

The New Islamists do not hesitate to interact freely and in variable ways, both competitive and cooperative, with other Islamist and non-Islamist networks. Not only the school itself but also the surroundings of which it is a part is thus constituted of diverse networks that are all undergoing rapid and unpredictable changes. Over several decades the school has evolved in this way as an elusive component of a broader environment from which it could be distinguished only with considerable difficulty, that is, it has the character of a difficult whole. While the New Islamists originate in Egypt and give Egyptian public arenas their major attention, the New Islamist School through its multiple connections has developed at once a national, transnational, and even global character, extending its influence, for example, to the important minority Muslim communities in the West.

By approaching participation in public life through the mechanism of such a school, the New Islamist School has been able to make the most of the limited opportunities of the political arena and civil society that emerged in the post-Nasser years in Egypt. It has done so, however, without making either political participation or engagements in civil society an end in themselves. Rather, the New Islamists consistently set their sites on the long term and can therefore survive the inevitable setbacks of the political and civil developments under authoritarian conditions. They focus on education and culture, critiquing the shortcomings of the national institutions and encouraging the development of alternatives in the interstices of official life.

For all of these reasons, the New Islamists have been able to accommodate ruling power without losing sight of long-term transformational goals. Thus, while the New Islamists have paid attention to the experiments of the growing number of activists of the Islamic wave in the political arena and in civil society (notably in the economic arena, in elections of professional associations, and in parliamentary alliances with non-Islamist political parties), their concerns are much broader. In their own activist interventions in public life, they reach beyond politics and civil society, and beyond Egypt's borders to address Islamic movements throughout the world in their remarkably diverse settings. They aim to

provide what they call a centrist *tarshid* (guidance) to the Islamic
Awakening in varied public arenas, including the new electronic public
spaces that have everywhere assumed major importance.

Tarshid: Harnessing the Power of Identity to Build the World

Quite explicitly, the New Islamists define the main task for Islamist
intellectuals in all public arenas open to them as a fearless interpretive
effort that aims at enabling centrist Islamic movements to address the priority challenges of the age. Tariq al-Bishri, for example, asserts the absolute
necessity in the new globalized conditions of accelerating changes for
an *ijtihad* that produces a new *fiqh*, consistent with these turbulent times
(al-Bishri 1996: 17). The required new *fiqh*, Yusuf al-Qaradawi explains, will
"welcome changes for the better, while preserving the best of the past"
(al-Qaradawi 2002 [2000]: 171–72). The Islamic world, al-Bishri adds, will
be at continued disadvantage unless the dramatic transformations that the
world is experiencing are analyzed and understood within an Islamic framework that assesses the new realities in the light of the core values and higher
purposes of Islam. He reasons that this essential work of *ijtihad* represents
the highest priority and most important *maslaha 'amma* of the Islamic world
(al-Bishri 1996: 17). From the *wasatiya*, the New Islamists inherited the principle mechanism to accomplish this central intellectual task of interpretation, the concept of *tarshid*, and the related notion of the mind–body that
connects the intellectual leadership to the followers of Islamist movements. An Islamist project identity necessarily relies on such linkage
between guiding élites and receptive masses whose channeled energies and
talents are essential for the social transformation that *istikhlaf* demands.

Calculated Inattention: The West and the *Wasatiya*

Centrist positions like those developed under the *tarshid* of the New
Islamists are now widely circulated throughout the Islamic world. In elaborating these positive stands, the individuals and groups of the mainstream
stand resolutely against Islamist extremists who violently attack the West
and speak for a retrograde political Islam. They clearly also provide an
improved basis for dialogue with the West, though this opening has yet to
receive the response it deserves.

The persistent inattention of Western policy makers and publics to the
record of the Islamic moderates requires considerable effort. For decades
Islam's centrists have been raising their voices in condemnation of criminal
political violence by extremists of all kinds, including those who hold abu-
sive power as well as those who oppose them. They are inspired by an inclusive vision of *istikhlaf* and the responsibilities it places on all humankind and
not simply Muslims. Such centrist groups do not hesitate in public forums

of all kinds to reject the worldview of the reductionist Islamic militants who set *dar al-islam* (the "house of Islam") violently against *dar al-harb* (the "house of war"). They champion a model of gradual social transformation that aims to preserve the best of what has been accomplished worldwide, including the West, while insisting that humankind can do better. They seek development with a strategy that begins with cultural and educational reform, based on reason and science. They speak out against the resort to violence in their own societies, whether by the regime or its opponents, as un-Islamic. They have been particularly effective in countering the distorted views that prompt militant assaults on the arts, women, and non-Muslims.

With the same forthrightness, the New Islamists have condemned the rise in violence around the world. In the face of the mass murders of 9/11, Islamic intellectuals speaking for the *wasatiya* issued timely and unequivocal condemnations of the killers. On September 27 Yusuf al-Qaradawi, Tariq al-Bishri, Muhammad Salim al-'Awwa and Fahmi Huwaydi issued a fatwa (religious ruling) that pronounced that "the terrorist acts . . . considered by Islamic law . . . (constitute) the crime of *hirabah* (waging war against society)" (al-Qaradawi et al. 2001). They are all part of the New Islamist School of centrist thinkers who have been active as critics of all forms of violence in very public ways in Egypt for decades. The influence of their views on this matter has expanded widely in the transnational Islamic world. Yet, the actions of these New Islamists for the most part remain unseen and their words fall on deaf ears in the West. Despite its very public character, their record leaves little trace on Western understandings of Islam or developments in the Islamic world. The very existence of such Islamic centrists is openly and repeatedly denied.[3]

This Western ignorance of the pursuit of peaceful remaking and repair in Islam's name can likely be explained by the fact that the New Islamists are strong advocates of a future for the peoples of the Islamic world of their own making, rather than copying the Western model or even forging a so-called liberal Islam. Moreover, their condemnation of the violence of the Islamic extremists does not translate into forgiveness for the violence of the West, particularly the United States and Israel (al-Bishri 2002). On a whole range of foreign political and economic issues, the New Islamists directly criticize currently existing Arab regimes for their failure to protect the right of self-determination of Arab Islamic peoples. They seize whatever opportunities existing public spheres provide to urge that when ruling regimes fail them, the peoples themselves should act directly through boycotts and other peaceful means to refuse destructive plans made by others for their future.[4] They have not hesitated to criticize all such excesses of Western and particularly American and Israeli power. Yet, as their total record indicates, the intellectuals of the *wasatiya* are neither pro nor anti-Western; rather, they stand emphatically for the peoples of the Arab Islamic world. They speak for a *maslaha 'amma* that is defined in Islamist civilization terms, vigorously defending their right to shape their own future in line with the higher purposes of Islam.

The neglect and misunderstanding of centrist Islamist voices derives not only from these political causes. It also has intellectual roots. Recognizing and grasping the importance of mainstream Islam in our global age provides a daunting challenge but not primarily for the reasons usually advanced. The focus of critical perspectives on surface misperceptions and misunderstandings or even the systemic distortions of an inherited Orientalist discourse underestimates the analytical task, despite the important contributions of such scholars as John Esposito and Edward Said. The more fundamental challenge today compounds two factors. The first arises from the astonishing and only dimly grasped complexity of the phenomenon of contemporary Islam itself, now more fully enabled by the new and as yet poorly understood conditions and logics of what Manuel Castells has usefully called "the network society" (Castells 1996a). The second is the exhaustion of the critical resources, what Mark Taylor has aptly labeled a "critical emergency," that would allow us to interpret Islam as a civilizational project that is successfully adapting to the new conditions of our time (Taylor 2001: 47–72). These two barriers to understanding are rarely considered in tandem, yet they are related in complex ways for those with eyes to see.

The *Wasatiya* as a Complex System and Difficult Whole

Complex systems, with their prototype in the globally dispersed production systems of the new economy, are emergent and self-organizing. They arise from particular circumstances and attain the capacity to achieve purposes without having rigid, fixed ends. They assume the character of "difficult wholes," that is, new networked structures that arise in the threatened conditions of chaos when old structures are weakened or collapse. They are not easily apprehended because their fluid forms and emerging structures cannot be "read" mechanically from past trajectories or rigidly anticipated futures (Taylor 2001: 36). It is precisely such a temporal and flexible character that allows the *wasatiya* as a complex adaptive system to operate as a whole without a totalizing effect. In effect, complex adaptive systems belie the fears that have driven and ultimately paralyzed the most promising, recent cultural criticism, such as Derrida's deconstruction, Foucault's social constructivism, and Baudrillard's theory of simulation.

Precisely at the moment when these despairing critical approaches that condemned all systems as ultimately totalitarian were capturing the most lively minds, a new economy and a new social and cultural world were taking shape. The Information Revolution and the resulting transformations gave the lie to the essential premise of the reigning cultural criticism of the last three decades of the 20th century. As Mark Taylor reports, "it is simply wrong to insist that all systems and structures necessarily totalize and inevitably repress." In a breathtaking *tour d'horizon* of complexity studies, Taylor succeeds in closing the gap between the sciences and humanities to disclose the history and logic of the natural, social, and cultural networks that are today transforming human life around the globe. Taylor brings into view precisely those structures that cultural critics have for three decades pronounced unimaginable, that is, non-totalizing systems that nevertheless act as wholes. Taylor shows how "important work now being done in complexity studies suggests that such systems and structures are not merely theoretically conceivable but are actually at work in natural, social, and cultural networks" (Taylor 2001: 65). Such complex, adaptive systems rest on flexible foundations and they assume the character of difficult wholes. The Islamic *wasatiya* functions in just this way, or to say the same thing more directly, mainstream Islam presents itself as a prototypical expression of "emerging network culture."

The New Islamist School as a Complex, Adaptive System

The particular realities, both predicaments and accomplishments, of the New Islamists exemplify the ways in which the Islamic mainstream or *wasatiya* is at work in the global age as a complex, adaptive system. The New Islamists have elaborated a noteworthy collective interpretation of Islam that manifests itself in ways subject to verification "in human acts that take place in human history and society" (Said 1997: 41). The issue here is not whether the Islam of the New Islamists is genuine or not in some abstract and unverifiable sense. Rather, the challenge is to recognize and assess this particular and fully human mainstream *ijtihad* of Islam that has left a record that can be objectively reviewed. At the same time, this accessible work of the New Islamists suggests the shape of an Islamic architecture of flexible yet comprehensive structures adapted to the "network society" that is everywhere emerging as the dominant social form (Castells 1996a). Their creative readings of the heritage, in Islamic terms their *ijtihad* of the center, represent a development of the cultural and intellectual legacy of the *wasatiya* that stands against the rigid and exclusionary thought of the violent militants.

Their school both responds to and reveals the logic of our global age, as much in the very character of their school as in the evolving interpretation of Islam that they are producing. In short, the New Islamists are actively and consciously creating new networks of Islamic moderation that are confirming the proposition that the *wasatiya* is making itself one with emerging network culture. Through their interpretive efforts in the public spaces available to them, the New Islamists are bringing into being an Islamic "network culture" of flexible meanings and structures responsive to the imperatives of the new world that is growing up around us.

The work of this vanguard of the *wasatiya* is so powerful because they have understood the essential reality of our time: the unprecedented speed of change that is transforming all aspects of our lives and they have responded accordingly.[5] They have correctly identified *taqlid* (imitation) and the rigidity of ideas and institutions it causes as the most destructive demon of the age of speed (Virillo 1986). Driven by this awareness, they have pioneered the development of alternative structures created out of flexible networks. In this sense, the New Islamists are actively translating their consciousness of the character of a new age into innovative systems that adapt successfully to it. Above all, the New Islamists have understood that ours is an age of transition and it is a dangerous one precisely for that reason.

We are only beginning to make sense of the changes brought by globalization. However, a few things are already becoming clear and the writings of the New Islamists indicate that they are aware in general of these most revealing developments. To understand the massive transformations we are experiencing, it will be necessary to look beyond the state and beyond civil society to locate the most important arenas where these changes are taking effect. What is emerging on a worldwide scale is the "network society," driven by the new, networking logic of its major institutions.[6] To be sure, the transformation from the world system built on the polarities of the Cold War opposition of two superpowers is far from complete and the long-term outcome remains uncertain. The network logic is generating new social wholes that are, in effect, networks of networks. These new network structures are born in conditions created with the collapse of old systems and before new formations bring new kinds of order, that is, they emerge and evolve in a transitional context poised between the rigidity of old orders that are giving way and the chaos threatened by their collapse.

This "moment of complexity," as Taylor describes it, creates the conditions for the emergence, evolution, and projection of the new social network formations and the identities they make possible. Whether or not the network logic driving these changes can create a world system and with what character remains unclear. However, the struggle to determine the shape of the future is clearly underway, taking its clearest form to date in the Middle East. More precisely, the two Gulf Wars, whose repercussions are only dimly understood, were opening battles in the struggle to determine the character of the new world order.

Paradoxically, the United States, the birthplace of the new network forms of social organization, has emerged as a conservative power interested in the preservation of the state-based system. As the sole superpower, the United States, particularly under the three Bush administrations, is defining its interests in the old state-centered way with an emphasis on global assertiveness in defense of its access to the most critical global resources and military keynesianism to stimulate a flagging domestic economy. Meanwhile, the most impressive forces of resistance to this U.S. strategy are not coming from the expected quarters of power politics. Neither Europe, young or old, nor China or Russia mattered much when it came to restraining George W. Bush from attacking Iraq. Rather, opposition is springing in unexpected ways from the new, worldwide networks of social forces, mobilized in flexible and adaptive ways. The space of appearance of these new forms of global political action is now emphatically the alternative media, originating in the internet and enhanced by satellite transmissions. This new electronic frontier, despite market and political encroachments, has become the most promising site of political creativity in the new conditions of globalization.

It is sometimes overlooked that the Information Revolution that made these electronic sites of opposition possible was itself a product of the same creative upheavals of the 1960s that gave rise to the sexual liberation, anticonsumerism, and antiwar movements. Still, it would be a mistake to allow the nostalgia in some quarters for the return of the "movement" to cloud appreciation for the radically new forms and prospects of contemporary resistance. The old forms of social movements, beginning with labor and ending with the classic antiwar movements, are being hollowed out as effectively as the nation-state. The shells and the memories remain. However, it is already clear that vital functions are moving into the new network systems of the electronic age.

The New Islamists are not overly concerned with the issue, widely debated in the West, of whether these effects of global economic and cultural processes represent a shift to some final stage of capitalist development or to a fundamentally new era in human development. Wherever we are going, they argue, it is clear that the traditional fabric of community life is weakening, as the condition of our neglected planet worsens through "the arrogance, tyranny, and ignorance" of a flawed humankind that has abandoned the values of "justice, humane betterment, and sense of balance" (al-Qaradawi 2001: 258). The rebuilding of community and repair of the earth is everywhere, and not just in the Islamic world, the challenge of the age.

The writings of the New Islamists also alert us to the fact that this time of dangerous transition has created the conditions for yet another threat every bit as ominous in its consequences for our species as divisive poverty and environmental degradation. In societies around the globe, they argue, we are now faced with a terrifying intellectual fundamentalism that inevitably leads to violence. Despite variations in its cultural forms and content, this deadly threat is recognizable for its futile longing to return to formalistic values and rigid structures. They read effects of such thinking in the slaughter by a criminal minority of thousands of defenseless civilians of a rainbow of colors, origins, and beliefs in the most cosmopolitan of world cities, in the devastating consequences of a rigid and inhuman market fundamentalism imposed by global financial institutions on the wretched of the earth, and just as clearly in the numbing spectacle of the world's only superpower waging war against an opportunistically defined "terrorism" and "axis of evil."[7]

On the ground of mainstream Islam, the New Islamists join enlightened intellectuals from other cultures to oppose such simplifications and the failure of moral and intellectual courage they represent. They insist on making distinctions and avoiding simplifications, notably even in their thinking about the threatening policies of the Bush administration. Recognizing that America under the leadership of George W. Bush has made itself the enemy of a scarcely understood Islamic world, Tariq al-Bishri nevertheless insists that Islamists recognize and embrace those within the United States who struggle against the abuses of unconstrained American power. Even in Bush's America, Bishri argues with compelling moral clarity, there are partners in the cause of peace and reconciliation (al-Bishri 2003). Similarly, in the Arab and Islamic world, the New Islamists have courageously faced down the extremist proponents of political Islam. They bluntly reject the equally terrifying simplifications of primitively thinking *amir*s who seek to hold back change with antiquated historical forms and a rigid and ritualized Islam.

The New Islamists urge "a leap into the time and space" of the new world they see emerging, insisting that the faith, understood through the nuanced prism of an *ijtihad* for a global age, calls on Muslims to learn to live creatively and humanely in the new world that the Information Revolution is creating with its transformations of the economy, society, and culture. Their record of public activities are crucial for understanding the dynamics of the contemporary Muslim public sphere; at the same time they provide important lessons that can contribute to our efforts to "provide an account of the distinctive operational rules and principles of networks" (Taylor 2001: 273). Making sense of these new cultural codes as they are being developed around the globe represents the most pressing political, intellectual, and moral challenge of the global age. In teaching these lessons, Islamist centrists also help explain the mystery of Islam's stunning adaptive capacities.

Moreover, the school is producing crucial work on issues related to social justice, human rights, the advancement of women and minorities, economic development, and democracy. In an authoritarian landscape beset by a dismal record of torture and other violations of basic human rights, and where they have by specifically targeted, these thinkers and public figures have left a public record of speaking and acting on behalf of reason and science, democracy and human rights, and economic development strategies that aim to close the gap between provocative wealth and the poor. This type of courage and resiliency can be favorably compared with Emanuel Kant's argument, in response to just the hint of imprisonment or censure, no longer to openly criticize his sovereign. Kant, we should recall, was one of the first articulators of the philosophical discourse surrounding civil society and the public sphere in Europe.

Thus, while support for the New Islamists comes primarily from the middle classes, they position themselves as spokespersons for the dispossessed in the name of Islamic justice. While women and non-Muslims still play only a limited role in their organizations, they project a self-critical vision of the necessity in the globalized world of the full inclusion of non-Muslims and women. More to the point, the positions the New Islamists take in existing public arenas emphatically aim to translate the promise of inclusion into new social realities. Clearly these "radicals of the center" have gone far toward demonstrating that Islam provides the cultural and moral resources to meet the challenges of the age.

These accomplishments are possible in no small part because the New Islamists never constituted the kind of direct political threat to the regime that would provoke their suppression. Their stature as distinguished and widely respected public figures with an unblemished reputation for personal probity also provides an important measure of protection as they undertake the tasks of guiding the Islamic wave toward their goal of a much broader national consensus. For a poor and backward country, as they describe Egypt, such a consensus would necessarily involve shared views on economic development. The New Islamists consequently devote corrective attention to the economic realm, recognizing it as the single area in which the thinking of the Islamic wave is least developed. Their innovative contributions on economic thinking and their interventions to defend the most instructive economic experiments illustrate more concretely the ways their intellectual project finds its way into existing public spheres.

If I have consistently used the word "school" to define the complex of personalities and discourses that comprise the *wasatiya* movement, I would like to take a moment to elaborate on the dynamics of this crucial mechanism within the contemporary Muslim public sphere. To accomplish their goal of establishing an independent public presence that could guide the Islamic Awakening without inviting repression, the New Islamists constituted themselves loosely as a "school" of Islamist thinkers rather than a mass movement or a political party. Their school had the following characteristics that distilled the lessons they had learned:

- a horizontal structure of a flexible network rather than a rigid hierarchy;
- a clear demarcation of the network, while leaving it permeable and open;
- it is self-created with the capacity for re-creation in other times and places;
- the school is infinitely adaptable while always remaining recognizable;
- it has a guiding intelligence but no leader;
- work is accomplished by procedures that mimic "parallel processing";
- the school interacts freely with other networks, both Islamist and non-Islamist;
- it simultaneously and with ease competes and cooperates with the networks with which it interacts;
- the school operates in an environment from which it can be distinguished but that environment is itself one of diverse networks that are undergoing changes as rapid as those of the school itself;
- the school is at once national, transnational, and global in character.

By approaching participation in public life through the mechanism of such a school, the New Islamists were able to make the most of the new opportunities of the political arena and enlarged civil society that emerged in the post-Nasser years in Egypt. They have done so, however, without making either political participation or engagements in civil society an end in themselves. They have set their sites on the long term and could therefore survive the inevitable setbacks of the political and civil development under authoritarian auspices. They focus on education and culture, critiquing the shortcomings of the national institutions and encouraging the development of alternatives in the interstices of official life. In all of these ways, the New Islamists have been able to accommodate ruling power without losing sight of long-term transformational goals. Thus, while the New Islamists paid attention to the experiments of the Islamic wave in the political arena and in civil society, their own canvass was much broader. They reached beyond politics and civil society. They envisioned fields of operation and development of the Islamic awakening in all sorts of public arenas, including the new spaces opened up by the revolutionary information technologies.

By acting as a "school" rather than as a "party" the New Islamists have never constituted the kind of direct political threat to the regime that would have provoked their suppression. Their stature as distinguished and widely respected public figures with an unblemished reputation for personal probity, despite occasional controversies, also provided an important measure of protection as they undertook the tasks of guiding the Islamic wave toward their goal of a much broader national consensus. For a poor and backward country, as they described Egypt, such a consensus would necessarily involve shared views on economic development.

The New *Fiqh* of Economics: Difficult Wholes of the *Maslaha 'Amma*

The impact of the New Islamist School extends far beyond political discourses of moderation and into the sphere of economic practice where, against both traditionalists and radicals of the Islamic wave, they argue forcefully that Islam offers no fixed model for the economy. Economic arrangements, they explain, constitute part of that "vast territory" left by God's wisdom for each generation to formulate in response to its particular circumstances and needs. Part of the charge of *istikhlaf* is the creation of suitable economic arrangements to meet human needs.

There are, of course, certain explicit but also very limited provisions in Qur'an and Sunnah that spell out some precise obligations and restrictions. Muslims, for example, are enjoined to pay *zakat* (the canonical alms) and to foreswear *riba* (illegal since effortless interest or profit). However, the New Islamists deny that such limited and circumscribed directives could possibly be described as a distinctive Islamic economic system. Moreover, they actively oppose all such misplaced efforts to create such a "timeless" system and to make it a requirement for all Islamic communities. Such a rigid model, they reason, cannot possibly be effective in the changing circumstances of the human condition. What Islam does provide is the articulation of the higher purposes and values to inspire creative work in the economic field as part of humankind's responsibilities from God to "build the world" and then the standards to evaluate what had been achieved.

Given their firm position that no fixed blueprint for the Islamic economy can or should be derived, the New Islamists argue that building an economy in particular circumstances necessarily involves self-directed experimentation rather than simple imitation of the experiences of others. If the New Islamists oppose the inclination of *taqlid* from the Islamic legacy, they are even more emphatic in speaking against the unthinking adoption of systems devised by other peoples in quite different circumstances. This attitude of mind does not, however, signal closed-mindedness. The New Islamists learn and even borrow from the experience of others; however, they insist that such appropriations must always be active and creative. That is, what is taken must be adapted to fit within a larger framework that the community designs to meet its own distinctive needs.

These open and experimental attitudes mean grappling with real problems and searching for practical ways to resolve them. Egyptian Islamists do rise to the challenge to innovate, as even their harshest domestic critics acknowledge. Their efforts do not go unnoticed on the Egyptian scene. Perhaps not completely innocently, secular critics point to the extraordinary variety of initiatives, very often in the economic realm, that Islamist activists launch. 'Abdu-l-Mun'im Sa'id, Director of the al-Ahram Center for Political and Strategic Studies, pronounced that "while others talk about civil society, the Islamists go about creating one, including economic institutions. They establish their companies and banks, they play an influential role in professional syndicates, and they build such social institutions as schools, hospitals, and even hotels." Sa'id concluded that "the Islamic trend is not satisfied to demand a civil society like the leftists do nor just calling for it like the liberals. They go about building it in their distinctive ways" (Ibrahim 1988a). Sa'd-al-Din Ibrahim, head of the Ibn Khaldun Center, made the implicit warning embedded in this "complementary" assessment explicit. He warned that "the real political parties in Egypt" were the banks and companies that were creating an independent and threatening source of social power for the Islamists (Ibrahim 1988b).

The New Islamists themselves never indulge in such exaggerated claims for the social power of Islamic institutions. Nor do they accept the unstated assumption that the variety of initiatives has a coordinated and intentional character. Rather, they see the spontaneous generation of new ideas and forms, without any directing intelligence. In particular, the New Islamists object to the notion that the social experimentation of centrist Islamist activists aims in some monolithic way to establish subversive Islamist cells as the nuclei of an alternative society. True, some extremist adherents of political Islam do indeed dream of building strength in this way for an eventual seizure of power. The New Islamists emphatically oppose those aspirations of a minority. This demurral does not mean that their own goals are not radical. They are as far reaching in their democratic consequences as the goals of the extremists who look to authoritarian outcomes.

Moreover, the New Islamists rule out the use of violence as a means to achieve them. Instead, they look to gradual social change as appropriate means to the democratic ends for which they strive. Occasionally, New Islamists such as Tariq al-Bishri speak about a "communal society" that might well emerge from the political, economic, and social experiments of the Islamic mainstream, suggesting an image of the society to come. Al-Bishri uses the term to amplify the Western notion of "civil society" by recognizing the constructive necessity of including Islamic social organizations within its purview.[8] However, for the most part New Islamist thinking is content with the notion of a loose Islamic framework of inspiration and evaluation within which wide-ranging experimentation can take place. This attitude of mind goes a long way toward explaining the extraordinarily adaptive character of their school in a period of unprecedented social change.

The New Islamists welcome the fact that Islamist efforts in the economic realm often emerge spontaneously and quite beyond the control of any organized force or movement. As a result, the new forms that take shape in the economic realm are unpredictable and not easily recognized as Islamic. On the one hand, such a process avoids the totalizing effect of most systems. On the other, the Islamic character of the outcomes is not easily apprehended, whether by opponents or supporters. Precisely for this reason, the New Islamists direct their own attention to discriminating critiques of shortcomings and guidance for their correction. New Islamist support for reforms does not mean automatic approval of the results of all such efforts. What count are positive results that advanced the general interest of the community in line with Islam's moral vision. Justice is central to this vision and elaboration of notions of the *maslaha 'amma* must always have social justice at their core. In the case of the notorious financial investment companies, the New Islamists recognized that, as their manifesto warns, opportunists and undesirables of all kinds exploit Islamic symbols and damage the community. In the end, the New Islamists recognized and criticized the unjust outcomes of these companies. In contrast, they aggressively defended the Islamic banks for their constructive and innovative contributions that advanced the aims of Islamic justice. These contrasting experiments and New Islamist evaluations of them merit a closer look.

The Islamic wave was heavily involved in the corruption story of the financial investment companies that dominated national attention in the late 1980s. In the popular idiom, the companies were considered "Islamic," as their founders obviously intended. The companies claimed that the unusually high dividends they paid did not constitute *riba* but rather represented a form of "Islamic blessing." Leadership of the largest and most visible companies aggressively marketed their services with Islamic symbols. In the end, the drama of the investment companies took on the dimensions of a national tragedy, involving the swindling of one half million investors with a capital estimated as high as LE 8 billion.

The New Islamist evaluation of the record of the investment companies confronted their disastrous consequences without apology or attempts to whitewash their disastrous consequences. However, their explanations for the phenomenon pointed to underlying economic and political factors rather than to any specifically Islamic causes. The possibility for fraud, as Fahmi Huwaydi explained, emerged from the generation of large quantities of investment capital from the remittances of Egyptians working in the oil rich Gulf. The government failed to provide suitable investment opportunities for these "petro-dollars" and corrupt elements organized themselves into "investment companies" to soak up these surplus capital reserves (Huwaydi 1988; see Baha-al-Din 1988 for a non-Islamic perspective).

Egyptian workers in the Gulf had lived for years in environments where a formalistic Islam held sway. Consequently, they were particularly subjected to appeals to deposit their holdings in institutions that had an ostensibly Islamic character. Beards, flowing robes, and Qur'anic citations proved enough to attract investors, who were then totally seduced by the high rates of return the companies initially paid. Behind the alleged miracles of "Islamic blessings" lurked the logic of pyramid schemes that, quite independent of cultural contexts yield the same effects everywhere ('Abdu-l-Fadil 1989).

Initially high interest rates are sustained by expanding the base of subscribers, rather than by any productive activity. As soon as the pool of would-be investors dries up, the companies can no longer extend these benefits and they inevitably collapse, ruining countless lives in the process. When the oil boom cooled, just such an outcome occurred. The New Islamists drew very clear conclusions from this failed experiment. Kamal Abu-l-Majd, for example, in outspoken public interventions on the matter declared unequivocally that there was no Islamic formula that could suspend fundamental economic laws. The investment companies had simply used an Islamic cover to defraud a vulnerable population. A new *fiqh* of economics, he concluded, was essential to protect the Islamic community from such fraudulent schemes (Abu-l-Majd 1988).

The New Islamists paid careful attention to such debates on critical economic issues in the public arena and injected themselves and their school into the most important of them. They understood that power in the Information Age resides in part in "the images of representation around which societies organize their institutions, and people build their lives, and decide their behavior." Consistently, they showed themselves to be skillful players in these new power games of the global age. In all these ways the New Islamists demonstrated that they understood that "the sites of this power are people's minds" (Castells 1996b: 359). Of complex, adaptive systems, the theorist Gell-Mann has written that they "operate through the cycle of variable schemata, accidental circumstances, phenotypic consequences, and feedback of selection pressures to the competition among schemata" (Taylor 2001: 207). In just this way, the New Islamists plunge into the social arena, not afraid to be identified with mistakes. They show themselves ready to learn and theorize, often in the most public ways, the lessons from such experience in order to elaborate more effective "schemata" to guide the work of their school. The New Islamists have no fixed or rigid view of where such communicative and social action on behalf of theory and practical social change should take place. When opportunities arise, they do pay attention to the possibilities of constructive action in the official political arena and in civil society. However, they do not have inflated expectations of what can be accomplished in those public arenas.

Western scholars have given a great deal of attention to the opportunities that official political activity offers. They have hotly debated the question of whether Islamist parties should or should not be invited to play the political game on the assumption that their inclusion would help democratize the Islamists. Interestingly, the New Islamists have a much cooler and more detached view of the political sphere. They understand accurately and fully how undemocratic the political arenas actually are throughout the Arab Islamic world, despite the appearance of opposition parties, newspapers that are modestly free to express opinions, and periodic elections. The New Islamists see too many ironies in the naïve idea that Islamists should angle for participation in the political process as a way to gain experience in democratic practices.

New Islamist Evaluations of Civil Society

More surprising, perhaps, is their parallel avoidance of developing any excessive hopes in the institutions of civil society. When openings occur to move into such civic spaces, they do take them. However, they again correctly recognize that the scope for civil society is sharply limited by the authoritarian character of the regime. Nongovernmental organizations are also highly susceptible to pressures from foreign donors who set agendas that do not reflect real national needs. Fahmi Huwaydi decries the distortions of national objectives when, for example, foreign financing leads nongovernmental organizations to an exaggerated focus on questions of minorities rather than more fundamental challenges to all Egyptians such as illiteracy, poverty, and health care (Huwaydi 2001: 31–32). Periodically, the regime cracks down on civil society and punishes those who have pushed the official limits on what is tolerable.

The New Islamists are always disinclined to make such developments an occasion for confrontation with the regime, preferring to search instead for other outlets provided by the Islamic Awakening for communication and acting on behalf of their goals of social transformation.

The New Islamist logic is more than pure and simple accommodation to an authoritarian regime, however. In contrast to their disinclination to exaggerate the importance of the "places" of politics and civil society, the New Islamists do look with considerable enthusiasm to the "spaces" that open up in network society, on national, transnational, and even international levels. To put the matter bluntly, the New Islamists know that the authoritarian regime exercises relentless repressive power over the Egyptian public sphere by its manipulation of the political arena and systematic containment and undermining of civil society, using "legal" as well as brute forms of repression.

Therefore, these public places are of very limited use for transformational purposes. In contrast, "spaces" are not geographically anchored and therefore are not as easily controlled for authoritarian purposes. For this reason, the New Islamists look with greater hope to the new electronic frontier and the uncharted spaces of opportunity opened up by the new information technologies. The New Islamists understand that knowledge is capital in this new world.[9] They and their ideas actively and productively cultivate all these new spaces. From Web sites to satellite television, New Islamist thinking makes itself felt in impressive ways that belie any easy criticism of their accommodation with the authoritarian regime at the expense of their project of long-term and peaceful social change on moderate Islamic ground. They are in fact quite successfully preparing the ground for radical transformation in these new spaces of the global age alongside the more circumscribed civic and political places.

Conclusion: *Istikhlaf* for a Global Age

The work of the New Islamist School illuminates the ways in which Islam lends itself to centrist interpretations, particularly well suited to the new social and cultural conditions of our global age. The mainstream Islam brought into view here is an Islam that has taken shape "at the edge of chaos." The New Islamist interpretation of Islam is delicately poised between the fixity of extremist Islam and the chaos that results when Muslims go so far in imitating Western models that they lose connection with their Islamic roots and undermine their Islamic identities.

There is no room in the usual mapping of Islam in the West for such "radicals of the center." A constant refrain in the West is that Islam wants to drive us back to the dark ages. Images of Islam evoke fixity or chaos and not the creative between. The openness of the New Islamist School to their environment is what makes it possible for feedback and feed-forward loops. The New Islamists reach back to draw on the Islam of higher purposes and values rather than specific institutions or particular behaviors. At the same time, the school extends itself forward into the new economic, social, and cultural realities created by the Information Revolution. New Islamist *ijtihad* yields an imaginative *fiqh* of text and a compelling *fiqh* of reality. Yet, their creativity cannot be read mechanically either from the heritage nor the environment. The feedback and feed-forward loops that their openness make possible accelerate, modifying schemata, taking account of accidental circumstances, assessing unintended consequences, and weighing alternative understandings, until things reach the "tipping point" where more becomes different. This is when emergence occurs and new forms—difficult wholes—take shape. These innovations, often involving unprecedented combinations of old and new systems as in the case of the Islamic banks, allow creative and adaptive understandings and actions. This way of seeing things involves both determination and chance. It enables us to understand how something emerges from, but is not reducible to, the interaction of parts. Thus, one avoids reductive analysis without slipping into explanations that invoke mere chance. In this sense, the *istikhlaf* of the New Islamists that is, their project of gradual social transformation, proceeds on foundations that are sufficiently flexible and adaptable to allow entry into "the vast new spaces of opportunity" of our global age (Taylor 2001: 65).

Notes

I would like to gratefully acknowledge the critical assistance I received in research for this chapter from my research staff at AUC, Cairo, directed by Ramadan 'Abdu-l-'Aziz. I am especially appreciative of the exceptional efforts of Mustafa Muhammad Sayyid, new to our staff, who helped clarify and sharpen my thinking on the theoretical dimensions of the relationship between Islam and the forces of globalization, especially in our discussions of the life chances of young people in the Arab world.

1. See the representative discussion of Fahmi Huwaydi (2001: 36).
2. The impact of the pervasive role of violence is assessed by Theodor von Laue (1987).
3. Thomas L. Friedman made this point repeatedly in his influential *New York Times* columns in the wake of 9/11.
4. This theme runs through al-Bishri's most recent work, *Arabs in the Face of Aggression*; see especially his assessment of the popular reaction to the official "peace" agreements with Israel (2002: 66–67).
5. This theme is sounded throughout the manifesto of the group (see Abu-l-Majd 1992 [1991]).
6. Castells 1996a is rich in empirical data on this issue.
7. See, for example, Tariq al-Bishri's assessment of the impact of the events of 9/11 on American official thinking (al-Bishri 2002: 55–57).
8. Tariq al-Bishri, personal communication, July 2001.
9. The notion of "huge space of possibilities" comes from Gell-Mann, cited by Taylor (2001: 207).

References

'Abdu-l-Fadil, Mahmud. 1989. *The Big Financial Trick: The Political Economy of the Tawzif al-Amwal Companies*. Cairo: Dar al-mustaqbal al-'arabi (in Arabic).

Abu-l-Majd, Kamal. 1988, *Sabah al-Khayr*, July 28.

———. 1992 [1991]. *A Contemporary Islamic Vision. Cairo*. Cairo: Dar al-shuruq (in Arabic).

Baha-al-Din, Ahmad. 1988. *al-Ahram*, August 10.

Baker, Raymond. 2003. *Islam Without Fear: Egypt and the New Islamists*. Cambridge, MA: Harvard University Press.

———. 2005. *Islam in the Moment of Complexity: Moving Foundations*. Cambridge, MA: Harvard University Press.

Bauman, Zygmunt. 1998. *Globalization: The Human Consequences*. New York: Columbia University Press.

al-Bishri, Tariq. 1996. *The General Features of Contemporary Islamic Political Thought*. Cairo: Dar al-shuruq (in Arabic).

———. 2002. *Arabs in the Face of Aggression*. Cairo: Dar al-shuruq (in Arabic).

———. 2003. *islamonline.net*, February 5.

Castells, Manuel. 1996a. *The Information Age: Economy, Society, and Culture*, 3 vols. Oxford: Blackwell.

———. 1996b. *The Power of Identity*. Oxford: Blackwell.

Habermas, Jürgen. 1985. *The Philosophical Discourse of Modernity*, trans. Frederick G. Lawrence, Cambridge, MA: MIT Press.

Huwaydi, Fahmi. 1988. *al-Ahram*, November 22.

———. 1989a. *al-Ahram*, October 17.

———. 1989b. *al-Ahram*, January 3.

———. 1990. *al-Ahram*, July 17.

———. 1992. *al-Ahram*, July 28.

———. 2001. *Egypt Needs a Solution*. Cairo: Dar al-shuruq (in Arabic).

Ibrahim, Sa'd-al-Din. 1988a. *Al Ahram*, April 29.

———. 1988b. *al-Jumhuriyyah*, June 4.

al-Qaradawi, Yusuf. 1988. *The Islamic Awakening: The Concerns of the Arab and Islamic Homeland*. Cairo: Dar al-sahwa (in Arabic).

———. 2001. *Nurturance of the Environment in Islamic Shari'a*. Cairo: Dar al-shuruq (in Arabic).

———. 2002 [2000]. *Our Islamic Community Between Two Centuries*, Cairo: Dar al-shuruq (in Arabic).

al-Qaradawi, Yusuf et al. 2001. *Fatwa*, Becket Fund for Religious Liberty, paid advertisement, *New York Times*, October 17.

Said, Edward. 1997. *Covering Islam*. New York: Pantheon Books.

Taylor, Mark C. 2001. *The Moment of Complexity*. Chicago and London: University of Chicago Press.

Virillo, Paul. 1986. *Speed and Politics: An Essay on Dromology*, trans. Mark Polizzotti, New York: Semiotext(e).

von Laue, Theodor. 1987. *The World Revolution of Westernization*. New York: Oxford University Press.

Waines, David. 2000 [1995]. *An Introduction to Islam*. Cambridge: Cambridge University Press.

Part II

Practice, Communication, and the Public Construction of Legal Argument

CHAPTER 5

CONSTRUCTING THE PRIVATE/PUBLIC DISTINCTION IN MUSLIM MAJORITY SOCIETIES: A PRAXIOLOGICAL APPROACH

Baudouin Dupret and Jean-Noël Ferrié

I s there any specific meaning to the notions of the "public" and "publicness" in Muslim majority societies? Is there anything that makes a situation characterized as public part of an "Islamic public?" This chapter argues for a multiple shift in perspective to address these questions. We claim that the private/public distinction and the very notion of a "public sphere" need fundamental reexamination, based on our argument that there is no such category as an "Islamic public sphere" outside those imagined and constructed by actors in Muslims majority societies in practice.

We ground this "praxiological" critique by demonstrating that "public" and "private" are contingent categorizations, always particular, contextualized, and not generalizable from one interaction to another even as people create meaning contextually and situationally. From a praxiological point of view, "public" is necessarily a redundant categorization simply because the analyst cannot take into consideration anything else but procedures and references that are shared and known as such—that is, public. We shall substantiate our analysis through the use of cases implicating moral characterizations during the course of daily exchanges. Indeed, morality is an activity that consists in normatively characterizing preferences in the thread of an interaction. As such, it is a public object, something that has no social reality outside its instantiation in public circumstances.

We also concentrate on cases in which judicial institutions are asked to adjudicate issues of morality. A trial, in this sense, is a paradigmatic instance of the fixation of moral preferences. It is a mechanism that is oriented par excellence to the production of a decision. In other words, law is a nonmoral mode of punctual reduction of moral indeterminacy. However, as far as the "public" is concerned, it does not correspond to some "public" intervention within a realm that is allegedly "private," since it consists only in a formalized reference whose sharing is explicitly taken for known and is known as constraining.

The Public, Islam, and Morality

In the reexamination that follows, we adopt a praxiological conception of the public and the corollary notion of the public sphere. Our conception considers the public as a practical, situated, contextual, and local accomplishment. According to this conception, the "private" is a categorization that exists only in a predicative way, in the course of interactions that are sustained by shared procedures and references; therefore, necessarily and by definition, these interactions are public. In that sense, the "private" exists only publicly. Thus, the "public" and the "public sphere" cannot be placed as a counterpoint to activities that are confined to some kind of private realm or space, which is too often conflated with the space of the "domestic."

The ubiquitous conflation between "the private" and "the domestic" in contemporary scholarship highlights how it has focused on the definition of "the private" as a place (i.e., the domestic), rather than on the identification of mechanisms through which people interact and circumstantially ascribe to some types of relationships the characterization of "private."[1] In a manner our argument echoes Eickelman and Salvatore (2004 [2002]), for whom the public and the public sphere receive their meaning through the action of members of a society. However, it diverges from this conception, for these authors seek to give the public sphere a specific *locus* that is external to the members' explicit orientations,[2] whereas our conception is radically situational, contextual, and bound to people's manifest action and understanding. It also echoes the position of LeVine and Salvatore (chapter 1, this volume) when they state that the vocabulary of social science theories can hardly capture the vocabulary utilized by Islamic movements, remaining external to the specific context of the latter. However, it diverges from LeVine and Salvatore's position in the sense that it does not seek to identify an alternative vocabulary, but it merely describes actual situations where people publicly characterize something as Islamic, or refrain from doing it.

We further question whether simply referring to an Islamic lexicon can determine if observed interactions are operating within a Muslim public sphere: For example: to answer *in sha'a-llah* does not pre-characterize the nature of our relationship with a taxi driver as Islamic; rather, in this context, it allows him (momentarily, at least) to ratify the direction that he is asked for. It is only if, later on, he ostensibly utters other formulations of the same type—*ma sha'a-llah, subhan Allah, bismi-llah*—that we shall be able to infer that he wanted to set the seal of religion on this interaction.

This clearly shows that words do not connote anything independent of a course of action. Whether a history of the use of these expressions and an etymology of the lexicon reveals its Islamic origin or not does not matter here, in the sense that most often people do not bear the entire weight of their history and tradition on their shoulders in the course of their daily, nonreflexive, and ante-predicative actions and interactions. We are not concerned with an archeology of language(s), because there is no way to show that its findings bear direct consequences on the practicalities of its actual uses.

We argue that an interactionist, contextual, contingent, and minimalist conception of the public *must* be adopted if any plausible investigation of "publicness" is to be conducted. The public must be understood as a publication device, that is, either (1) "a set of practical operations that regulate, during the time of their enfolding, the problems posed by the organization of speech exchanges during conversation" (Relieu and Brock 1995: 77) or (2) the embedding and the coordination of action within an institutional frame that is explicitly recognized as such by interacting people, or (3) the nominalization (ibid.) that constitutes the public as a collective entity to which people orient. These are the three possible ways to conceptualize anything like a "public" from within an ethnomethodological perspective. We must note that the third meaning does not correspond to a conceptual elaboration that the praxiological perspective builds on the notion of "public," but rather to an objectivization that is produced by actors, both professionals and lay people.

From a praxiological point of view, the "public" is this and only this. This article aims at showing that all the attempts that seek to substantiate the "public"—outside (1) the collective character of a specific situation, (2) its embedding within an explicitly institutional context, or (3) its being an actors oriented object—come under the theorizing endeavor proper to the social sciences professionals. In this article, we shall not try to systematically observe and describe "public" situations in these three senses. We will rather try to document this contention as against the prevalent abstract theorizations (or more precisely, the overt disposition toward abstract theorizing) concerning the "public" and the "pubic sphere."

We also contend that morality is a phenomenon of order. This moral order is performed by operations of category ascription in which the idea of normality is central. Garfinkel, in his description of the case of Agnes, a transsexual, exhibits the practical conditions for displaying the category of "woman" allowing Agnes to exhibit the features making her a "natural, normal female" (Garfinkel 1984 [1967]: 185). Hence, categories on which members of a population are distributed according to their sexual orientation are at the same time objective configurations produced by these members' practices and schemes orienting these practices (Quéré 1994: 33). In another study devoted to the analysis of a famous case of rape,[3] Matoesian shows how the mobilization of a category (the one of "rapist" in this case) somehow naturalizes the normative expectations that are linked to it (it is normal to be frightened by a rapist) and makes it possible to question the belonging to such a category (he cannot be a rapist since you weren't frightened by the idea to meet him) (Matoesian 1997). Normalcy here corresponds to these situations that share a family resemblance and from which one can expect the reproduction of their particular features. Thus normalcy constitutes the reference point of practical legal reasoning.

There is no way to give morality and the moral order any kind of meta-definition. Like religion, morality is what people orient to as such in a given context, that is, what they contextually and situationally take as true and fair. It means that norms do not impose themselves because they belong to the nature of things, but on the contrary belong to normalcy because people collaboratively impose them as such. In other words, practice is making norms, not the reverse. Moral norms enjoy what one may call a status of "unquestionability" because they are supposedly known and expected by the many members of a given context, express what everyone supposedly knows, and contain "pious allusions to presumed, deep, pre-existing moral commonalties" (Moore 1993: 1) that catapult the normative version of reality into a state of public acceptance.

This is made possible through the action of institutional settings and languages such as law. Law is one major realm where the "normalization process" takes place: this is where things of nature and the nature of things are made normal and consequently binding. There is a legal claim to morality, that is, a tendency to make appear as a legally and institutionally sanctioned norm what was a supposedly socially sanctioned norm. Category ascription is here a circumstantial operation aiming at orienting the debate by labeling an object and thus ascribing it a cluster of rights and duties that do not belong to the category as such but to the relational configuration it sets up. For instance, characterizing a female as an "Islamic woman" does not refer her to a preestablished set of permanent rules (e.g., the eternal rules of female modesty in Islam) but puts her in a definite membership categorization device (e.g., being an Islamic woman) implying that all her activities are evaluated according to the rights and duties (e.g., modesty) associated with this category (cf. Dupret 2001).

A Praxiological Conception of the "Public" and the "Private"

Amongst the most influential discussions of the "public sphere" are the ones found in the works of Habermas (1989 [1962]) and Koselleck (1988 [1959]). According to these two scholars, the "public sphere" corresponds to the inflating of private spaces into a sphere of rational discussion about collective issues. Such a discussion concerns topics of general interest, serious and nontrivial, and it implicates the existence of a "list" of commonly admitted themes belonging to the "public" and others belonging to the "private." The list is not at stake in the discussion. The main consequence of this division is that the procedures that are recognized so as to evoke "public" problems are not deemed to be the same as those aiming at dealing with "private" problems. Henceforth, we observe a triple disqualification: not all conversational interactions belong to "communicative ethics" (Habermas 1984 [1981], 1987 [1981]); not all places of interaction belong to the limited space within which discursive rationality can enfold; not all interacting people are endowed with the hermeneutic "sagacity" and "tact" allowing to get access to the elite of communicative action (Cayla 1996).

Like Messick, we contend that "Habermasian categories as 'public sphere' and 'civil society' cannot be unproblematically applied in understanding a situation such as obtains in contemporary [Muslim majority] societies" (chapter 8 by Messick, this volume). But if it is true that "versions of such categories are in global circulation" (ibid.), one must stress that they circulate only in a locally and situationally achieved manner. In other words, people orient to the public sphere and give it an objective dimension in a contingent and contextually defined way, which cannot be captured in any kind of general theory of the public sphere and communicative action. Contrary to the Habermasian attitude, from our point of view, interactions are phenomena that are always public and publicly available, and so are also trivial and transparent, whatever the occasion that gives rise to them (Watson 1998). "Trivial," because the hierarchy of the themes does not govern the intrinsically normative character of interactions; action and cognition are thoroughly moral phenomena (Heritage 1984). "Transparent," because the "private" that is suggested in the Habermasian distinction does simply not exist, insofar as the quest for any private instance floating in a vacuum, outside the public realm, is a quest for chimera that ignores the important fact that the procedures used to describe any such private instance must be totally embedded in language (Watson 1998: 215). This is true "whatever the occasion that gives rise to them," because interactions—however futile their object may be—are necessarily moral. In fact, interactions are based on the intersubjective sharing of types and categories and proceed in that sense from an idea of what is "normal." The relationship between the token and the type is interpreted in terms of congruity and incongruity, that is, in an evaluative perspective (Heritage 1984).[4]

Let us tell an anecdote. During engagement or wedding parties, it is common practice, in small Moroccan Middle-Atlas cities, to ask female dancers who are sometimes also prostitutes (*shikha*) to entertain the guests. Although such parties express respect for a moral order that is grounded on the public and stable character of exclusive sexual relationships, these female dancers are nevertheless an indispensable feature of their success. How can it be that a part of these women's activities, which is known to everybody, does not impugn the morality of the participants? In one instance, the housewife, the bride's mother, could only gather five *shikhat*, whereas the minimal number of dancers whose participation is necessary to form a group is six. Therefore, she asked one of her friends, some respectable woman of the neighborhood, to come and participate as the sixth member of the group. Actually, this woman used to practice the profession of *shikha* before her marriage. This anecdote gives us the opportunity to relate a series of interactions that do not particularly contrast with normal, daily life: marriage, party, organization problems, neighborhood relationships, all constitute a set of routine events.[5]

To begin with, we can observe that asking this neighbor to dance meant to make "public" her sexual (through the indirect reference to her former, nonexclusive sexual relationships) and biographic (through the "public" reference to her past) intimacy. However, the fact that it could be done without prejudice for her suggests *a contrario* that the practice of prostitution proceeds from a certain kind of normality. Moreover, the mere fact that she was invited as a dancer and that by so doing she did a favor directly excluded the reference to the double profession of the *shikhat*. Everybody knew that she had been a prostitute, but they also knew that she was one no more and that she will not be one anymore; it is on the basis of this shared knowledge that people could see her dancing with the other *shikhat* in a way that did not harm her respectability. In that sense, it is the interaction that makes available the conditions of its intelligibility by the participants. The interaction is therefore transparent. Concerning the evaluative perspective, it is noticeable that the presence of the neighbor among the *shikhat* is interpreted with regard to a goal that makes it impossible to make any inference from what is known of her past activities on her present actions. It would be incongruous and incorrect. The moral evaluation is done with regard to a typified activity—to do a favor to a neighbor—and it would be incongruous to evoke something that would step aside from the normal features of this typification.

Through this anecdote, it becomes clear that the notions of public and private, the concept of the public sphere, and their relationship to an Islamic predicate are inappropriate. First, the idea of an ante-predicative separation between the "public" and the "private," that is, a separation that has not been the topic of a judgment prior to the interaction, does not fit the situation: the sexual past of the neighbor is indirectly invoked in a "public" situation without being presently used to characterize her "private" life. Second, it is obvious that the reference to Islam—that is manifested through the "public" ritual of marriage—does not determine the interaction order.

We can now follow up with an Egyptian anecdote. In the district of Heliopolis, a police operation led to the arrest of several women accused of prostitution. Some men were also implicated. Although interactions are, phenomenologically speaking, always "public"—be it in front of a "limited" public—interacting people subjectively proceed, according to the circumstances, to characterizations of the situation in which they interact in terms of "public" and "private." During the operation, the policemen noted that an unmarried couple was staying in a closed room. Thus, this situation, subjectively private, became immediately characterized "publicly," compelling the couple to position itself in a configuration henceforward subjectively "public." Therefore, the characterization depends on the accidental course of the interaction, in the sense that the policemen's intrusion is external to the story that conducted this man and this woman in this room. However, even though there is nothing in this room but a man and a woman, the policemen's intrusion retrospectively characterizes the relation constitutive of this couple as an intimate relation "publicly" blamable. From this point of view, there is nothing private or public outside the police operation. In other words, the police operation is a categorizing action that creates the distinction between the "public" and the "private" within the course of an action oriented to a practical goal: enforcing the "public" morality of "private" life. If the definition of the "public" and the "private" follows the hazards of interaction, it necessarily means that it is action that defines them and not that action is defined by them.

With regard to the Islamic dimension of the situation, we must simply stress that these categorizations are not religiously indexed. It will perhaps be objected that the public morality that must be enforced is itself "Islamic." To this objection, we answer that if it is action that defines categories and if action is oriented to a practical goal, one cannot insert in its constituent features anything but what does explicitly manifest itself, under pain of ascribing mental operations that cannot be documented to interacting people.

Moralizing Preferences

Morality is essentially public. It has no existence outside its public accomplishment. Indeed, it accompanies every activity and it consists of normatively characterizing preferences in the course of interaction. In one sense, morality is a special domain in scholarly philosophical investigation. In another, more common sense, it is an evaluative modality that takes place in the daily course of action. Any interaction involves operations of categorization and hierarchization, that is, operations that evaluate and normatively express a preference. This is what John Heritage calls the "morality of cognition." Let us take his example of a greetings exchange. Mahmud meets Ghassan in the doorway of a research institute where both work. Mahmud looks away and does not greet Ghassan back. Many interpretations are open to Ghassan: "Mahmud didn't see me"; "Mahmud didn't hear me, he must be worried"; "Mahmud expresses his dissatisfaction by not greeting me back"; "Mahmud has bad manners, he doesn't answer to those who greet him"; "Mahmud doesn't have to greet me back since he's the director," and so on.

These concrete cases, which are of a very trivial nature, simply illustrate that there is no interaction that is not the object of an evaluation. By "evaluation," we mean a process that starts from the categorization and comes out with the ascription of a normative value to beings, things, or situations. When telling himself that Mahmud is the director and that it is well known that directors do not have to greet their subordinates back,

Ghassan categorizes the person of Mahmud (as a "director") and his conduct (that he does not greet) in a way that allows him to consider that Mahmud is "arrogant" more than "rude." Although it was possible to contemplate a priori a scope of rules that might be applied to this interaction, it was in no way possible to say which one had to be effectively applied outside its actual performance. From Mahmud's point of view, it is not even sure that the absence of reciprocity in the greetings proceeds from a feeling of superiority that is inherent to his directorial function. He might have wanted to just express to Ghassan the contempt with which he takes him as a colleague. Far from having to be necessarily considered as the many particular instances of a single rule, similar actions can be performed on the basis of different particular rules that are defined in a contingent and contextual way in the course of one same interaction. In other words, the rule is not teleological: it does not consider *ex ante* the whole set of its instances; and the interaction is not retrospective: it does not look *ex post* to the rule it was deemed to follow.

Action cannot be referred to any moral theory that grounds and organizes the entirety of its possible forms on the basis of abstract rules. That is, there are no abstract rules sufficient to all possible instances of an action that would impose a necessary coherence upon it. This is why Mahmud's conduct cannot be morally characterized as long as it is not documented in itself and in its own right. However, it can be said that an interaction can be referred to an open series of rules that are used to support its interpretation and that could be used to support its performance. The rule is a referring point that can be used *ex ante* and *ex post*. In this sense, assuming the existence of a rule allows one to consider as virtually intelligible—and therefore to a certain extent "normal"—conducts that cannot be said to be effectively grounded on a precise rule (Heritage 1984: 99). It implies a rejection of the postulate of moral coherence: the different moments of an interaction are always morally characterized, but this is a characterization that does not take place, with a few exceptions, in a congruent and stable manner, that is, through the reference to a system of moral obligations continuously determining the courses of action of one same interacting person (Williams 1985, 1993). In this perspective, the impossibility to decide by reference to which rule the other interacting person acts implies not only that there is a rule that remains to be identified, but also that there can be a plurality of possible rules, divergence on the rule that has to be applied, and discontinuity of the rules of reference in the course of interactions (Livet 1994). It means that the interaction imposes its dynamics on the moral deliberation and, symmetrically, that the latter determines the former.

We now come back to an anecdote, the story of Hasan and the twin sisters. Hasan is married to Hayat, his first cousin. He also has sustained adulterous relationships, and Hayat is aware of it without knowing with whom. One day, she is informed by a phone call that her husband uses their former flat to meet his mistress Na'ima. She directly heads to this place and on the doorstep she hears a monologue that sounds like a phone conversation and a series of sounds suggesting some sexual activity. Hayat starts hitting the door while shouting her husband to come out. She insults him and threatens to call the police. Worried by the fuss, the doorkeeper comes and tries to calm Hayat down by telling her that the neighbors might alert the police. Hayat stops crying and just keeps on knocking on the door, asking her husband to open, which he eventually does. Hayat enters and realizes that there are two women, twin sisters who are the nieces of one of Hasan's friends. She insults them and everybody comes back home. At home, Hayat calls her mother and sisters, packs her bags, and goes to her father's house. Later on, after many episodes, the two spouses are reconciled. Various interpretations combined with new details circulate in the family. The twins' aunt is said to be responsible for the phone call that alarmed Hayat so as to avenge herself upon Hasan's brother who used to be, briefly, her lover. Whether Hasan was the lover of the twins or of Na'ima remains uncertain. A couple of months later, the twin sisters appeared in a commercial ad for some olive oil. Each time she watched it Hayat and Hasan's daughter would say: "these are dad's girlfriends."

It must be stressed, to begin with, that adulterous relationships are criminally prosecuted in Morocco. In other words, Hasan risks questioning by the police if they are asked to examine the case. It seems that this is precisely the outcome that Hayat was looking for. However, the fear arising through the doorkeeper's intervention to see the police effectively intervening induces a substantial change in her attitude. The direct fear of a precise sanction is not equivalent to the direct threat of some virtual sanction. Here, action transforms itself directly and quickly according to some incidental interventions. That is to say, Hasan risks the police's intervention insofar as this intervention remains potential. This is what the doorkeeper's interference makes clear: it compels Hayat to adapt her conduct with regard to its possible consequences. One could imagine, at first, that the idea of a sanction was linked to the gravity of the accusation itself, that is, that Hayat was activating a legal categorization and was seeking to prosecute Hasan criminally by doing so. However, she stepped from one repertoire to another at the time when the sanction became effectively more precise. One can therefore state that the hazards of interaction designated the normative repertoire that was used to characterize actions. In this sense, interactional contingencies index morality (Garfinkel 1967). We are in a situation of "moral luck" (Williams 1981). What is meant by moral luck is that the moral characterization of an action does not depend on what this action is in any substantial and absolute manner, but on what this action becomes according to circumstances.

When asked about the morality of this story, Sara, Hayat's sister (and Hasan's first cousin) firmly opposed her husband, 'Umar, who was suggesting that Hasan was the lover of the two sisters. 'Umar's suggestion was grounded on the fact that the reaction to the twins' appearance on the TV screen was about "dad's girlfriends." There was no distinction between

Na'ima and her twin sister Sharifa. Although Sara did not express any trenchant judgment concerning Hasan's infidelities, which were considered as a blamable though rather common behavior, she felt that the mere idea that Hasan might be this "man-who-sleeps-with-two-sisters-who-sleep-with-the-same-man" was unbearable. The double incongruity, that is, a man sleeping with two women and two sisters sharing the same lover, prompted the moral condemnation of this attitude which took the form of denying the possibility of such an action. Sara was scandalized by the mere possibility of such a suspicion. In a euphemistic way, she shifted the blame from Hasan to 'Umar.

This story of blame, which arose from the incongruity of the ascription of an incongruous sexual behavior to somebody, suggests a hierarchy in blame allocation: the blame for blamable though banal conduct and the blame for blamable though non-banal conducts. A "man-who-sleeps-with-a-woman-who-is-not-his-wife" belongs to the former category, whereas a "man-who-sleeps-with-two-sisters-who-sleep-with-the-same-man" belongs to the latter. According to the category, the blame turns on different objects: on the one hand, on marital infidelity; on the other, on sexual aberrations. It can also be said that, in the first case, the moral indexation is founded on an institutional membership categorization device (to be husband and wife), whereas in the second case it is grounded on a natural membership categorization device (to be a man and a woman).

The blame that is attached to the breach to the duties specific to the institutional device implicates some reference to the notions of engagement, intention, and reciprocity, whereas the blame proceeding from the natural device indicates the existence of a matter of fact, independent of any engagement and intention. In other words, the natural device is grounded on the idea of stain (Douglas 2002 [1966]), that is, an evil independent of the intention to harm others (Williams 1993). The institutional device is instead grounded on the idea of impersonal (i.e., not related to any specific person) and reciprocal obligation. Without entering into too much detail, it must be stressed that these devices are never free of any reciprocal influence. For instance, it is hard to understand why marital fidelity constitutes an obligation if any idea of stain is excluded. The story of Hasan and the twin sisters shows us how much normative positions and references oscillate in the course of interaction and according to categorization devices that are distinct but operate simultaneously. In that sense the dramatic unfolding of any interaction gains its coherence from successive, indexical, and reflexive adjustments (Ferrié 1998; Dupret 2001).

The situation described above is one where categorization devices sustain "thick" ethical concepts (Williams 1985). For instance, the standardized relational pair (Sacks 1972, 1992; Watson 1994) husband/wife sustains the concept of infidelity. The identification of this concept operates through some "documentary method of interpretation" (Garfinkel 1967),[6] that is, the mundane method through which the interacting people are referring to an underlying and supposed scheme of interpretation. It means that the various ways to consider fidelity, reciprocal engagement, sexuality, parental responsibilities, and others refer to the underlying scheme of a normal couple's life. Ethical principles slip into the life of people. The taking of an overhanging position claiming the possibility to identify these principles ante-predicatively would contradict their phenomenologically contingent character."

The Judicial Stop to Moral Indeterminacy

Phenomenologically speaking, normative indexation can appear as an endless process. Considering that moral judgments function by inductive inferences, they are necessarily dependent on circumstances, interacting people, and conventional adjustments. In this configuration, inferences are always revisable and nothing implicates any stable agreement between interacting people who can initiate in a relatively autonomous way revision procedures that are partly intelligible by others but whose consequences are not necessarily shared (Livet and Thévenot 1994).

Contrary to this, legal characterization stops the revision process through a broad restriction of indeterminacy. Indeed, the process is constrained at three levels: formal, procedural, and institutional. By formal level, we mean that characterization must be performed according to a legal taxonomy. In other words, legal actors must produce legally relevant statements, that is, statements that are recognizable by, and intelligible for, other effective or potential legal actors. It operates a sorting between possible characterizations and implicates a substantial impoverishment of the situation's features. It cannot be denied that law is endowed with an open texture that authorizes and even requires interpretation. However, this does not mean that interpretation operates in an arbitrary manner: the interpretive field is necessarily constrained by the choice of the definition's wording and its ordering (Hart 1961). For instance, in Egypt, law no. 10 of the year 1961 represses "prostitution" (*da'ara*). However, it does not give any definition of prostitution, which at least opens the field of interpretation. The Court of Cassation, in its ruling of March 2, 1988, stipulates that "prostitution" means the committing of an indecent action (*fahsha'*) with somebody else without distinction, independently of any repetitive character of this action. Such definition allows much but not all. Indeed, the term "indecent action" cannot be applied but to actions of a sexual nature. It is the constraint induced by the selection of the words that comes here to the surface. The selection of one term instead of another brings out the activity that is commonly designated by a language family, that of sexually immoral actions whose signification is understood by "everybody."

By procedural level, we mean that characterization can only be embedded in a judicial sequence partly predefined and that the compliance to this constraint is sanctioned. The Public Prosecutor to whom a prostitution case is referred must treat it with regard to, and in accordance with, the law of 1961. Moreover, he must necessarily frame his actions within the trial sequence, which means that he must lean on former procedural actions (police reports) and anticipate forthcoming procedural actions (the reading of his work by the judge who will issue the ruling). This procedural dimension involves a set of standard mentions testifying to the validity of the measures taken in the course of investigation, prosecution, and judgment. It takes place in a sequence whose ordering is not free (investigation, searching authorization, searching, arrest, police record, routing to the Public Prosecution, etc.). At every step of this sequence, it must be mentioned that all procedural requirements were formerly followed and that the professional is now, in one's turn, satisfying these requirements that are specific to the current step and will be necessary to ground the validity of the following step (e.g., the policeman, in his report, must mention that the searching was done pursuant to a warrant in proper form and he must state the identity of every person he examines so that no procedural flaw can be opposed later in the trial).

By institutional, we mean that the participants in the trial occupy positions specified by the judicial frame and that these positions restrictively limit their capacities of action. The parties do not have the same status and are not endowed with the same rights and duties. They are therefore engaged in asymmetrical relationships. If there is a system of speech turns allotted to the various participants, this system is partly determined by some pre-allocation of these turns (one asks and the other answers), by the initiative of and the control on the content of exchanges (one chooses the topic, the other cannot deny its relevance), by the uneven distribution of legal knowledge and the capacity of one of the participants to orient to a precise goal that the other can guess and whose damaging effect can anticipate and sometimes avert but not determine. Although the accused person is never deemed to contribute to his/her own incrimination, the institutional organization of turns and exchanges puts him/her in the obligation to collaborate and this confronts him/her to a series of dilemmas whose solution can never be entirely propitious to his/her interests (Komter 1988). This is how suspects, in a police investigation, are led to answer to facts that were already characterized in a former record by the police. Their alternative is between showing their willingness to cooperate to some extent—but this cooperation, even though it allows them to amend the presentation of some facts according to their own interests, presupposes their consent to the general economy of the legal narrative— or refusing any kind of cooperation (their right to keep silent)—but this attitude, even though it protects against self-incrimination, makes him/her lose any control on the characterization of the facts and is often interpreted as an implicit confession of guilt (Komter 2001).

Here follows the police record in an Egyptian case of prostitution:

Information came to the police station that suffices to state that the called Fawqiyya Mahmud Ghunaym, living at No. 4 al-Sa'ada str., Roxy, behind the

Helio Lido club, district of the Misr al-Gadida police station, runs her lodging for purposes of prostitution, procuring and exploitation of depraved women whom she finds for prostitution purposes in return of some pecuniary advantage. The investigation we conducted and the secret scrutiny conducted under the direction of the police station's chief, in his capacity, confirmed that the called Fawqiyya Mahmud Ghunaym, living at No. 4 al-Sa'ada str., Roxy, behind the Helio Lido club, district of the Misr al-Gadida police station, ground floor, runs her lodging for purposes of prostitution, procuring and exploitation of depraved women, among whom her relative, for prostitution purposes, and that some male and female taxi drivers assist her in this matter, among whom this who is called Ahmad, who drives a Peugeot cab, who worked to decoy men looking for sexual pleasure to the above mentioned, like the called Fatin and the called Amina, so that they assisted the above mentioned to supply the depraved women while she herself undertook to present them to the men looking for sexual pleasure, among whom Arabs and Arab Orientals, in return of some pecuniary advantage which they gave to her. One has observed, during this scrutiny, frequent visits of men and women to the lodging of the above mentioned so as to commit adultery inside the lodging of the above mentioned or, with regard to men looking for sexual pleasure, to get the company of women whom the above mentioned made work and exploited for prostitution purposes.

Also consider the following excerpt of the examination conducted by the police in the same case:

Question of the police officer: Since when have you practiced prostitution?
Answer of the accused: For three years
Q: Did you get used to practice prostitution with men without retribution?[7]
A: Yes
Q: How many times did you practice prostitution?
A: More than once but I don't do it a lot and I do it monthly once or twice because I don't like doing like that
Q: When was the last time when you practiced adultery?
A: About two weeks ago or a little bit less
Q: Did you commit adultery today?
A: Yes
Q: Who did push you into doing these things?
A: This whom I told you about before who is called Fatna who has a known name and she kept on calling me at the doctor where I work and asking me to come and sleep with this who was with her and these are Egyptian and she settles up with me and then I leave
Q: Did the above mentioned undertake to facilitate and exploit your prostitution?
A: Yes
Q: When was the last time when the above mentioned undertook to exploit your prostitution?
A: About one month ago
Q: What financial advantage did the above mentioned get in return of this?

A: She sat with the client and it was her who gave me the money and I don't know how much she took from the client

Q: How did you know about the presence of the called Ja'far in Cairo at the domicile whose searching was authorized?

A: It is Fawqiyya who came to my home yesterday and told me that Ja'far was with her in the flat and asked me and she told me to stay with her because he desired me hard and she told me this time or I understood that she didn't want to let me speak with Ja'far about the question of his marrying me because she wasn't in the mood to do that

Q: Did the above mentioned get from you a financial advantage from all this?

A: I'm like her I take from the one who sleeps with me and she naturally she takes a part of this

Q: Are there other women who use to frequent the lodging whose searching was authorized at the home of the called Fatna and her friend Amal so as to commit adultery inside?

A: There are other girls than me who go there and I know it but they don't leave more than one man in the flat because this who's called Fawqiyya she's scared and she prefers to go out and to leave the flat because she's scared

Q: Did you already get arrested before?

A: No

Q: You're accused of exposing yourself to prostitution with men without distinction in return of retribution

A: I do it actually and our Lord will punish this who's the cause of this

Q: Do you have something else to say?

A: No

Through the reading of this record, it appears that the incriminating party orients the exchanges toward the legal specification of facts: place, circumstances, concerned people, and especially toward the examined person's confession. There is no "normative overload" insofar as the incriminating party seeks only to get a clear, coherent, and facts-centered narrative and refrains from evaluating facts from a moral point of view. Thus, the accused person is not even asked about her feelings when doing what she did. It is up to her to use her own answering turns, which follow precise questioning turns, to add a few words stating her moral position. To the question, "How many times did you practice prostitution," she answers, "More than once," and specifies, "but I don't do it a lot," which aims not at giving a periodicity, but at indicating the limited character of her punishable practice. Then, she specifies the periodicity: "I do it monthly once or twice," which serves as a preface to the expression of a moral positioning that was not elicited by her interlocutor: "because I don't like doing like that."

The same technique is used after the formulation of the blame by the incriminating party. The accused person takes advantage of this formulation and uses it as if it introduced a speech turn even though it did not address any invitation to her to introduce a formulation designed to excuse her from at least part of the blame: "I do it actually and our Lord will punish this who's the cause of this." This formulation is abstracted from any procedural order, since it designates an anonymous or even virtual responsible entity and a divine intervening entity, who are not relevant in the legal ascription of blame. Neither does this formulation conform with the institutional order, since the accused person's speech turn does not follow a question but precedes it and since the incriminating party does not nod approval to this statement and asks immediately after the question that might have directly followed the completion of the accusation. This bracketing of a statement that is not really processed as a statement (despite its being consigned in the record) suggests the incongruity and uselessness of this type of exit from the procedural (where only facts that can be legally characterized are processed) and institutional (where the accused person is not supposed to intervene outside the incriminating party's invitation) orders.[8]

The accused person gives a moral response to a legal accusation that makes her bear the responsibility for a misdemeanor that she patently perceives as a moral blame, even though there is nothing of this kind clearly manifested in the incriminating party's formulations. There is place for neither moral order nor divine order in the characterization enterprise conducted by the police officer. It occurs only and at best in an interstitial manner, in a totally asymmetrical relationship, without having been elicited and without any consequence on the outcome of the ongoing procedure. However, the accused person, despite the fact that it is never asked of her, has set her heart on the expression of her possessing a moral identity in front of an accuser who, in the routine accomplishment of his work, takes no further interest in this moral dimension. It can be inferred from all this that legal normativity can function independent of moral normativity, even though, from a commonsense point of view here expressed by the accused party,[9] the two go hand in hand.

Conclusion

A proper genealogical investigation into the boundaries between public and private would reveal how much this boundary is external to this or that tradition, appeared in specific historical circumstances, and takes a quasi-metaphysical dimension when referred to by scholars as an invariant. In this chapter, we argued, although in a very different way, that the drawing of this boundary has a totally contingent character and is situationally achieved. It does not mean that such a boundary, whatever the shape it takes, must be drawn. It only shows that, in just the contexts we described, the participants in the interactions oriented their behavior to sexual morality, religion, and law in a way and with a lexicon that punctually and situationally pointed to the boundaries they drew between public and private situations or that did not entail any kind of distinction. This is what a praxiological inquiry can achieve, whereas a genealogical analysis misses the phenomenon of what people actually do when practicing dancing, marrying, chatting in a wedding party, shouting their anger, threatening to call the police, prostituting themselves, writing reports, interrogating, and answering questions in specific contexts.

In the different cases we described, the reference to Islam is embedded in courses of action that are not determined by Islam. The meaning is four-fold: (1) The reference to religion has no signification other than what is given to it by interacting people in the course of interaction when they ori-ent to it; in other words, religion is nothing but what people do and say when referring to something they designate as such; (2) Even when people turn to a lexical repertoire of a religious nature, it must be said that its use is embedded in sequences of action that are not logically oriented to a religious performance; (3) It is not the religious reference that modalizes the context but the context that modalizes the religious reference; (4) There can be something called a public sphere and it can even be char-acterized as Islamic, but all this has no meaning outside what people iden-tify as such in a course of action; the reference to Islam is dependent on what they orient to (and what they orient to can have nothing to do with Islam), and both the signification and the range of this reference are strictly limited to the contingencies of the context in which it is embed-ded. There are only punctual and contingent uses of a lexical repertoire of a religious nature whose signification is irremediably bound to the context of its use. There can be Muslim publics in various contexts, but the mean-ing of the reference to Islam has a locally achieved and constrained char-acter, that is, it is not defined a priori by the recourse to a supposedly Islamic lexicon or attitude, but through the explicit orientation of the peo-ple participating in the situation toward Islam as the reference around which they organize their interactions in public.

With regard to normative orders, one must observe that the reference to Islam does not impose, because of its mere mobilization, a kind of hier-archy among the many normative orders to which people refer. In other words, the preference orders are not ante-predicatively determined and the revision of preferences is indexically referred to the context in which it is embedded. In that sense, we partly oppose the working hypothesis of this volume, according to which the Islamic character of determined dis-courses is constructed according to contexts linking social practice to hegemonic contests. This is certainly the case in certain contexts, but it cannot be generalized so as to become the underlying interpretive scheme. The preference orders are dependent on the courses of action, that is, they are in a situation of equivalence outside these courses of action—insofar as such a generalization is possible. It is only their use that creates a dis-tinction between them; it is only their use that determines the potential revisions of their hierarchy. This claim is consistent with Wittgenstein's position according to which symbols have no intrinsic meaning. And, according to Williams, there is no essential hierarchy of axiological norms, but only situations in which some of these norms are luckier than others.

Notes

We wish to express our gratitude to Hussein Agrama who carefully read the first draft of the text and made invaluable comments and corrections. Our thanks also go to Armando Salvatore for his many useful suggestions.

1. We must note here that what is "private" in some circumstances can be "public" in others, depending on the context of interaction. For example, the same person might expose his or her sexual life during a TV show yet refuse to do so at an evening among friends.
2. "When not limited to modern secular settings, the public sphere is the site where contests take place over the definition of the obligations, rights and especially notions of justice that members of society require for the common good to be realized" (Salvatore and LeVine, Introduction, this volume: 6).
3. That is, the Kennedy Smith rape trial. See also Matoesian 2001.
4. See in particular his chapter 4: "The morality of cognition." It must be noted here that the terms "moral" and "normative" have in this type of perspective a very close meaning.
5. One may wonder why there is no direct reference made here to the work of scholars who anthropologically studied *shikhat*, like Kapchan (1996). To put it briefly, it must be emphasized that the singular phenomenon we observed largely differs from the general picture overloaded with folklorism, symbolism, and interpretivism with which she provides us. One of the main tenets of the praxiological perspective we advocate consists precisely in refraining from constructing grand schemes that eventually miss the phenomenological dimension of every singular situation.
6. The title of the chapter is "Common sense knowledge of social structures: the documentary method of interpretation in lay and professional fact finding."
7. The meaning of this sentence is contradictory. It can be attributed to some mistake in the transcription process.
8. In that sense, we consider that the statement of Norman Calder (1996: 995–96, quoted by Messick, chapter 8, this volume), according to whom, whereas *fiqh* does not dominate society as it once did, the inspirational power of *sharïa*, although devoid of detail or specificity, has increased, although right in its general formulation, misses the phenomenological specificity of the reference to Islamic legal and moral principles in every singular, specific, contextual, and local, situation.
9. Nothing allows us to say that the accusing party does not subscribe, independent of his professional activity, to this commonsensical point of view.

References

Calder, Norman. 1996. "Law." In *History of Islamic Philosophy*, ed. S. H. Nasr and O. Leaman, London and New York: Routledge.

Cayla, Oliver. 1996. "Droit." In *Dictionnaire d'éthique et de philosophie morale*, ed. Monique Canto-Sperber, Paris: PUF.

Douglas, Mary. 2002 [1966]. *Purity and Danger: An Analysis of Concepts of Pollution and Taboo*. London: Routledge.

Dupret, Baudouin. 2001. "Normality, Responsibility, Morality: Virginity and Rape in an Egyptian Legal Context." In *Muslim Traditions and Modern Techniques of Power*, vol. 3 of *Yearbook of the Sociology of Islam* 3, ed. Armando Salvatore, Hamburg: Lit; New Brunswick, NJ: Transaction, 165–83.

Eickelman, Dale F., and Armando Salvatore. 2004 [2002]. "Muslim Publics." In *Public Islam and Common Good*, ed. Armando Salvatore and Dale F. Eickelman, Leiden and Boston: Brill, 3–27.

Ferrié, Jean-Noël. 1998. "Figures de la moralité en Egypte: Typifications, conventions et publicité." In *Urbanité arabe. Hommage à Bernard Lepetit*, ed. Jocelyne Dakhlia, Arles: Actes Sud/Sindbad.

Garfinkel, Harold. 1967. "Practical Sociological Reasoning: Some Features in the Work of the Los Angeles Suicide Prevention Center." In *Essays in Self-Destruction*, ed. Edwin S. Schneidman, New York: International Science Press.

———. 1984 [1967]. *Studies in Ethnomethodology*. Cambridge: Polity Press.

Habermas, Jürgen. 1984 [1981]. *The Theory of Communicative Action*, vol. I, *Reason and the Rationalization of Society*, trans. Thomas McCarthy, Boston: Beacon Press.

———. 1987 [1981]. *The Theory of Communicative Action*, vol. II, *Lifeworld and System: A Critique of Functionalist Reason*, trans. Thomas McCarthy, Boston: Beacon Press.

———. 1989 [1962]. *The Structural Transformation of the Public Sphere*, trans. Thomas Burger, Cambridge: Polity Press.

Hart, Herbert L.A. 1961. *The Concept of Law*. Oxford: Oxford University Press.

Heritage, John. 1984. *Garfinkel and Ethnomethodology*. Cambridge: Polity Press.

Kapchan, Deborah. 1996. *Gender on the Market: Moroccan Women and the Revoicing of Tradition*. Philadelphia: University of Pennsylvania Press.

Komter, Martha. 1998. *Dilemmas in the Courtroom: A Study of Trials of Violent Crime in the Netherlands*. Mahwah: Lawrence Erlbaum Associates.

———. 2001. "La construction de la preuve dans un interrogatoire de police." In *Le droit en action et en contexte. Ethnométhodologie et analyse de conversation dans la recherche juridique*, special section of *Droit et Société*, ed. Baudouin Dupret, 48: 367–93.

Koselleck, Reinhart. 1988 [1959]. *Critique and Crisis: Enlightenment and the Pathogenesis of Modern Society*, trans. Maria Santos, Oxford: Berg.

Livet, Pierre. 1994. *La communauté virtuelle. Action et communication*. Combas: Editions de l'éclat.

Livet, Pierre, and Laurent Thévenot. 1994. "Les catégories de l'action collective." In *Analyse économique des conventions*, ed. A. Orléan, Paris: PUF.

Matoesian, Gregory. 1997. " 'I'm sorry we had to meet under these circumstances': Verbal Artistry (and Wizardry) in the Kennedy Smith Rape Trial." In *Law in Action. Ethnomethodological and Conversation Analytic Approaches to Law*, ed. Max Travers, and John F. Manzo, Aldershot, UK: Ashgate.

———. 2001. *Law and the Language of Identity: Discourse in the William Kennedy Smith Rape Trial*. New York: Oxford University Press.

Moore, Sally F. 1993. "Introduction." In *Moralizing States and the Ethnography of the Present*, ed. Sally F. Moore, American Ethnological Society Monograph Series, No. 5.

Quéré Louis. 1994. "Présentation." In *L'enquete sur les catégories*, ed. Bernard Fradin, Louis Quéré, and Jean Widmer, Paris: Editions de l'EHESS.

Relieu, Marc, and Franck Brock. 1995. "L' infrastructure organisationnelle de la parole publique. Analyse des réunions politique et des interviews télédiffusés." *Politix* 31: 77–112.

Sacks, Harvey. 1972. "Notes on Police Assessment of Moral Character." In *Studies in Social Interaction*, ed. David Sudnow, New York: The Free Press.

———. 1992. *Lectures on Conversation*, 2 vols., Oxford: Blackwell.

Watson, Rodney. 1994. "Catégories, séquentialité et ordre social. Un nouveau regard sur l'oeuvre de Sacks." In *L' enquete sur les catégories*, ed. Bernard Fradin, Louis Quéré, and Jean Widmer, Paris: Editions de l'EHESS.

———. 1998. "Ethnomethodology, Consciousness and Self." *Journal of Consciousness Studies* 5, 2: 202–23.

Williams, Bernard A. O. 1981. *Moral Luck: Philosophical Papers 1973–1980*. Cambridge: Cambridge University Press.

———. 1985. *Ethics and the Limits of Philosophy*. London: Fontana.

———. 1993. *Shame and Necessity*. Oxford: University of California Press.

CHAPTER 6

COMMUNICATIVE ACTION AND THE SOCIAL CONSTRUCTION OF SHARI'A IN PAKISTAN

Muhammad Khalid Masud

Introduction

The shari'a, in common Muslim usage, refers to a comprehensive concept of law, which includes ritual and dietary rules, as well as laws about family, commerce, and social relations. The shari'a had been almost marginalized in the public sphere emerging during the colonial period in the 19th century. Most Western experts on Islamic law saw no future for shari'a in a modern society, which was conceived of as essentially secular, and which had no place for religion in public affairs. But shari'a reappeared in the emerging postcolonial public spheres in a number of Muslim majority societies in the 20th century. This trend raises a number of questions about the conception of the public sphere: specifically, does the emergence of a public sphere necessarily presuppose a secular society? Is it not possible to speak of public sphere in Muslim societies? Does the revival of shari'a reflect the decline of public sphere?

In this chapter I explore these questions with reference to the revival of shari'a in some major public controversies in Pakistan, in 1961, 1979–1985, and 1990–2000.

The Public Sphere and Communicative Action

Before proceeding to the analysis, let me explain my understanding of what social scientists and philosophers define as the "public sphere" (for an analysis and critique of standard definitions, see chapter 1 by LeVine and Salvatore, and Eickelman and Salvatore 2004 [2002]). With reference to Pakistan, I would like to define the public sphere as a space that the modern media and mass education have helped to create and where public debates on issues of common concern are taking place. The existing public sphere reveals at least two characteristics of publicness: a plurality of voices, and a fragmentation of traditional authority. In Muslim majority societies the public sphere is where debates on religious issues increasingly take place, no longer restricted to or monopolized by the specialists. It is not only the 'ulama as experts of shari'a, but also "lay" members of the society who publicly discuss shari'a related matters. In these discussions, some crucial questions about shari'a and traditional religious authorities are raised. Where a critique is formulated, it is formulated through a religious discourse. However, while it is not a secular critique, it is certainly not led or dominated by the religious "orthodoxy" either.

"Publicness" may be understood differently, depending on the specific social environment. In my view, the secularity of the public sphere is a condition that was specific to the European experience and it need not be a definitive characteristic in non-Western publics. The presumption of an inevitable exclusion of religion, and specifically of shari'a, from the public sphere in Muslim societies derives from the particular strategy adopted by Enlightenment thinkers in Europe. In order to construct a new vision of reason, these thinkers embarked on the deconstruction of the authority of tradition, church, metaphysics, and others. This deconstruction was a strategy, not the objective of the Enlightenment; the real goal was to institute the primacy of human reason and the autonomy of the individual. A unilateral emphasis on this strategy hostile to organized religion, however, reduces the importance of other essential elements of a public sphere. Recent experience in Muslim countries (e.g., secular but undemocratic regimes in Turkey, Algeria, and now Uzbekistan) suggests that secularism by itself cannot ensure democracy, or for that matter, a well-functioning public sphere, if it aims at the deconstruction of only one type of traditional authority, based on religion.

It is, therefore, more meaningful to redefine the public sphere by focusing on ideas such as the individual autonomy of the self and public reason, rather than putting an emphasis on a deconstruction of religious authority. Excluding religion from the public sphere in societies like Pakistan means keeping large segments of the population out of the public sphere and restricting it to some élite groups. In this regard, Habermas's theory of communicative action is specifically relevant, as it lays a primary stress on the autonomy of self and on the open and rational character of public discourse (Habermas 1996 [1992]: 3–5).

The theory of communicative action focuses on how individuals communicate on the basis of their individual interests and come to agree through rational discourse on common interests. The emphasis here is on discourse, rationality, and universality as necessary ingredients of consensus. It clarifies universality not as cosmic or metaphysical like traditional discourse, but rather as derived from common grounds of understanding among the participants in the discourse. The norms created by this discourse in the public sphere reflect an ongoing consensus based on the reflexive self-positioning of individuals. These norms are assumed to faithfully mirror pluralism and autonomy, which are very basic to modern life. This elaboration makes it possible to see that the Western experience may not be universally normative. The societies whose political economies differ considerably from those of the West may practice communicative action and construct public reason differently from the West.

Claims to universalism, without the underlying communicative action, tend to imply a kind of historical determinism: a process of social evolution, ultimately ending in the triumph of universal values of democracy. The determinist view of universalism leads Muslim reformists to believe that change in a specific direction is inevitable, and need not pass through discursive mediations. Consequently, they overlook the significance of communicative action and prefer to rely on reforms by law. Their discourse's targets are the educated middle classes. They believe that mass education by itself will incorporate the masses into this change. They, therefore, feel justified to carry out these reforms, without building a consensus. This sense of complacency among the reformists prompts the conservative to build resistance to change. The theory of communicative action helps us to understand that a popular consensus achieved through this type of action is more effective than by enlightened coercion. Laws can help facilitate public discourse and consensus, but cannot replace it. This facilitative recourse to law, not intended as a purely coercive force, may fit into Habermas's category of "strategic action." I elaborate on this point further below.

Law

Legal positivism rightly focuses on man-made law as a modern law, but the positivist approach, together with the theory of state's sovereignty, undermines the role of the individual as well as society in raising normative claims and in participating in law-making activity. The positivist notion of law does not seek normativity outside of the legal system; its normativity comes from within the system, for example, from the command of the sovereign or in the form of constitutional laws. The problem is that this notion of law overlooks the participation of individuals in the process of the social construction of normativity. Often, positivist lawyers distinguish law from a normative order, which is founded on a sense of morality in a certain society. This distinction does not solve the basic problem.

Habermas's theory of communicative action is relevant as it seems to overcome these shortcomings of legal theory and helps to understand how the process of construction of normativity takes place in the public sphere in the form of discourse.[1] Habermas distinguishes between communicative and strategic action. A communicative action makes a validity claim not only using language, but also nonlinguistic means in order to arrive at an understanding and, further, at consensus. Strategic action is required to facilitate this consensus. Law supports and often constitutes a strategic action. Law has, therefore, a dual character: through communicative action it establishes rationally acceptable norms, and through legal rights and statutes it performs a strategic action to create a stable social environment in which persons can form their identities, pursue their individual interests, and regularly communicate.

The problem, here, is how to imagine the autonomous individual. In fact, individual interests are interconnected with each other. Individuals, therefore, continuously form groups and subgroups to negotiate over their overlapping interests. Furthermore, these interests keep changing under the given circumstances. In the end, universality, which is an essential characteristic of this construction of normativity, is constantly relativized. Law then provides the environment in which universality may be negotiated discursively.

The Social Construction of Shari'a

With this discussion of communicative action, normativity, and law in mind, let us turn to an analysis of the restoration of shari'a in the Pakistani public sphere. The social construction of shari'a between 1960 and 2000 varied considerably in Pakistan and thus provides interesting material to investigate communicative action in the public sphere.

By "social construction of shari'a" I mean a process that enacts communicative action, including the strategic action that facilitates discourse. The construction process eventually reflects a particular frame of reference in which the relationships between religion—in this case Islam—and society, between individuals and society, and among individuals, are defined. I prefer to call this process "social construction" because it comes about as a result of social discourse, rather than by state action. In this sense, the social construction of shari'a is not essentially a modern phenomenon, but the emerging public sphere in Muslim societies has certainly made it more transparent.

Islamic law is generally understood as a sacred law and hence it is believed that no discourse is allowed by it. In fact Islamic law in history developed as a discursive tradition and the present debate on shari'a in Pakistan is also a discourse; it is diversified even on the question of what constitutes the shari'a. The Urdu speakers use three terms for "Islamic law": *shari'at* or *shar'* (*shari'a*, i.e., God's willed normativity), *qanun* (law), and *fiqh* (jurisprudence). Often they are used interchangeably, but sometimes they are distinguished to stress certain meanings. For instance, in order to stress the legal dimension, one calls it *islami qanun*, that is, "Islamic law," but when emphasis is on its sacredness, it is called *shari'at*.

The History of Islamic Law

Looking back at the history of Islamic law, we find that in the early centuries of Islam there developed several sources of normativity: local customs, Qur'an and the *sunna* (the teachings and practice of the Prophet and his companions). Local practices in various cities like Medina and Kufa generated diverse legal doctrines and gradually produced more than nineteen schools of law (*madhhab*); about seven still exist today. The doctrines of these schools came to be called *fiqh* (i.e., jurisprudential understanding of the shari'a) or *madhhab* (school doctrines). In its formative phase, *fiqh* was not regarded as sacred or immutable. Gradually, however, it came to be closely identified with shari'a, probably for two reasons: to establish the authority of the schools, and to deny attribution of immutability to *qanun*, the laws enacted by the rulers. In order to institutionalize the authority of the schools, the jurists expounded the doctrine of *taqlid*, which instituted these schools as authorities of jurisprudence and called for law practitioners' strict adherence to one of them.

Until reformist trends, such as the one headed by Ibn Taymiyya (d. 1328), launched a vigorous attack on this doctrine, *fiqh* also continued to be regarded as being as sacred and immutable as shari'a. The doctrine of *taqlid* crystallized authority but also promoted the diversity and pluralism of the law. Muslim judicial systems continuously recognized the legitimacy of these schools as diverse subsystems of Islamic law. The people were allowed to go to the court of their choice. It is not surprising, therefore, that the emphasis on *fiqh* as pluralist and in a sense personalized law created a tension between shari'a (as enacted by *fiqh*) and public law, especially criminal law. As a compromise, *fiqh* recognized the parallel existence of state law enactments in several areas of public law, like criminal, fiscal, and administrative laws. Practically, shari'a came to be restricted to religious and personal matters. This may also explain why the marginalization of shari'a during the British colonial period took place without much protest: shari'a had already been "privatized" before colonialism. But, then, why did shari'a regain significance in the 20th century? Answers to this question need to be explored through examining the reformist trend in the 14th century.

This century was marked by critical studies of Islamic law by reformist thinkers like Ibn Taymiyya (d. 1328), Ibn Qayyim (d. 1350), Ibn Khaldun (d. 1382), and Abu Ishaq al-Shatibi (d. 1388). These reformists began analyzing the basic assumptions in Muslim legal thought. Stressing *ijtihad* (the use of individual reasoning without exclusively relying on the doctrines of the schools of law), they questioned the validity of the doctrine of *taqlid* (adopting the doctrines of a school of law). Ibn Taymiyya called for a return to the preschool period of Islamic law. He singled out *sunna* (the practice of the Prophet) as the only basis of the normativity of shari'a, all other norms and practices being *bid'a* (invalid religious innovations). Later revivalist movements in the 18th and 19th centuries were greatly influenced by Ibn Taymiyya.

In the 13th century, Ibn 'Abd al-Salam (d. 1263), in his treatise *Qawa'id al-ahkam fi masalih al-anam* ("The foundations of laws in the interests of the masses") had already expounded that *maslaha* (common good) and *huzhuzh* (self interests) were the bases (*qawa'id*) of shari'a laws (Masud 2000 [1995]: 146–48). Abu Ishaq al-Shatibi (d. 1388), in his book *Al-Muwafaqat fi-usul al-shari'a* ("A synthesis of the principles of shari'a") developed a philosophy of shari'a focusing on the purpose of law. Contrary to the hitherto prevalent deductive method that used analogical reasoning, Shatibi employed an inductive approach. He insisted that the universal principles must be inferred by an inductive analysis of all the verses of the Qur'an, rather than by deducting rules from selected verses. He concluded that the main objective of shari'a was the protection of human interest (*maslaha*), articulated in the following five basic areas: person (self), reason, religion, family, and property.

Based on the protection of these interests, he expounded a theory of *maqasid al-shari'a* (objectives of the law). Particularly relevant to our subject, he also elaborated that shari'a is in its essence *ummiyya*, a term that is difficult to translate, since it lays stress on various aspects of communication, including the universal understanding of a word among the speakers of a particular language, and also the conceptual level as it is universally apprehended by speakers of all languages, for example, when translated. The focus of Shatibi's analysis of the communicative role of the language is on the understandability of laws for common man. The communication is thus not only based on shared cultural understandings, but also has a specific discursive dimension (Masud 2000 [1995]: 169–81). To stress this aspect Shatibi also analyzed the term *huzhuzh*. Since laws are meant to protect the general, common human interest (*maslaha*), he wanted to stress individual self-interest (*hazhzh*) as the root of *maslaha*. In this way, Shatibi underscored the role of the autonomous self in universalizing his self-interests into collective interests.

Shatibi refuted the idea that shari'a is to be obeyed only as a command of the lawgiver (i.e., God), and that it is free from personal interests. He stressed that the universal interests such as the protection of property and religion are interconnected with human natural desires, pleasures, and pain. They are built on the passions that motivate a person to protect these interests or to demand them as rights. Even penal laws are eventually meant to protect self-interests, since if there are no penalties for those who violate these rights, these interests could not be protected (Masud 2000 [1995]: 196–99). Shatibi emphasizes the significance of self-interests in the communicative process of laws; if the people do not find their personal desires fulfilled and their self-interests protected, the law has failed in its basic communicative function.

The tradition of critical evaluation of Islamic law was carried forward by Muslim reformists during the 18th and 19th centuries. As illustrated by the movements led by Muhammad b. 'Abd al-Wahhab (1703–1792) in the Arabian Peninsula, Usuman dan Fodio (1754–1817) in territories corresponding to today's Nigeria, Sayyid Ahmad Barelwi (1786–1831) in lands corresponding to today's Pakistan, Umar Tall (1794–1864) in West Africa, and Muhammad b. 'Ali al-Sanusi (1787–1859) in Libya, they were greatly influenced by the 14th century critique of Islamic law, in particular by Ibn Taymiyya and his critique of *taqlid*. These movements are sometimes called revivalists or *salafis* because they called for the revival of the authority of *sunna* upheld by *al-salaf al-salih*, the pious ancestors or the early generation of Muslims, against the authority of the founders of the schools. They also attacked the pluralism of Islamic laws and called for the unification of law based on the Qur'an and *sunna*, but pluralism, as entrenched in the schools of law, survived their assaults.

The Colonial Period and the Marginalization of Shari'a

This legal pluralism in Muslim societies was also rigorously questioned by the Western legal discourse, when it came to the Muslim world through the colonial penetration in the 18th and 19th centuries. The colonial powers favored centralized, uniform, and state-controlled legal systems. The colonial legal systems, however, recognized the validity of customs, and Islamic law, therefore, came to retain a place as customary law. Also, claiming not to interfere in the personal and religious matters of their subjects the colonial regimes also treated Islamic law as personal law. Ironically, the traditional ideas of personality and plurality of law in the Muslim tradition facilitated the marginalization of shari'a, as the traditionalists had no objection to the restriction of shari'a to regulating personal status in a non-Muslim, since colonial state.

The marginalization of shari'a went unnoticed also due to a growing disenchantment with traditional authority. Laws and statutes enacted by the colonial state accelerated the fragmentation of authority. Nevertheless, shari'a never became irrelevant. It became rather an increasingly significant constituent of identity in nationalist movements in Muslim societies in the late 19th century. When, during the struggle for independence from the colonial rule, political leaders decided to seek the support of the 'ulama for their cause, the guardians of the Islamic law began to restore the authority of shari'a—and of themselves as its legitimate representatives.

The Case of Pakistan

After attaining independence in 1947, unable to govern the political and economic problems of the new nation-state, the ruling groups in Pakistan resorted to politicize the position of the 'ulama in order to exploit the religious sentiments of the people. This situation generated debates about the 'ulama's positioning in society and, consequently, about the relevance of shari'a. Within these discussions, various groups and subgroups were created. Two trends stood at the two extremes of the spectrum of those participating in the public controversy: for the sake of convenience, and at the cost of simplifying their views, I call these two trends the "revivalist" and the "modernist." The revivalists called for the revitalization of shari'a as they saw it enshrined in early Islam, while the modernists asked for a reconstruction or reinterpretation of shari'a. The traditionalist 'ulama who supported a restoration of the shari'a of the precolonial period, namely a shari'a based on the consolidated doctrines of the various schools of

Islamic law, stood somewhere in the middle of the two extremes, but were frequently overwhelmed by the revivalists. Let me elaborate on the traditionalist view first.

Most traditionalist Sunni groups, including Jam'iyyatul 'Ulama Islam (Association of the 'Ulama of Islam) and Jam'iyyatul 'Ulama Pakistan (Association of the 'Ulama of Pakistan) equate shari'a with the *fiqh* of the Hanafi school, the legal system developed by the followers of the 8th century jurist Abu Hanifa. These two organizations represent respectively the Deobandis and the Barelwis: the former denouncing a number of beliefs and rituals that the latter practiced. For instance, *milad* (the celebration of the Prophet's birthday) is a religious obligation for the Barelwis, and a *bid'a* (an undue innovation) for the Deobandis. They also form subgroups within the larger, majority Sunni community that adheres to the Hanafi school. Like the Sunnis, shi'a organizations such as Tahrik Nifadh Fiqh Ja'fariyya (Movement for the enforcement of the *fiqh* of Ja'fari school) define shari'a in terms of their *fiqh*.

In contrast to the traditionalist groups, revivalists including Jam'iyyat Ahl al-Hadith (Association of the people of Hadith) and Jama'at Islami reject the doctrine of *taqlid* as a *bid'a*, and call for returning to the Qur'an and *sunna*, instead of adhering to *fiqh*. They distinguish *fiqh* from shari'a, which is identified with the Qur'an and the sunna. The Jama'at Islami, a religious political party founded by Abul A'la Mawdudi in 1941, differs from other religious groups as it is not organized on a sectarian basis. It has gradually come to champion the revivalist cause of shari'a. Due to its more efficient organizational structure, it has assumed the leadership over all other religious groups, including the traditionalists. In the 2002 elections in Pakistan, the Muttahida Majlis Amal (MMA), the alliance of the religious political parties, was headed by the Jama'at Islami. The revival of shari'a has now become the common platform of all religious groups. This political collaboration has not, however, diminished the adherence of the traditionalist groups to different schools of law, or erased the differences among various groups in the definition and formulation of shari'a.

In addition to organizing themselves as social and political groupings, the revivalists also adapted traditional instruments of communication like the fatwa (jurist's opinion), and the *khutba* (the Friday sermon in the mosque) to the modern media of press, radio, and public meetings. They were quick to adapt to the needs of a new communicative language and corresponding means to connect to the masses. The illiterate masses found the discourse of the traditionalist 'ulama inaccessible and were increasingly influenced by the revivalist groups.

The modernists are an even less homogenous group than the revivalists. They even agree with some revivalist groups like Jam'iyyat Ahl al-Hadith and Jama'at Islami that the bulk of Islamic law is a product of jurists' activities and does not constitute shari'a. The modernists, however, disagree with the idea of the revival of shari'a as formulated by both the schools of law or by the revivalists; they call for its reconstruction. Some of them, like Ghulam Ahmad Perwez, even question the authority of its primary sources, for example, the *sunna* and the *ijma'*, that is, the consensus of the ancient jurists. It is noteworthy that in order to justify legal reforms or reinterpretations of shari'a, Muslim modernists need not claim the secularity of Islamic law by denying its origins in revelation. In fact, relying on the distinction between the divine and the human in Islamic law, they are able to challenge the authority of tradition. Separating *fiqh* as man-made jurisprudence from shari'a as the sacred norm, they have been able to stress the role of human reason in the development of Islamic law and to justify the necessity of its reform.

The modernists did not promote mechanisms for an effective communicative action to provide an alternate religious authority. They did not establish their own *madrasa*s (institutions of religious learning), social organizations, or a political party; they mostly depended on public sphere mobilization and state support. On the other hand, the modernists could not always enjoy the support from the state. Instead of coherently relying on the modernists to mobilize the masses for reforms and modernization measures, the state often resorted to shortcuts, like appealing to traditional authorities, that is, landlords, 'ulama, and *pirs* (shaykhs of Sufi brotherhoods) to legitimize its top-down, factually undemocratic policies. In order to safeguard their own interests in Pakistani society, these traditional authorities on the one hand supported the revivalist groups, but on the other hand continued to promote their traditional construction of shari'a. To summarize, the definitions and constructions of shari'a in Pakistan are subject to variations, although the discourse tends to be polarized between two extremes.

The above brief survey shows that pluralism in the form of varying legal schools has persisted throughout Muslim history, and that Pakistan is no exception. The emerging public sphere has reemphasized this pluralism of Islamic law, indeed a pluralism of method, not only of content. Even the conservative doctrine of *taqlid*, which is presumed to aim at creating conformism, has in fact fortified legal pluralism. Since the state had no role in the development of *fiqh*, the Islamic legal tradition has been essentially discursive. In the current debates over shari'a in Pakistan, however, the discursive nature of this tradition appears to be increasingly overshadowed by a power game between various groups. We can witness various social constructions of shari'a contending for political influence. Consequently, the public sphere in Pakistan has failed to produce a common understanding of shari'a. Borrowing from Habermas, we find that in these modern discourses there has been more stress on strategic action than on communicative action, or at least that strategic action was not put at the service of communication action. In the rest of this chapter I suggest that the social construction of shari'a requires, especially with reference to its communicative dimension, three elements: normativity, rationality, and acceptability. Let me explain how in Pakistan an insufficient consideration of theses elements has hindered the process of consensus and let the social construction of shari'a serve group interests.

Normativity

The Stand of Western Legal Theory

The term "normative" is generally used to indicate accepted conventional ways of accomplishing a task. The semantic field of this term denotes a standard that is binding, authoritative, and regulatory. The usage of the term is, nevertheless, ambiguous. On the one hand it is a statement of justification: "P is normative" means that it conforms to a norm, a standard. On the other hand, it is a statement of obligation: "P is normative" means that it is obligatory. The use of the term normative in the discourses on shari'a is even more complex. In modern debates on law the issue of normativity arises in two ways. First, in contemporary usage, shari'a is described as a normative set of rules in order to distinguish it from law in the positivist sense. The positivist distinction between law and morality, the latter being normative, suggests a problematic view of normativity. It is claimed that the law enforced by the state is not normative. Does it mean that normativity is a social construct and state law is not? As mentioned earlier, the legal positivist fixation on the deconstruction of traditional authority and the separation of law from morality has unnecessarily resulted in a denial of normativity outside positive law. Legal philosophers have defined normativity in terms of collective interests, and the law is assumed to regulate individual interests in order to serve those collective interests. Normativity is thus conceived in terms of the common good, while self-interest was regarded as a manifestation of selfishness and contrary to the purpose of common good. Legal positivists like Hart (cf. Lloyd 1979: 267) could not sufficiently explain the conflict between the common good and individual interest and how this conflict was resolved and allowed to create "rights."

Shifting the emphasis to individual autonomy, modern legal philosophers like Rawls (cf. Lloyd 1979: 165) have assigned a more active role to the individual and have demystified the concept of normativity. Yet, the conflict between individual and collective interest or common good seems unresolved. The concept of right necessitates an institution, for example, the state, to enforce rights, otherwise only the mighty will be able to exercise their rights. By dismissing the common good as a source of normativity, these theories have added to the ambiguity of the role of the individual in creating norms. Habermas's theory of communicative action provides an intermediate solution to these dilemmas, in that it explains how through discourse individuals form interest groups and subgroups. These groups continuously develop agreements among themselves by further discourse. The consensus reached in this way creates norms that can provide a basis for law.

However, the positive idea of law suited very well the legal needs of the modern nation-state that claimed sovereignty over the law. The colonial regimes and newly emerging nation-states developed new legal systems on these bases. This view of normativity provides a justification for state law but it fails to explain why people obey laws. The only reason for obedience appears to be the power of the state to punish law-breaking. Benefiting from Habermas's analysis of the relationship between facts and norms, we can explain that an individual obeys the law, at least in an ideal framework of modern law, because self-interests are the starting point in the creation of norms. Individuals arrive at universal norms in a discursive manner to secure their individual interests.

In Islamic legal thought, the problem of the source of normativity arose quite early in the 10th century as the question whether human reason can discover the values of good and bad by itself or if they are known only through divine revelation. The Mu'tazila, a rationalist school of Muslim theology, claimed that the values of good and bad are inherent in things and are known by human reason. They also argued that the revelation is not contrary to human reason because God is just, which means that His laws are just as well as rationally justifiable. The Asha'ira, another school of theology, opposed this view by declaring that the knowledge of what is good and bad is based only on revelation (and therefore on shari'a). It would be anachronistic to compare the Mu'tazila with the modern rationalist philosophers. They did not say that these values are known only by human reason. However, they claimed that divine justice could not be explained if we don't admit that human mind can understand these values independently.

Significantly, theology (*'ilm al-kalam*), which dealt with the question of the nature of revelation and divine attributes, and Islamic legal theory (*usul al-fiqh*), which discussed the principles of reasoning and morality, shared a basic concern about the nature and sources of knowledge. Both interacted so closely in the formative period of Islamic thought that George Makdisi describes Shafi'i's *al-Risala*, which is popularly regarded as the first treatise on Islamic jurisprudence, as "juridical theology" (Makdisi 1984). The 14th-century proto-sociologist Ibn Khaldun calls this particular method to approach jurisprudence from a theological perspective "the method of theologians" to distinguish it from the method of jurists who focused more narrowly on legal reasoning than on theological issues (Ibn Khaldun 1989: 456).

The question of the sources of normativity was a major one within Islamic jurisprudence. Early developments of shari'a were closely connected with customs and local practices (Wheeler 1996). The jurists defined the *sunna* as the practice of the Prophet Muhammad. However, a large number of practices in that early period were assimilated into the *sunna* under the category of sunna *taqriri*, indicating the approval of a local practice by the Prophet by not objecting to it. The jurists also discussed the normativity of the practices of the Prophet's companions and of pre-Islamic religious traditions as an integral part of shari'a norms. The Maliki School, one of the four canonical Sunni schools of law, argued in favor of the normativity of the practice (*'amal*) of Medina. Later, when other Muslims from non-Arab cultures joined the Muslim community, their customs and practices also came under discussion, hence the place of *'urf* (customs) and *'adat* (habits) was investigated by the jurists. The Hanafi School is particularly known for its recognition of the normativity of customs (Ibn Abidin 1884). Muslim jurists never fail to emphasize that customs played a very vital role in family law. The Qur'anic injunctions regulating family affairs were largely based on the pre-Islamic Arab practices.

The previously mentioned Shatibi, along with Shah Waliullah (d. 1762), an 18th-century Muslim thinker from Mughal India, and several other jurists open their discussions about the philosophy of law (under the heading of "the secrets of shari'a") by raising the question about the nature of legal obligation. This is also a key question in raising the issue of normativity in general. Answering the question provides a framework for understanding why humans obey laws, according to these jurists.

Maslaha *as a Source of Normativity*

Abu Ishaq al-Shatibi, as mentioned above, expounded the doctrine of the purpose of law, explaining that laws were for the common human good (*maslaha*), not for the benefit of God. He defined *maslaha* as "that which concerns the subsistence of human life, human livelihood, and that what emotional and intellectual faculties require of human beings in an absolute sense" (Shatibi 1975 [1883] II: 25; Masud 2000 [1995]: 151). Shatibi's definition gestures toward a view of *maslaha* not alien from, but indeed residing in an individual self-interest. Communicative action can easily turn this individual interest into a "common good" because *maslaha* is a commonly shared interest, that is, it is a type of individual interest that can only be attained through interactive and mutual accommodation, if individuals discuss these interests among themselves. Habermas's theory of communicative action seems meaningful with reference to this classic notion of *maslaha*.

Muslim jurists traced the term *maslaha* to the Qur'an. Shatibi explained that *'adat* (social customs and practices) defined what was good and evil in human experience and that the shari'a endorsed that social understanding. He elaborated that *maslaha* or good did not exist in a pure and absolute form; it was always found mixed with discomfort, hardship, or other painful aspects because the world of existence is created as a combination of opposites. Human experience determines what is good or bad in view of what is predominant in a given matter or situation. If the good elements are overwhelming, it is called good. The shari'a endorses these criteria and confirms the findings of human reason (Shatibi 1975 [1883]: 307). Shatibi argued that the five basic values of the shari'a (i.e., protection of religion, life, reproduction, property, and reason) were universally recognized among all other nations (Shatibi 1975 [1883]: 2–10).

The Indian Shah Waliullah also refuted the conception of shari'a as the commands of a master intending only to test his slave's loyalty and sense of obedience. He argued that the shari'a laws were issued not merely for the sake of obedience, but have human welfare as their inherent goal (Waliullah n.d., I: 4). He explained prophecy and the revelation of divine laws as a process of reform. The prophets examined the laws in practice. They retained most of them and reformed only those that had lost the aspect of human good due to changes in social practice. Discussing the Islamic laws of marriage, Shah Waliullah explained that the Prophet Muhammad retained most of the pre-Islamic Arab practices such as engagement before wedding, dower, and wedding feast. Similarly the Prophet confirmed the pre-Islamic penal practices, which Muslim jurists assimilated into Islamic law under the heading of *hudud* (penalties in Islamic law) (Waliullah n.d., I: 124). Shah Waliullah stated very clearly that customs constituted the major material source of shari'a. He clarified in particular the pre-Islamic Arab bases of the Qur'anic laws.

The above two examples explain the pivotal significance of the question of normativity in the social construction of shari'a. The interpretation of shari'a must take into consideration the changing social norms. Further, the new interpretations must be grounded in already accepted social norms. In other words, an action may be defined as "good" in itself, but it should be predicated in terms of "utility" based on self-interest, and in terms of "normativity" to the extent individuals in a group share this approbation of it as good and find it necessary in the common interest. In Habermas's theory of public sphere, if reinterpreted with reference to the notion of *maslaha* in Islamic legal theory, the normativity of an action is developed by communicative action among the individuals who discuss their self-interests (*maslaha*) with regard to a particular action and reach an understanding about common interests. This process implies "rationality" and "acceptability" as necessary elements in communicative action. Let me elaborate on this point in the following section.

Rationality and Acceptability

The second major dimension of the social construction of shari'a is rationality. In Islamic law, the issue of rationality was discussed at least from three perspectives. First, the jurists debated whether reason is a source of law. Theological debates in early Islamic history influenced the development of shari'a. Second, the rationality of law means its extendibility to new situations. Therefore, jurists developed methods of legal reasoning to discover the normative basis (*'illa*) of each shari'a provision and assign to it a legal normative value (*hukm*). Third, the rationality of law means that it can impact reality and is understandable to each individual. The jurist perspective on obligation (*taklif*) seeks rationality on two levels, first by ensuring that law is reasonable and within human physical capacity to perform, and second that it does not demand more than the average or even below-average individual can do.

Strictly related to rationality is the dimension of acceptability. The jurists found that if people do not believe in and therefore accept the laws, they cannot be effectively forced to obey them. The observation of processes of social construction makes sociologically explicit this stress on the social acceptability of the sharī'a. Acceptability in this regard is a necessary corollary of both normativity and rationality, since it articulates them in terms of the essential intersubjectivity of human life and social relations. Not unlike the scholars of most other religious and philosophical traditions, almost all Muslim thinkers characterize human beings as social animals. Law to them is a social institution that comes into being at a certain level of social development in order to define and regulate social interactions. Acceptability thus means the mutual understanding of the significance of the social bond and therefore the need to commit to laws one can obey with only a limited degree of coercion. The obedience to law comes from an inner reason rather than due to a fear of external pain. In this regard law comes very close to social norms and practices. Shah Waliullah, for example, expounded the theory of evolution of society in four stages and found that custom played a central role in the evolution of laws (Waliullah n.d. I: 49).

The perspective on the social construction of sharī'a facilitates the process of renewing acceptability by introducing new social institutions and practices or by reforming the existing ones. For instance, the authority and authenticity of the sharī'a are defined in the educational sector through the selection of teaching materials and the construction of syllabi and courses. This process is not always conducive to openness and renewal. Hierarchical societies develop social stratifications reflecting the system of authority, and educational systems reinforce these stratifications by defining expertise and valued knowledge. Close societies define limits of acceptability by excluding some segments of the society and by censoring certain teaching materials. Analyzing the growth of *madrasa* as an institution of learning in the 12th century, Makdisi has argued how the colleges and the guilds of lawyers were created to increase the prestige of the sharī'a education and to limit the popularity of theology, philosophy, and rational sciences (Makdisi 1991, II: 5–47). Theology, a very important political tool for the Abbasid and Fatimid caliphs in the 11th century, continued as an extracurricular subject, but philosophy was relegated to private teaching.

Moments of the Social Construction of Sharī'a in Pakistan

The social construction of sharī'a in Islamic history restricted the interpretative authority of the *fuqaha'* (jurists). The emergence of the public sphere in Muslim societies gradually broadened the base of discourse on shari'a in many ways. Despite the divide between various trends, the debates in the public sphere have been able to slowly shift the focus of authority from the jurists to the texts of the Qur'an. Such a process started with groups such as the above-mentioned Ahl al-Hadith, who opposed *taqlid*, which underpinned the personal authority of the jurists. The process was also evidenced by the transformation in the use of the institution of fatwa, when the people asking for a jurist's opinion requested him to cite his sources. Debating contemporary issues on religion and science, including social problems like those affecting gender equality, the 'ulama have been forced to explain their view rationally, which according to them meant going beyond the traditional sources. Mawlana Ashraf Ali Thanawi's book *An Answer to Modernism* (*al-intibahat al-mufida*) and Qari Tayyib's *Islam and Rationalism* (*Islam awr aqliyat*) are examples of this genre of literature. Modern public debate, thus, succeeded in putting the traditionalists, and especially the 'ulama, in a defensive position. In the following lines I analyze three different moments and fields of contention within the process of social construction of shari'a in Pakistan.

Family Law Reforms and Their Critique (1961–1971)

Let me begin with the first major shari'a legislation in Pakistan, in 1961. This legislation was characterized at that time as a reform of Islamic law, similar to attempts undertaken in other Muslim majority countries such as Egypt, Algeria, and Tunisia. The Pakistani family laws reform dealt with the issues of polygamy, age of marriage, triple divorce (according to which the husband pronounced the formula of divorce three times to render it effective), the registration of marriages and divorce, the inheritance of orphaned grandchildren, dower, and maintenance. I need not go into the details of these law reforms as they have been extensively discussed in various studies (Mahmood 1972, 1987; Anderson 1976; Pearl 1979; Nasir 1986). They were meant to ameliorate the status of women. My goal here, however, is to put in evidence their dimension of social constructedness.

This legislation was enacted as an ordinance by a martial-law government in 1961, but it was preceded by a decade of debates on the status of women and their rights. The voice of the 'ulama who opposed the women movement for law reforms was not yet very strong in the early years of Pakistan. The media was dominated by liberal voices, mainly belonging to *Taraqqi Pasand Tahrik*, that is, a "progressive movement" that had taken shape in India as a reformist trend in Urdu language. It was prominent in the government press and radio, and also published its own newspaper. The political background was predetermined by the army's interference in the political process. General Ayyub Khan had declared the martial law in 1958 and abrogated the 1956 constitution. He introduced reforms in the country at several levels. The Family Laws ordinance was one of these reforms intended to modernize personal status laws in the country.

Before the ordinance was issued, the government established several institutions and encouraged public debates on the main issues at stake. These discussions appeared in the daily press and were aired on radio. At the educational level, a new subject of Islamic Studies was introduced in universities and colleges. This subject reflected a very modern approach to the shari'a, when compared to the teaching of Islamic disciplines in the *madrasa*s. Moreover, the government grounded the Central Institute of Islamic Research (later renamed the Islamic Research Institute), headed by Fazlur Rahman, in Karachi, the Institute of Islamic Culture, directed by Khalifa Abdul Hakim, in Lahore, and the Islamic Academy, headed by Abu'l Hashim, in Dacca. The government also constituted a Council of Islamic Ideology to discuss and advise the legislative assembly on matters related to Islam. Fazlur Rahman, Khalifa Abdul Hakim, and Abu'l Hashim were Islamic modernists, who wrote on issues of family law and were quite active in promoting reforms in this field. Rahman and Abu'l Hashim were also members of the Council of Islamic Ideology. These institutions presented variants of a modernist construction of the shari'a in their journals and publications. Finally, a commission, consisting of judges, lawyers, representatives of Pakistani women associations, and 'ulama was constituted to draft the new Family Laws. In each forum the opinion was divided, although the modernist view remained dominant. The draft prepared by the commission was eventually released as The Family Laws Ordinance in 1961 and was welcomed by liberal groups and especially by women.

Opposition to these and other reforms, taken as a threat to the Islamic tradition, came from various 'ulama groups and the Jama'at Islami. They made full use of the media, gradually monopolizing discussions on shari'a, while they also started to publish daily newspapers, weekly journals, and special magazines for women, students, and children. The leading Islamist theorist Abul A'la Mawdudi, who had begun his career as a journalist, developed a special rhetoric style that appealed to the growing educated middle class, in contrast to the 'ulama, who still wrote in a style specifically addressed to their peers. The only rival to Mawdudi's capacity as an emerging leader in the public sphere where shari'a was reconstructed was Ghulam Ahmad Perwez, but Mawdudi discredited him. Perwez gave a modern interpretation of Islam and called for a critical approach to *hadith* (reported sayings and deeds of the Prophet with the value of legal sources). He maintained that *hadith* literature was generally unreliable, and therefore set criteria for its selective acceptance. Perwez was also a member of the commission for Family Law reforms. Mawdudi, along with leading 'ulama, effectively campaigned against both Perwez and other reformists like Fazlur Rahman. The journals of the Islamic Research Institute published articles in favor of these reforms. The Urdu journal *Fikro Nazar* dealt with the issues of child marriage, divorce, and similar topics, upholding reformist arguments. The *Bayyinat*, a monthly journal from Karachi, published refutations from the point of view of the 'ulama. The various journals of Jama'at Islami also joined *Bayyinat*.

This debate was particularly beneficial for strengthening the public authority of Mawdudi, because in his earlier writings he had antagonized the 'ulama by his harsh criticism, while they had challenged him on the allegation of his lacking credentials as a religious scholar, even issuing fatwas against him. Mawdudi took up the opportunity offered by the new public dispute in order to win the favor of the 'ulama by joining them in their opposition to the reforms. He gradually succeeded to be regarded as the champion of the Islamic cause in Pakistan. Mawdudi overshadowed other religious leaders and also succeeded in getting the support of the 'ulama against Perwez and Rahman, who were declared apostates.

Attempting to interpret the public contentions on shari'a in this period, we see that the process was initiated by Islamic modernists with the support of the government. However, reforms were not produced in a democratic way. The modernists could not extend their influence among the masses because mosques and *madrasas* stayed outside of their area of influence. Jama'at Islami and the 'ulama proved more effective in their communication strategy over Islamic matters than Islamic modernists, also by entering the politics of student and trade unions. They succeeded in launching a mass movement against Ayyub Khan, and finally another general replaced him by imposing the martial law. Pakistan went through a phase of political turmoil, also due to the war with India and the independence of Bangladesh in 1971. In the brief interlude of the elected government of Zulfiqar Ali Bhutto, the Jama'at Islami led the religious parties against the ruling party who stood for Islamic socialism. The constitution of 1973 restored the Islamic provisions and soon the alliance of religious political parties was able to bring about a mass movement against Bhutto. This alliance called for a Nizam Mustafa ("order of the Prophet") and ushered in the third martial law called by General Ziaul Haq in 1977. Clearly, the capacity to win public disputes in the shari'a field and to mobilize consensus, on the one hand, and the democratic process, on the other, did not clearly coincide.

Underneath the surface of this ongoing public dispute on reform, no political leader paid due attention to the actual content of the teaching of Islamic studies. Khurshid Ahmad, a prominent member of the Jama'at Islami compiled the prescribed texts, since writings by the 'ulama were too technical and complex for the college and university students, and there was no other reading material available on Islamic subjects. Jama'at's ideas about the Islamic state and shari'a gained currency among the young graduates in this period. This situation paved the way for another stage of the public reconstruction of shari'a.

Islamization of Laws (1979–1985)

Apart from the fact that the program of Islamization provided legitimacy to the martial-law regime, the program was also the culmination of the ongoing battle for the reconstruction of shariʿa that the ʿulama had been fighting since after their challenge of the Family Law reforms. The ʿulama's position was buttresed by their support of the martial-law regime of Ziaul Haq and their condemnation of Bhutto as a secular and a socialist.

The ʿulama managed to take over the lead in the shariʿa field by building mosques and *madrasa*s as spaces sharing in the public sphere. This strategy gained élan also due to geopolitical factors. First, the Cold War between the United States and Soviet Union entered a new phase when the communist parties took over in Afghanistan and invited the military inter- vention of the Soviet Union. The opposition against communism received active support from the Western governments, especially from the United States. The Jama'at Islami along with other religious groups in other Muslim countries launched a *jihad* against the Soviet Union in Afghanistan. Ziaul Haq supported this move that succeeded in throwing the Soviet forces out of Afghanistan. This enhanced Zia's prestige and legitimized his Islamization program. The second important factor was the dawn of the 15th century of Islam, accompanied by messianic hopes and fears, sup- ported by world events like a rebellion in Saudi Arabia that ended in the siege of the Kaʿba in 1979. In the same year, an Islamic revolution took place in Iran. Several Muslims took these events as signs of a revival of Islam, and Zia's Islamization could be interpreted as the specific form the revival of Islam was taking in Pakistan.

Ziaul Haq undertook a comprehensive project of Islamization of law, economy, and education in 1979. He began with promulgating a series of ordinances enforcing the *hudud* (Islamic penal laws), which had hitherto never been implemented. These ordinances prescribed the penalties of cutting hands for theft, lashing for drinking of liquor, and stoning to death for unlawful sexual offence. The following year, the government of Pakistan introduced two traditional taxes: *zakat* (an annual 2.5 per cent levy on cash and wealth savings) and *ushr* (an annual 10 per cent tax on agricul- tural produce). The *ushr* was ineffective because the landlords resisted its implementation. However, the *zakat* began to be deducted immediately from bank saving accounts. A *zakat* fund was established to distribute the tax collected for religious purposes, that is, to *madrasa*s, as institutions of religious learning. It was contrary to the doctrines of the Hanafi School to pay *zakat* to *madrasa*s but the ʿulama justified it on the basis of *ijtihad*, that is, the free reasoning that they did not disdain to exercise on a point that immediately affected their interests. Islamic banking laws were also intro- duced, in order to regulate bank transactions according to Islamic law. A Federal Shariʿa Court was established to administer cases according to Islamic law. In 1984, an ordinance was promulgated to introduce the Islamic law of evidence. In 1985, a law prescribed death sentence for the offence of blasphemy against the Prophet Muhammad and the Qur'an. A specific shariʿa ordinance defined in general the jurisdiction of shariʿa, and allowed shariʿa courts to examine existing laws and declare them invalid if they did not accord with Islamic law, with the only exemption of *riba* (usury) transaction, fiscal laws, and so on.

It is important to point out that this wave of Islamization of laws was undertaken in haste and promulgated without debate or scrutiny. The ordinances were criticized by lawyers, women's groups, and human rights organizations. The regime also launched a programme for the Islamization of education. An Islamic university was established in 1980, which in addition to teaching Islamic traditional subjects also introduced Islamic economics and management, along with degrees in shari'a. Two academies undertook the training of imams, preachers, attorneys, and judges. Reforms were also introduced in the curricula. Islamic studies was made a compulsory subject, even in professional courses such as medicine and engineering. During this period, thousands of new *madrasa*s were established in Pakistan, patronized by Ziaul Haq: their numbers rose from 137 in 1947 and 210 in 1950 to 1896 in 1982 (Malik 1996: 180). The graduates from these *madrasa*s strengthened the ranks of religious political parties like Jam'iyyat Ulama Islam and Jam'iyyat Ulama Pakistan. These graduates also supported the *jihad* in Afghanistan. This Islamization accelerated militancy among the youth. Almost every religious group developed a youth group, representing their respective political parties as student wings in colleges and universities. They staged street demonstrations and election campaigns.

Similarly, older *madrasa*s also developed student forces. These formations often clashed with their rival student groups representing other political parties, some of them organized along ethnic and linguistic, not religious lines. The clashes generated a militant culture. This situation overlapped with the Sunni–Shi'a conflict, enhanced by the tension between Iran and Saudi Arabia. Several clashes among militant groups generated sectarian violence in which a number of 'ulama were killed from both sides.

This period witnessed the introduction of hundreds of new religious magazines and newspapers, in representation of almost every single religious group. These new writings had an impact on Pakistani society without however enhancing the dynamics of the public sphere, because each group was talking to its own members. The public reconstruction of shari'a relied heavily on the state, as it was informed by a certain concept of Islamic state that made the shari'a a responsibility and an asset of the state. The Jama'at Islami, that was the main supporter of Zia's regime, was a primary influence of this shari'a politics, which no liberal organization was able to challenge in the public domain. Political formations such as the Pakistan People Party or the National Awami Party opposed the Jama'at and other religious groups, but only at a purely political level, thus neglecting the level of public discourse. In other words, they did not offer any alternative reconstruction of shari'a. The only real opposition and alternative construction were offered by the women's action groups who entered the public sphere to expose the prevailing understanding of shari'a as particularly unjust to women.

Public Debates on the Shari'a (1990–2002)

The public opinion on shari'a continued to be divided but the range of actors in the debate widened. Besides the 'ulama, now Islamists who were not trained as 'ulama, and a number of lay persons were also voicing their views on shari'a. No doubt, Islamist speech was louder, yet there were also other voices to be heard. Let me give three examples from the last decade of the 20th century to illustrate how the socio-political process produced different reconstructions of the shari'a. In 1990 the government of Pakistan promulgated an ordinance implementing the Islamic legal principles of *qisas* and *diyat*. *Qisas*, literally meaning retaliation (*lex talionis*), prescribes the death sentence for murder and the same injury in case of injurious assault. Furthermore, it provides the right of retaliation for the heirs of the victim. It also allows the right to pardon or to receive compensation (*diyat*). The ordinance obliged the public transport drivers to pay huge amounts of blood money and damages in cases of traffic accidents. Transporters in Pakistan protested against the ordinance. Their opposition generated a public debate, which reflected at least three different conceptions of the shari'a. The transporters argued that this shari'a-based law was not practicable, thus basing their view on a notion of practicability. For the government legislators, *qisas* and *diyat* were integral to the shari'a, and therefore the government was obliged to implement them: this was a perspective of almost pure normativity. A number of writers in the daily press distinguished the shari'a from *fiqh*, as we have mentioned above, thus giving historicity to the construction of shari'a. They argued that details of *qisas* and *diyat* evolved in the framework of the concept of liability in tribal systems. Muslim jurists of the past based the corresponding legal provisions on the foundation of this generally accepted social norm in those days, in order to make the law more effective. The transporters held a nationwide strike in Pakistan protesting against this ordinance, and the government had to withdraw it under the pressure of public opinion. It was a victory of practicability and historicity against the abstract normativity of state legislators in their construction of shari'a.

In 1991, the assembly of the state of Punjab blocked the passage of a bill that obliged the landlords to pay the above-mentioned *ushr*, a religious tax amounting to one-tenth of their income from agriculture. Again, in the dispute we see two different conceptions of the shari'a. The government legislators felt bound to implement the shari'a laws. The landlords argued against the duality of the fiscal system, by evidencing that if they were to pay the shari'a taxes, then other taxes should be abolished. Interestingly, public opinion voiced in the press doubts whether the landlords paid any taxes at all. However, since a majority of the legislators were landlords, both government and opposition benches easily united to defeat the bill.

In 1994, the government of Pakistan abolished the Frontier Crimes Regulations—the so-called tribal laws introduced by the British during the colonial period—in order to bring the tribal areas into the national legal system. Under the British, different systems of judicial administration operated in these areas. For instance, in the princely state of Swat, the judge (*qadi*), and in other areas the Jirga (tribal tribunal) settled disputes among the people. The British government did not interfere, and the system was perpetuated until after the independence. Only in 1994 the government decreed its end. Several groups protested against the abolition of the old system. In their midst, a movement, Tahrik Nifadh Shari'at Muhammadiyya, arose in Malakand, calling for the immediate enforcement of the shari'a in those areas. Various groups joined this claim under the leadership of a local religious leader, known as Sufi Muhammad. The movement gained momentum to the extent that its militias clashed with government forces in 1996. After three weeks of skirmishes and hundreds of casualties, the government was able to restore law and order, and promised to introduce the shari'a in the area. A package of shari'a laws drafted by the government bureaucracy was announced, but the movement refused to accept it. During a visit in 2000, I was informed that several interest groups supported the movement. The landlords (*khans*) hoped that the shari'a would restore their property rights, which had been restricted by the land reforms. They believed that land reforms were not supported by shari'a. Smugglers and businessmen also supported this approach because they believed that shari'a does not prohibit smuggling, and its application exempts them from paying custom duties and other taxes. These and other similar calls for the shari'a reflect the semantics of very different, at times divergent understandings of shari'a of various social groups.

Conclusion

The above analysis of variations in the public reconstruction of shari'a in Pakistan illustrates, first, that shari'a depends on an ongoing interpretative struggle based on the different positioning of social actors, and, second, that this reconstruction depends on the discursive arsenal well defined by the concept of communicative action examined at the beginning of this chapter. In the process of communicative action, social actors introduce certain interpretations of shari'a laws, claim them as normative, and argue that they are in the general interest of the community. Optimally, the process should entail an emergent tendency to seek a consensus by discussion. However, the above examples have shown that this communication is inevitably accompanied by some "non-communicative" actions like political strategies, educational reforms, and legislation, which are used to support the communicative dimension of social action. Though it is true that the public reconstruction of shari'a has been generally discursive, it cannot be ignored that the discourse has been often restricted to certain groups that were expected to hold the authoritative means and competence to influence public opinion. In modern times, emphasis on public opinion as an autonomous factor of influence has certainly increased, but the burden of authority has not disappeared.

It needs no explanation that language plays a very essential role in this process. In the past, a very complex use of language in the shari'a writings confined the discourse to expert milieus. In modern times, when the 'ulama had to communicate with the masses, this complex language created problems in their attempts to reach the lay person. It is often complained that even a person learned in other sciences finds it difficult to read a shari'a text. Consequently, lay people were advised to consult jurists even in reading the books that the 'ulama wrote for the general public. In one of his treatises on the issue of judicial divorce, Mawlana Ashraf Ali Thanawi, who is known for his efforts for promoting education among Muslim women, advised readers not to read the book unaided by an expert and pious Muslim (Masud 1996: 199). For sure, shari'a writings share this problem with legal language in general. It is thus not surprising that in modern times the writers who have been able to gain popularity in public contentions over shari'a were either journalists or authors who began their careers by writing in journals. The public sphere in modern times has questioned this closed expert approach to law and stressed the need for a more communicative language.

Mass education and new communication media have enhanced the need and role of communicativity. The new media have introduced new voices in the public debate on shari'a, which is clearly no longer the exclusive domain of the religious scholars. Engineers, medical doctors, and non-shari'a lawyers are also participating in the debates. The debate is no longer confined to mosques, *madrasa*s, and scholarly publications: shari'a issues are being discussed in the press, on television, in public forums, assemblies, and on the Internet.

However, the jurists retain a special place by continuously responding to debates on social norms and public morality. They now refer to *'urf* (customs), *'adat* (habits, social practice), *bid'a* (religious changes), *sunna* (accepted social practice), *ijma' sukuti* (unarticulated consensus), to justify the normativity of certain laws. The underlying assumption in the doctrine of *tardy* (gradual legislation) is that it is difficult, if not impossible, to expect humans to suddenly change their ways. The jurists recognize the significance of debates (*khilaf*) and difference of opinion (*ikhtilaf*). Optimally discussion leads to consensus (*ijma'*), which is often silent (*sukuti*). This negotiation presumes the capacity of human beings to understand what obligation means in both psychological and linguistic terms, as much as the above-mentioned medieval Andalusian jurist and theorist of law Shatibi characterized shari'a as *'ammiyya* (understandable at a general level) and as *ummiyya* (understandable by lay persons). These characteristics also define legal obligation on the scale of the lay person. From this perspective, the norm or standard is set on the minimum scale measured according to the capacity and comprehension of a common man.

The public reconstruction of shari'a is also based on ideas of common good, a notion that remains very general and abstract unless it is measured by the interests of the common man. It becomes normative when a society comes to accept it in concrete terms, which are incorporated in the ongo-ing formation of consensus. Communicative action presupposes the idea of common good, but its details are continuously defined in discursive terms. Their acceptability depends on how a society comes to define *maslaha/masalih*, that is, the general interest and the particular interests that specify it. Accepted practice is in fact the result of discourses that help to construct this practice. Discourse requires the participation of nonexperts, otherwise it is a mere convention or a special ritual of a group of experts. Communicative action is not a sufficient, but a necessary con-dition to bring about acceptability, as it defines normativity, and explains how a certain practice is reasonable.

Political power can facilitate the construction of shari'a by a certain group but such power relations do not become normative unless other groups also find that construction suitable to their interests and are con-vinced, at least to some degree, through communication. Various other strategies in the form of education and the enactment of laws create a favorable environment but a consensus, even if a silent one, develops after a negotiation among various interest groups. The public reconstruction of shari'a is not an exception to this rule of communicative action, but rather proves it quite nicely.

For sure, modern conceptions of law are different from their premod-ern counterparts: while the latter sanctified law as sacred, modern con-cepts stress law's capacity to protect the interests of individuals in a human society. It is true that no legal system operates without coercive power, as also maintained by Shatibi, but a construction of law cannot be normative in the sense we have discussed unless its normativity is based on its wider acceptability in a society. In the above discussion we have seen that both liberal and Islamized constructions of shari'a were introduced with the help of state power: in fact both by martial law ordinances. They were not initiated by public discourse. However, state power facilitated the respec-tive constructions, but it could not build a wider base of acceptance. The state can create the environment for a socially constructed view of shari'a but it cannot provide sufficient conditions for acceptability, rationality, and normativity, which can only be delivered by communicative action.

Note

1. I read Habermas's theory through Korsgaard's study (1996) of normativity as emerging through notions of voluntarism, realism, reflexive endorsement, and appeal to autonomy, and through the analysis of Habermas's theory of communicative action by William Rehg (1996) and Manuel B. Dy Jr. (1998).

References

Anderson, J.N.D. 1976. *Law Reform in the Muslim World*. London: Athlone Press.
Austin, John. 1954. *The Province of Jurisprudence Determined,* ed. H.L.A. Hart, London: George Weidenfeld and Nicholson.

D'Agostino, Fred. 1996. *Free Public Reason: Making it Up as We Go*. Oxford: Oxford University Press.

Dy, Manuel B. Jr. 1998. "The Ethics of Communicative Action: Habermas's Discourse Analysis." In *The Humanization of Technology and Chinese Culture*, ed. Tomonobu Imamichi et al., Washington: Council for Research in Values and Philosophy.

Ehrlich, Eugene. 1936. *Fundamental Principles of Sociology of Law*. Cambridge MA: Harvard University Press.

Eickelman, Dale F., and Armando Salvatore. 2004 [2002]. "Muslim Publics." In *Public Islam and Common Good*, ed. Armando Salvatore and Dale F. Eickelman, Leiden and Boston: Brill, 3–27.

Habermas, Jürgen. 1996 [1992]. *Between Facts and Norms: Contribution to a Discourse Theory of Law and Democracy*, trans. William Rehg, Cambridge: Polity Press.

Ibn 'Abidin. 1884. *Nashr al-'urf fi bina ba'd al-ahkam 'ala al-'urf*. Damascus: Dar al-ma'arif.

Ibn Khaldun. 1989. *Muqaddima*. Tehran: Intisharat Istiqlal.

Korsgaard, Christine M. 1996. *The Sources of Normativity*. Cambridge: Cambridge University Press.

Lloyd, Dennis 1979. *Introduction to Jurisprudence*. London: Stevens and Sons.

Mahmood, Tahir. 1972. *The Family Law Reform in the Muslim World*. Bombay: N.M. Tripathy.

———. 1987. *Personal Law in Islamic Countries*. New Delhi: Academy of Law and Religion.

Makdisi, George. 1981. *The Rise of Colleges*. Edinburgh: Edinburgh University Press.

———. 1984. "The Juridical Theology of Shafi'i: Origins and Significance of *Usul al-Fiqh*." *Studia Islamica*, 59: 5–47.

———. 1991. *Religion, Law and Learning in Classical Islam*. Hampshire: Variorum.

Malik, Jamal. 1996. *Colonization of Islam, Dissolution of Traditional Institutions in Pakistan*. New Delhi: Manohar.

Masud, Muhammad Khalid. 1996. "Apostasy and Judicial Separation in British India." In *Islamic Legal Interpretation: Muftis and Their Fatwas*, ed. Muhammad Khalid Masud, Brinkley Messick, and David S. Powers, Cambridge, MA: Harvard University Press, 193–203.

———. 2000 [1995]. *Shatibi's Philosophy of Islamic Law*. Kuala Lumpur: Islamic Book Trust.

Mehdi, Rubya. 1994. *The Islamization of the Law in Pakistan*. Richmond: Curzon.

Nasir, Jamal. J. 1986. *The Islamic Law of Personal Status*. London: Graham and Trotman.

Pearl, David. 1979. *A Textbook on Muslim Personal Law*. London: Croom Helm.

Rawls, John. 1999. *The Law of Peoples*. Cambridge, MA: Harvard University Press.

Rehg, William. 1996. "Translator's Introduction" to Jürgen Habermas, *Between Facts and Norms: Contribution to a Discourse Theory of Law and Democracy*. Cambridge: Polity Press.

Schwartz, Richard D. 1986. "Law and Normative Order." In *Law and Social Sciences*, ed. Leon Lispon and Santon Wheeler, New York: Russel Sage Foundation, 63–107.

al-Shatibi, Abu Ishaq. 1915. *Al-I'tisam*. Cairo: Mustafa Muhammad.

————. 1975 [1883]. *Al-Muwafaqat fi-usul al-sharïa*, 4 vols. Cairo: al-Maktabat al-tijariyya.

Waliullah, Shah. n.d. *Hujjatullah al-baligha*, 2 vols. Lahore: al-Maktabat al-salafiyya.

Wheeler, Brannon M. 1996. *Applying the Canon in Islam, The Authorization and Maintenance of Interpretative Reasoning in Hanafi Scholarship*. Albany, NY: State University of New York Press.

CHAPTER 7

IS THERE AN ARAB PUBLIC SPHERE? THE PALESTINIAN INTIFADA, A SAUDI FATWA AND THE EGYPTIAN PRESS

Dyala Hamzah

In the spring of 2001, Saudi Arabia's Grand Mufti issued a fatwa condemning suicide attacks in the name of Islam. In the Egyptian press, the fatwa was perceived as a desecration of the icon of Palestinian resistance (the martyr or *shahid*). An "Arab public opinion," voicing its concerns over the jeopardized interests of the community (*umma*), was soon staged in its daily columns. In this chapter, I explore a debate that laid bare the contemporary procedures by which consent is manufactured. For that purpose, I address the *reception* of the Saudi fatwa in the Egyptian press, the *argumentation* construed in favor or against it, and the *explanations* put forth to make sense of the acts it sanctioned.

The main outcome of the analysis is that the specialized opinion of the 'ulama is given precedence over nonspecialized opinion and gains the legitimacy of being both "public" and "Arab." I argue that the consensual (mis)representation of the Saudi fatwa that resulted from the debate is proof not of the existence of an Arab public opinion and thus of an Arab transnational public sphere, but rather of its absence. I conclude with a critical assessment of the application of the Habermasian concept of public sphere to the Middle Eastern context of this study.

This investigation primarily addresses the Egyptian press[1] for a case study of "Arab public opinion." The sheer size of the Arab press makes it impossible to conduct a systematic review at a macro level. The Arab Press surveys published by the Israeli organization, the Middle East Media Research Institute (MEMRI) could have offered an alternative to extensive research, were it not for its problematic handling of the material.[2] Reference to it was therefore kept to a minimum. But there was an organic reason too for this choice of Egypt—namely, its self-posturing as recipient, and amplifier, of an "Arab voice." The self-conscious representation of this country's political weight and cultural centrality in the region is a constant of its national press and was restaged on the occasion of this particular debate.

Chronology of a Pre-9/11 Debate

On April 21, 2001, the London-based Saudi daily *al-Sharq al-awsat* released a major interview with Saudi Arabia's Grand Mufti, shaykh 'Abd al-'Aziz ibn 'Abdallah Al al-Shaykh.[3] In the front-page summary of the interview, the mufti's corporate stance regarding the prerogatives of religious scholars (the 'ulama) was affirmed alongside considerations over recent violent militancy. The few lines devoted to suicide operations soon came to be known in the Egyptian press as the "stray fatwa"[4] or the "bomb-fatwa,"[5] provoking a heated debate over the legitimacy of Palestinian "martyrdom operations" against Israel. Lasting in intensity from April 22 till mid-June 2001, the controversy had largely subsided by the 9/11 attacks on the World Trade Center and the Pentagon and was not to recover momentum subsequently. The Egyptian press then focused on the "War on Terrorism," leaving momentarily in the background the Second Intifada, about to enter its second year.

The few articles debating the virtues of martyrdom after 9/11 did so by drawing a distinction between terrorism, on one hand, and heroism and legitimate defence, on the other. At stake for such observers was the manipulation, by violent proponents of Islamic militancy, of the reformist reinterpretation of the *jihad* doctrine as a concept of international law and of the equation of *jihad* with the concept of *bellum iustum*. Egyptian thinker Muhammad Salim al-'Awwa wrote:

> The allegations that Arabs are terrorists or that they practice terrorism against Israel are nullified by what is recognized in international law and in the United Nations charters and successive resolutions, i.e., by the distinction between the right to resist the occupying enemy and terrorist acts against civilians. What happened in New York and Washington on September 11 is a terrorist act without any doubt.[6]

However, with the sudden intensification of Palestinian suicide operations in December 2001 leading to the unprecedented measures taken by Israel against the Palestinian Authority and Yasir 'Arafat, the debate floundered in response to the needs of the actual political agenda.[7] Though the issue of suicide bombings cannot be considered specific to the Second Intifada, the Egyptian debate reveals that these operations started to be assessed in clearly dichotomous terms (martyrdom versus suicide) in the wake of the Saudi fatwa that refused to qualify a suicide (*intihar*) attack as martyrdom (*istishhad*), and asserted that such attacks contravened Islamic law.

This dichotomization was confirmed locally and transnationally. Public opinion polls carried out at regular intervals among Palestinians since the start of the Oslo process have shown the dramatic increase of support of suicide operations as an adequate or legitimate means of resistance to the occupying forces. On the other hand, Egyptian press observers, both "secularist" and "religious," have echoed a quasi unanimous celebration of the glorious martyrs. Religious writers have dominated the debate as they issued innumerable condoning fatwas, after the initial Saudi fatwa ignited the controversy. How the debate picked up again and how it changed after the first suicide attack perpetrated by a woman,[8] are matters beyond the bounds of this contribution. The value of this study transcends the political contingencies of those months and offers insights into the ambivalent emergence of an issue-oriented public discussion in an Arab context that the post-9/11 war scenario has not allowed since.

Of Contemporary Fatwas

While it was expected that the fatwa that sparked the debate would mobilize *en masse* the specialists of that legal genre, it is less obvious why the discussion remained under their control. In the modern era, the upsurge of that specific legal genre called fatwa[9] in times of crisis has been acknowledged by recipients and practitioners of Islamic consultation (*ifta'*), so as to refute earlier scholarly findings that had declared the institution obsolete (Tyan 1960). This fatwa revival has received recent scholarly attention[10] and the institutional transformations of *ifta'* are now well documented. Noteworthy among those who have attested to the vitality of this legal practice and literature in modern days are Masud, Messick, and Powers (1996) on the one hand, and Skovgaard-Petersen (1997) on the other. They have stressed how *ifta'* has been decisively revived and transformed by print culture and the development of mass media.

Umlil (1996) seems to attribute to the Islamic resurgence of the 20th century the responsibility for this renewed role of the fatwa. His stress on an emerging type of "non-official," "fundamentalist" fatwa,[11] puts in evidence its loosened ties with the vast corpus of "jurisprudential precedents" (i.e., the mass of volumes of collected fatwas). The fact that this type of fatwa readily addressed modern social issues[12] probably influenced the institutional fatwa in style, content, and even frequency. But a focal point in the debate here under scrutiny is the fact that the "stray fatwa" and the major counter-fatwas all came from the most official and orthodox (Sunni *and* Shi'a) institutions, up to the point that the debate is saturated with considerations of status, legitimacy, and justification.

The Saudi Fatwa

The Front-Page Summary

Under the heading "Saudi Arabia's Mufti: the Excommunication (*takfir*)[13] of Muslims is a Dangerous Matter," 'Aqil al-'Aqil, *al-Sharq al-awsat*'s correspondent in Riad cursively referred on the front page to shaykh 'Abd al-'Aziz ibn 'Abdallah Al al-Shaykh's long interview in the inside "religion" page, summarizing it through four apparently unrelated issues: (1) the prerogatives of 'ulama in matters of excommunication (*takfir*); (2) the scholarly prerequisites of Islamic consultation (*ifta*'); (3) the illegitimacy of suicide attacks and the fact that they do not pertain to *jihad*, and (4) the illegitimacy of airplane hijacking. While this front-page summary is only a partial reconstruction of the Grand Mufti's words, it must be noted that it is to this truncated and reconstructed text that all participants in the debate would later refer. This made it possible: (1) to ignore or bypass the jurisprudential arguments put forth by the mufti, which are truncated in the summary, and (2) to question the authenticity of his sayings, since the interview framework was absent from the front-page summary.

The Text of the Interview

The text consists of three distinct parts. Starting with a biography of the shaykh, it proceeds to summarize the content of the subsequent interview—in an order of subjects that differs from the one on the front page—before parading the 12-question-and-answer-long interview. The length and complexity of the questions are such as to suggest either their prior formulation by the mufti himself or the assumption by the journalist of the role of *mustafti*' (the individual or institution soliciting a legal opinion), a point I later give more attention. As to the 12 questions, they dealt with diverse issues amongst which: suicide operations and their relation to *jihad* (question no. 1); the issue of *takfir* ("excommunication") and who is allowed to pronounce that legal statute (no. 5); the current passion for and competition over Islamic consultation (no. 6); airplane hijacking (question no. 7); the official representation of Islam (no. 12). While the title of the interview took up the topic of the seventh question/fatwa ("Airplane hijacking and the terrorizing of passengers is illegitimate"), its subtitle bore: "*Takfir* is a dangerous matter which Muslims ought to abstain from and leave to established scholars—in the absence of qualification, Islamic consultation is greater [a crime] than polytheism." The title seems to point to a specific recent event whereas the subtitle focuses on two of the major challenges that official Islam has had to contend with in the last decades of the 20th century, as Islamist groups strove to capture religio-political authority through *ifta*' (Willis 1996).

Discrepancies

Nowhere in the article does the condemnation of suicide operations appear in headlines, although this issue is the first to be tackled in the interview and the first point to be summarized in the peculiar introductory part of the interview following the biography of the shaykh. That short reconstructed front-page text displays yet another problematic feature when compared to the original: it does not make clear whether some of its four fatwas were issued at the spontaneous initiative of the mufti himself while others were issued as an answer to the questions of the journalist ("[The mufti] emphasized . . . And in an interview with *al-Sharq al-awsat*, he considered . . ."). But since the Egyptian opinion makers would single out that short column instead of the original interview, a close look at its apparently unrelated contents is in order. It reveals a subtle, albeit artificial, editorial articulation, where, of the four fatwas listed above, (1) appears to be a species of (2) while (3) and (4) are concrete applications of the former.

In substance, the front-page column ran as follows:

> While all muftis are 'ulama, not all 'ulama are muftis since *ifta'* belongs only to those deeply versed in the science of *fiqh* as well as in worldly affairs. Not all who have been driven to impiety, fornication, unlawful innovation would be judged accordingly: better the Muslim public (*'umum al-muslimin*) keep their tongues to themselves and leave these matters to the 'ulama. A mufti is a *'alim* with knowledge and understanding in worldly affairs and in the situation of the questioner. He is bent on averting harm and promoting benefit, and endeavors in the exercise of *ifta'*, in order to strike a balance between the benefits and the harms entailed when these are in contradiction in the situation which is the object of the fatwa.

What the front-page summary does next is to give a definition of *'ilm* and *'alim*, before delivering the condemnation of suicide attacks and hijacking. In the process, it transforms fatwas 1 and 2 into meta-fatwas, and fatwas 3 and 4 into concrete applications: in this case, of legal opinions on novel social issues:

> The mufti sees that the suicide operations have no legitimate cast and are not part of *jihad* for the sake of God. And he expresses his concern lest they be a form of self-killing while stating that the killing of the enemy is an obligation, though it is an obligation which is determined in its modalities. As to airplane highjacking and the terrorizing of passengers (*aminin*: those entrusted to), it is contrary to the *shari'a* due to the aggression on women it breeds and to what is entailed by the breach in security.

The Context of the Saudi Fatwa

Whether we revert to the original interview or stick to its truncated version, the salient characteristic of these fatwas remains their self-assertiveness and defensiveness. The reported speech adopted by the journalist to illustrate them (as opposed to the interview frame whereby the questions are clearly formulated), adds to the aloofness of the statements. This is retroactively corroborated, however, by the subsequent silence of the mufti in the ensuing controversy.

Without delving on the domestic Saudi turmoil since after the first U.S.-led war against Iraq, which issued in protests against the presence of American troops on Saudi soil and demands for reform,[14] it seems reasonable to think that both "empirical" fatwas were prompted by recent events related to Saudi Arabia. Fatwa 4 addresses the Chechnian hijacking of a Russian plane that occurred on March 17, 2001 and ended, in Medina, with the death of one hijacker and of one female passenger at the hijackers' hands. Fatwa 3, on the other hand, which was understood by the Egyptian public opinion as concerning the Palestinian suicide operations against Israel, is however susceptible of a double interpretation. Despite the quite explicit formulation of the journalist's question, the fatwa could have addressed the USS Cole missile destroyer's suicide bomb attack, which killed 17 U.S. sailors and injured 39 in Aden on October 12, 2000 and in which Bin Laden, notoriously an ex-Saudi national, was incriminated. However, the time span separating this fatwa from the attack (six months) is quite long. Moreover, the adamant retreat of the mufti after the controversy erupted does suggest the inclusion of Palestinian suicide attacks in the circle of prohibition. What counts for the follow-up debate is that in a manner typical of fatwa rhetoric, the case at hand is stated in an impersonal and general tone. While the mufti knows the particulars of the case, the fatwa is stated as applying in general, "given such and such events and presuppositions."

That the fatwa should be politically motivated comes as no surprise. The position of Grand Mufti in Saudi Arabia is a state appointment. The Supreme Council of 'ulama (founded 1971), headed by the Grand Mufti, is also an integral component of the apparatus for the state's religious legitimation. As to the members of organizations promoting violent forms of Islamic militancy, they are first-rate rivals of this institutional and "statist" Islam. The mufti shares a "class" interest with state officials and protects his prerogatives when addressing the *'umum al-muslimin*, a rhetoric qualification formally designating the ordinary and peaceful laymen, but here most specifically singling out the violent revolutionary contenders of religious and political authority.

The Saudi regime's commitment to the Israeli-Palestinian peace process initiated by the 1993 Declaration of Principles has been consistently displayed at the diplomatic as well as at the financial levels,[15] and the regime's interest in the establishment of a Palestinian state is consistent with late king Faysal's successful transfer, during the 1970s, of the Arab-Israeli conflict from the Arab plane to a broadly Islamic one. This move prompted most Arab states, including Syria, Egypt, and Libya, to accept this redefinition of the conflict after the 1973 war. In 1973 as in 1993, the stakes from the Saudi point of view were the survival, in the case of Saudi Arabia, or the emergence, in the case of Palestine, of a nation-state claiming guardianship over the three holiest shrines of Islam and the assertion of its legitimacy over the contending pan-Arabism of the 1960s and early 1970s or the Islamism of the 1990s and of today.

The Counter-Fatwas and Other Responses

The Reception: Asserting the Transnational Umma

The reception of the Saudi fatwa in the Egyptian press ranged from outright rejection to unequivocal agreement, with some intermediate degrees of tentativeness. As we map the different reactions, the traditional divide in the "Arab public opinion" between "secularist" and "religious" voices is significantly redrawn.

Incredulous Denial

Among those who rejected the Saudi sanction of suicide operations were those who did so incredulously, by refusing to believe that such a fatwa could emanate from such an orthodox authority as the Saudi mufti and blaming the media for distorting or even faking it. Others offered inadequate interpretations, saying that the fatwa referred to internal events in Saudi Arabia or applied only in times of peace. Al-Azhar's shaykh Tantawi's initial reaction was indeed one of sheer denial,[16] while Hamas's Rantisi and other religious figures[17] were said to have rejected it prudently.[18] In one occurrence reminiscent of conspiracy theory, a journalist considered three hypotheses: (1) such a fatwa was "insinuated" to *al-Sharq al-awsat*, which lacked the time to carry out the necessary verifications, a hypothesis that is not very plausible given the absence of any official denial by the Saudi mufti and the reputation and wide circulation that the newspaper enjoys; (2) the "insinuated fatwa" (which is examined notwithstanding) raises suspicions as to its timing: aren't the latest suicide operations close to defeating the enemy, after they made clear that no peaceful coexistence can be achieved without returning the land to its owners in Palestine? (3) such a fatwa was issued by the mufti but only after he was driven to it, intentionally or not, by *al-Sharq al-awsat*'s journalist, who wanted to make a scoop without considering its negative impact on the morale of a people who suffers continuous missile attacks and has no alternative except turning their sons into human bombs.

Condemnation

Another modality of rejection was through debasing the Saudi mufti by describing him as incompetent or corrupt. A representative of the first opinion was the Egyptian Muhammad 'Imara, who did not question Shaykh 'Abd al-'Aziz's erudition as *'alim* but only his credentials as mufti, while offering the only term-to-term refutation of the Saudi mufti's meta-fatwa on the conditions of *ifta'*. Among those who embark on *ifta'*, said 'Imara, some might be knowledgeable in the "legal statutes" but are ignorant of reality. And we must be aware of the actors' intentions, lest we become bookworms, repeating what we find in books without being aware of the reality we live in.[19]

'Abd al-Rahman al-'Idwi (professor at al-Azhar in Cairo) was among those who upheld both types of hostile opinions and so delivered the probably sharpest condemnation of the Saudi mufti. Such sayings, 'Idwi stated, can come only from our enemies who are bent on weakening our will. As to the ubiquitous and popular, Egyptian-born and Qatar-based Muslim Brother shaykh Yusuf al-Qaradawi, he was among the first to voice criticism and one of the few to do so consistently throughout the debate,[20] but his condemnation, as far as we know, never ventured outside the bounds of scholarly argument.

On the front of denial, religious and secular arguments combined to counter a legal and authoritative opinion that was deemed harmful to the self-representation of the "Islamic community" (*umma*). Indeed, denial often sustained by an assertive "we," by the rhetorical, albeit proud, appropriation of the martyrs and self-martyred heroes, of "our" children of Palestine. As Qaradawi summed it up: "What our children in Palestine are doing arouses pride," describing them as "those lion cubs with whom the community glorifies itself." This is a good illustration of the way in which Palestine was inscribed at the heart of the *umma* and consecrated as an icon of Arab nationalism, even for what are otherwise, in Raymond Baker's words (see chapter 4) moderate or *wasatiya* figures.

Elsewhere this icon even assumes the quality of a substitute for national action, as in the Lebanese Shi'a mufti's statement that "the Intifada is the ultimate weapon of the Arabs . . . its endurance is a revivification of the Arab dignity and were it to be defeated, God forbid, we would be left only with collective suicide."[21] A far cry from empty nationalistic slogans, the statement of the Shi'a mufti rather situates suicide bombings in historical perspective: his statement responds to the journalist's question whether the unilateral withdrawal of Israel from Southern Lebanon after two decades of occupation and a relentless resistance by Hizbullah, history would repeat itself in the Palestinian territories.

Political Agreement and Doctrinal Support

If the denial of the fatwa was carried out in the name of the *umma*, the few religious and political figures who agreed with it did it in the name of the nation-state. Remarkably, however, this agreement, whether delivered by politicians or 'ulama, did not find its way into the Egyptian press. However these voices are significant and so is the fact that they can be found in the Palestinian and Saudi press,[22] that is, in the two national contexts that are central to the debated issues and that one would assume were being narrowly monitored in Egypt, given the Egyptian press's claim to voice Arab opinion. The political and doctrinal support that the Saudi shaykh was granted highlights the significance of omissions in the manufacture of a national public opinion (the Egyptian one) poised as a transnational Arab voice.

Those who de facto agreed with the Saudi fatwa by condemning suicide attacks, were mostly Palestinians involved in the construction of the Palestinian state: the head of the Palestinian Authority Yasir 'Arafat and the journalist Muhammad Masharqa,[23] the Jerusalemite lawyer Jonathan

Kuttab,[24] and academicians like Musa Budeiri and Rema Hammami.[25] But what characterizes the reception of the Saudi fatwa by this quite hetero-geneous set of observers is not a real reception, but a condemnation of sui-cide operations in the name of political opportunism ('Arafat), morality and political expediency (Budeiri/Hammami), or antireligious nationalist legitimism (Masharqa), sometimes driven by a keen understanding of international opinion (Kuttab). This approach never addressed the fatwa or the person of the mufti whether directly or indirectly. This might also explain why these opinions never found their way into the Egyptian press.

Among the notable non-Palestinian exceptions who lent, de facto or de jure, their support to the Saudi fatwa, were the Lebanese journalist Samir Qassir,[26] who saw in suicide attacks the suicide of a nation, and the Moroccan *'alim* shaykh Muhammad al-Hajj Nasir,[27] an expert member of the International Academy of Islamic Jurisprudence. No mufti seemed to have as flatly and unambiguously agreed with the Saudi Grand Mufti as he did, in such rigorous doctrinal terms, with such discriminating notions as to appear ultra-orthodox if compared with the authority he was support-ing. We cannot, says the shaykh, assign to any Muslim who dies in a nationalist struggle the attribute of *shahid* if only because, by doing so, we might confer this status upon someone in disagreement with religion; and we may not even declare martyrs those whose Muslim virtues are not in question and who die, because it is not up to us to confer the status of mar-tyr upon he who dies in pursuit of an authentic interest. We may only pray God that He accepts his martyrdom. Nationalist struggle, therefore, does not produce martyrs *sui generis*. Martyrdom is preconditioned on integrity; it is not to be gained through action alone. Religion is not to be subsumed under politics. The fatwa by shaykh Nasir was not only meant to assert some kind of orthodoxy but it also seemed to want to score a point against one of its fiercest mediatic contenders: the above-mentioned shaykh al-Qaradawi. Published in *al-Sharq al-awsat* too, this contestation of Qaradawi's arguments against the Saudi fatwa produced no response from the latter in the Egyptian press; neither did it attract other contenders or defendants of the Qatar-based Egyptian shaykh.

Religious Lip Service

While many journalistic statements point to the contrary, no mufti, except shaykh Nasir of Morocco, really came directly to the rescue of Saudi Arabia's Grand Mufti. Others paid some ambivalent lip service. Shaykhs al-Sadlan and al-Albani, the alleged front-line supporters of the Saudi mufti according to *al-Sharq al-awsat*,[28] delved each on details in what appears as a diversion for expressing a diluted disagreement. For al-Sadlan, the matter really boiled down to three possibilities, each of which he examined without ever designating names or groups: (1) he who engages in a battle whose fatal outcome is certain is committing suicide; (2) he who engages in a battle in order that Right may dawn and Wrong be annihilated and who dies doing so is a martyr; (3) he who engages in a battle whose issue is uncertain is not committing suicide. Then follows a statement to the effect that those people who commit such acts are a variety and that some who commit a "suicidal self-sacrificial act" (*'amal fida'i intihari*) are probably indoctrinated into thinking that they are fighting for a principle or a cause; those who die under these conditions are not to be described as having committed suicide and so they are pardoned. While Palestinian suicide bombers would certainly not fit in (3) but most definitely in (1), they are morally "saved" by the construing of (2), which is meant to qualify the condemnation, and, as "indoctrinated" individuals, they are furthermore pardoned while the blame seems to lie with their "indoctrinators," the Hamas and Jihad organizations. While initially presented as supportive, the fatwa of al-Sadlan is in fact all to the contrary. The same is also true, though to a lesser extent, of shaykh al-Albani's fatwa, entitled in the article "the suicide operations carried out these days are permitted and not permitted": in an Islamic regime, they are allowed if they emanate from a caliphal or military command. The Caliph or army leader must be well versed in Islamic *jihad*, otherwise these operations would not qualify as permitted. Only a legitimate Islamic authority can guarantee the intentions of the self-martyred. Without it, how would one know whether they all pray and whether there are no communists among them?

Another half-condoning stance was that of shaykh Tantawi of al-Azhar, who supported the operations as long as they did not target civilians. However, Tantawi's opinion was not weighed so much against that of the Saudi mufti as against his own preceding opinions on the legitimacy of suicide operations, which oscillated, between 1998 and 2001, from one side of the spectrum to the other.[29]

Has the public forum afforded by specialized religious debates contributed to remap the traditional divide between "secular" and "religious" voices? While the overwhelming predominance of the religious personnel would lead to answer negatively to the question, a closer look at the arguments deployed might yield a different picture.

The Arguments: Asserting the Public Interest

The arguments developed by the actors in the debate ranged from intra-jurisprudential to extra-jurisprudential, while also offering the occasional mix. The recourse by the layman to jurisprudential arguments and, conversely, the use of extra-jurisprudential arguments by 'ulama is one of the most interesting characteristics of the debate. A second noteworthy feature is that whatever the type of argument used in defence of or against the fatwa, the objective was mostly the assertion of some national form of public interest.

Intra-Jurisprudential Arguments
The intra-jurisprudential arguments sought to refute the correspondence established by the Saudi mufti between martyrdom and suicide in the case

of Palestine: the stakes were high since suicide is generally considered as a grave sin in Islam, disapproved by the Prophet himself who refused to recite the customary prayers for a suicider, and entailing terrible consequences in the afterlife. As they sought to distinguish martyrdom from suicide, actors in the debate, religious and nonreligious alike, did so by resorting to analogous situations of "suicidal martyrdom," which they endeavored to find in the early history of Islam.[30] But they also did so by discussing the notions of objectives and intentions (*niyyat*)[31] in self-inflicted death, in relation with the purposes of the Law (*maqasid al-shari'a*).[32] It was found that those operations were invariably carried out for the love of one's fatherland, or in self-defense and defense of religion and the fatherland (Nasr Farid Wasil[33]), or in defense of land, rights, and dignity (Qaradawi[34]), or in defense of land, honor, and the weak (al-'Idwi[35]), or in defense of land, self, and worldly goods (Kamal Imam[36]).

Since it was ascertained, according to the declarations of an unexpected participant, that "the martyrdom of those who are fighting for Palestine does not mean giving up on life, but rather protecting its meaning" (Saddam Hussein),[37] the suicide bombers were qualified as martyrs and a prophetic *hadith* was called in support: "he who is killed stripped of his religion, his worldly goods and his honor, is a martyr." Those acts were seen as promoting the interest of the nation and/or the *umma*: the superior interest of victory (*maslahat al-intisar*: al-Hajj Nasir); the benefit of Muslims (*manfa'at al-muslimin*: al-Qaradawi); the public cause (*al-qadiyya al-'amma*: 'Imara). In another instance, support for the operations in conjunction with a radical critique of the religious disagreement was uttered, through the plea that the 'ulama stay away from politics for "peoples have interests that are dictated by circumstances and change."[38]

Reading the debate through the prism of the emerging notion of a superior collective interest allows yet another revisitation of the traditional divide between secular and religious actors: a *'alim* arguing in favor or against the operations would do so, not so much in the name of doctrine as in the name of immediate national interests. Qur'anic invocations of a transcendent order are subsumed under the national interest: there is no higher expression of *jihad* than self-sacrifice for one's fatherland. If the overlapping of discourses does not achieve "communicative action" (cf. chapter 6 in this volume by Masud), could it be that the jurisprudential concept of *maslaha 'amma* ("public interest") was bridging over the divide? Could it be that this notion, through the historical transformations it went through, was providing ground for the foundations of a common language? Or is it that the notion was employed through a powerfully integrating mechanism that Bourdieu (1971) has described as "l'effet de double-entente," whereby the *same concept* takes on *opposite meanings* when it serves to express different social experiences? It should suffice here to point to the fact that the Egyptian press was on the same wavelength as the Saudi and Palestinian dailies as far as invocations of the general interest were concerned. This in turn would lend support to the idea of an emerging, common, trans-Arab political discourse, thanks to the migration of concepts from jurisprudence to "common sense."

An eloquent illustration of the possible migration of the category of *maslaha* across the religious/secular divide was when *al-Ahrar*, a self-declaredly liberal newspaper, published a suggestive criticism of the Western economicist notion of interest as it was allegedly developed by Samuel Huntington's "faulty and dangerous representations" of the issue of Jerusalem in *The Clash of Civilizations*. This unsigned criticism summarizes a series of interviews with four scholars on the problem of the "judaization" of Jerusalem.[39] The conclusion is basically that the danger of Huntington's theory lies in its misrepresentation of sensitive issues. One of them is the misconstruction of Jerusalem as a sentimental issue, rooted in religion and culture, that is, devoid of political and economic interests. The conclusion goes on to say that it is the error of maintaining Israeli settlements in Jerusalem, in contradiction with the peace process and Islamic sentiments, that has led to a consensus among the *umma*'s 'ulama on the clinging onto Jerusalem, despite the fact that most of the Islamic countries have no political or economic interests in it. Muslims consider the sacred city as a religious, cultural, and therefore political affair of utmost importance: there lies their disagreement with the West. The assertion of identity politics over economics, the defining of national interest as having firm religious and cultural roots is indeed a definition that seems to be shared across the religious/secular divide.

On the other hand, intra-jurisprudential arguments were not able to sustain the legitimacy of suicide attacks on the sole basis of historic precedents and national interest. Indeed, they had to cope with the killing of civilians. In order to repel possible counterarguments to the effect that though the intentions are noble (fighting occupation), the means are ignoble (targeting civilians instead of the military), the rectitude of the suicide bombers' intention had to be established and this was carried out through legal analogy (*qiyas*). Since the killing of enemy soldiers and the targeting of the military is what wars are all about, and since Israel is a militaristic society through and through, the suicide bombings are in fact never carried out in the midst of civilians, since civilians simply do not exist in Israel.[40] And as if *qiyas* was not enough, Qur'anic verses are mobilized to justify the killing of civilians, the most quoted of which was *al-Baqara*, 194: "Those who assault you, assault them the way they assaulted you."

Extra-Jurisprudential Arguments

Resorting to extra-jurisprudential arguments is a key feature of contemporary fatwas that rely more and more on all sorts of scientific expertise (Masud et al. 1996). This increasing dependence has raised questions about the nature of the opinion thus being produced. One such example was the fatwa of Muhammad Ibrahim al-Fayyumi, member of the Islamic Research Academy of al-Azhar, who based his ruling throughout on "international legality," referring to the United Nations Security Council resolutions on

Palestine and especially resolutions 232 and 348, to the 1993 Declaration of Principles, and to the 1998 Wye Plantation Agreement. In his support of suicide operations, Fayyumi refers, like many other scholars, to the right to legitimate defense, a "human and religious right" that is recognized by international law.[41]

Other extra-jurisprudential arguments elaborated on international public opinion, whether local or international. This trend was present mostly among Palestinian actors, including the already mentioned lawyer Jonathan Kuttab and Hamas leader 'Abd al-'Aziz al-Rantisi. As they engaged in a polemic in December 2001[42] over the role of international public opinion in exercising pressure on Israel and pushing for conflict resolution, the two entered a rare direct exchange across the secular/religious divide. While Kuttab praised the virtues of nonviolence and the sense of community-building that had prevailed during the First Intifada (when all sections of the Palestinian society and not only "small non-representative armed groups," were partaking in the resistance to the Israeli occupation), he also registered how badly the slaughter of unarmed children and youths was impacting on Western public opinion. How, indeed, nonviolent actions were more "marketable" than suicide operations. Rantisi would question sarcastically whether "non-violent activists" really thought that the only thing that could mobilize the West was that the Zionist military apparatus massacred thousands of Palestinian children? And whether these "pro-American Palestinians" thought that this would prompt such an emotional reaction as to lead ultimately to the grounding of a Palestinian state?

The Dichotomous Frame of the Argumentation and the Question of Terrorism

Following the issuance of the Saudi fatwa, all those who entered the debate over the Palestinian suicide bombings did so by systematically and prudently sticking to the suicide/martyrdom dichotomy imposed by the fatwa.[43] The dichotomous frame offered an unexpected arena for celebrating the virtues of the bomber while denouncing the vices of his foil (he who commits suicide "for his own benefit," in the curious wording of Qaradawi). It also provided an exit out of the debate on terrorism. While some opinions did touch upon the legitimacy, according to the shari'a, of "terrorizing the enemy," they usually took great care never to address seriously the stigmatization through their "enemy" 'of the attacks' organizers and perpetrators as terrorists. A few notable exceptions did, but in ways, contexts, and timings so different that it is hardly possible to ascertain any pattern. Among them, the first was the opinion of al-Qaradawi, who as early as April 25, 2001, that is, four days after the Saudi fatwa had been issued, made the sharp statement that "these operations are the supreme form of *jihad* for the sake of God, *and a type of terrorism that is allowed by the shari'a.*"[44] Another exception was Muhammad Salim al-'Awwa's refutation of the allegations of wholesale terrorism charges against Arabs: but this was a post-9/11 opinion and thus will be read by related standards rather than by the dispute on Palestinian attacks and on the fatwa that condemned them. A third such exception, which came as a *billet d'humeur* under the title "How is an Israeli ideological terrorist created," tackled the question only by reverting it.[45] Answering that such an ideological terrorist is processed in Israeli schools and through rituals of commemoration, the author actually calls for the creation of a Palestinian counterpart to fight this war on equal footing: the Palestinian terrorist is yet to come!

Apart from these opinions, the vast majority of the participants managed to evade the question or indeed to answer it on another plane: that of the state of war. The Palestinian society is at war with an enemy within (the occupier), whose military strength is incomparably superior, slaughtering civilians every other day, resorting to political assassinations, and now bent on destroying an eight-year-old process of state-building after having devastated Palestinian economic life. Its answer to this onslaught is nothing less, but nothing more, than an act of war. War being the referential context of all opinions supporting the suicide attacks, the question remains as to why their authors felt the need to justify the reasons and explain the acts of the suicide bombers. To put it differently, if the act of the suicide bomber is morally, politically, and legally self-sustained (it is an act of war, an act of legitimate self-defence, of sacrifice "in the name of") why then is this act constantly pitted against its foil, that is, the act of he-who-commits-suicide-out-of despair—that anomic act described by Durkheim (1960 [1897]) as being characteristic of "Western suicides," and paradigmatically opposed by Khosrokhavar (1993) to Islamic self-martyrdom? Why this recourse to psychological and sociological categories alongside the religious, the legal, and the political? Is it because the accusation of terrorism is so overwhelming as to prompt the public to produce an all-out assertive discourse on self? Or, to put it in another way, is it because the community feels threatened, its official discourse on self-identity notwithstanding, by the revolutionary potential of these individuals?

The Explanation: Individual and Community

The framework in which the suicide operations were to be "correctly" construed was that of *jihad* against the infidel, and only in that particular instance when it is transformed from *fard kifaya* (collective obligation incumbent on the few who are apt or willing to carry it out, but whose benefits accrue to the whole community) into *fard 'ayn* (individual obligation), in situations of occupation or invasion. However, instead of functioning as an articulating and integrating process of individual and community, *jihad* as a *fard 'ayn* is reportedly operating as a distorting social factor on the ground, breaking down the community into scores of ready-to-die individuals: "For the first time we are unable to absorb all the applicants," a Hamas military official declared in September 2001, while a Jihad leader added, as if in explanation: "Nobody wants to die because he or she likes death, this is a normal human feeling, but when life is no longer possible and becomes worse than death, death becomes desirable."[46]

Paradoxically, however, the breaking up of social ties, exemplified by this collective atomization as well as by children's disobedience are positively related to community building: the suicide bomber, by morbidly asserting his individuality and the children, by disobeying their parents for the sake of *jihad*, participate in the struggle and thus serve the interest of the community (as in a question addressed by Qaradawi). Similarly, the death of a child or a youth, through martyrdom or self-martyrdom, is presented as a joyful event prompting the parents to smile out of pride at their achievement.[47] General and especially psychological explanations are put forward in lieu of sociological insights and this is significantly facilitated by the blurring of the conditions of reporting.

Indeed, those articles that assert the joy of the parents at the death of their martyred child are not based on interviews. It is not clear whether the reporter is a correspondent reporting the incident or whether he is reconstructing it from press agencies material. The epic or inflated rhetoric and the hagiographic tonality given to the youth's biography take the place of sociological insight and support the psychological justification. That any explanation is deemed necessary after the religious obligation has been asserted does signal that an "iconographic discourse" is being produced to cover up social morbidity and anomization.

This iconographic (as opposed to argumentative) discourse fixes an unbearable event (the death of a child; the suicide of a youth) into a serialized strand of events by dissociating it from its historical genealogy and from its social and human consequences: the dead child belongs no longer to his family but to a glorious martyrs' *galérie de portraits*, and is mourned collectively, not just parentally. The suicide bomber, likewise, and his portrait in religious setting, his inscription in the chain of heroes in a war of liberation, is radically dissociated from the consequences of his act: he has not wrought death and wreckage as he was violently pushed to his tragic end.

It is in this context of a superlative *jihad* that one must resituate those fatwas that were so detailed about the conditions of *jihad* or those countless fatwas that compared the martyr to he-who-commits-suicide, as if in an effort to state clearly the perils entailed in self-inflicted death for he-whose-determination-and-intention-are-not-firm-enough. Their purpose was less an explanation of those suicidal acts than an attempt at averting the revolutionary (from the viewpoint of religious orthodoxy) potential of such acts and of the reasoning on which they were seemingly based (unbearable life/desirable death). Indeed, "this reasoning seems to find increasing, even overwhelming acceptance among all the strata of the Palestinian society, an acceptance transcending political and even ideological orientations." Hussein al-Tawil, an erstwhile member of the Palestinian Communist Party, described martyrdom operations as representing "the highest revolutionary level among humans."[48]

Therefore, the obsessive dichotomy imposed by the debate, the insistence on the conditions to be fulfilled in order to be a real *shahid*, the endless particularizations—all seems to address and to circumscribe this upsurge in morbid voluntary work, so to speak, with all its macabre imagery, celebrating the dislocation and maiming of bodies: a work that is sensed as being less religious than dictated by a rationale of despair. Hence the recourse to the psychological-religious category of *hope*, which averts the accusation of suicide: "He-who-commits-suicide kills himself for his own benefit, while he-who-commits-martyrdom sacrifices himself for the sake of his religion and his nation. While someone who commits suicide has lost hope with himself and with the spirit of God, the *mujahid* is full of hope with regard to God's spirit and mercy."[49]

Averting the notion of suicide and despair ultimately serves to prevent the martyr's act from signifying resignation from life and assertion of the self in death: as in the case of the Bassidji, the Iranian youth enrolled in the martyrologic defence of the Islamic revolution (Khosrokhavar 1993), who is paradigmatically transferred onto the Palestinian scene (Bucaille 1998). The psychological explanation serves the purpose of avoiding such readings, in which the suicide bomber despairs of the effectiveness of the revolutionary utopia and of his ability to assert himself as a social actor. In the Palestinian context, the wreckage of the revolutionary utopia corresponds to the end of the nationalist struggle, brought about by the peace process.

Conclusion: Of Public Opinion and the Public Sphere

The Doxic Substitution in the Egyptian Public Opinion

The Egyptian debate over the Saudi fatwa that allegedly condemned Palestinian suicide operations has yielded a peculiar "middle-of-the-road" picture of Egyptian public opinion. A remarkable fact is the absence of the extremes: no voices from the radical militant Islamist constellation (notably, *al-jama'a al-islamiyya*) were heard—at least none reached the Egyptian national press. At the other end of the spectrum, no big figure from among the secular, nationalist intellectuals engaged the "martyrdom versus suicide" dichotomy, the format, and the consensus lines of the debate. The "national consensus" was mostly the making of co-optation by the state (whether "liberals" like al-Azhar's Tantawi or moderate Islamists like the Qatar-based Muslim Brother Qaradawi) and of 'ulama engaging jurisprudential as well as non-jurisprudential rationality. On the other hand, the recourse to jurisprudential arguments by the "lay" could signal its appropriation of religious argumentation more than its questioning of the legitimacy of such argumentation.

However, the migration of certain jurisprudential concepts (such as *maslaha*) into common sense (cf. chapter 1 by LeVine and Salvatore) needs further systematized investigations: future research should replot this debate against other discussions in order to determine whether recourse to *maslaha* signaled the emergence of a common public language bridging over the divide or manifested the mechanisms of Bourdieu's "double entente," that is, an extreme polarization of the secular and the religious clad through a consensual use of words. The reception and amplification of non-Egyptian voices was discriminate and traveled along the ambivalent line between the defense of the *umma* and the safeguard of the nation-state. The exclusion of Palestinian or other non-Egyptian voices who agreed with the Saudi fatwa in the name of Palestinian national interest is a sign of how foreign indeed Egyptian public opinion is to another Arab national interest, which it nonetheless asserts to support and whose symbols it appropriates in its calls for the defense of the *umma*. More perplexing is the lack of an ample public resonance to the numerous religious voices in Palestine who took the same stance as their Egyptian counterparts.[50] One explanation could be the self-consciousness of Egyptian journalists of Egypt's prominent position in the realm of Islamic consultation (*ifta'*), prompting them to play down competing non-Egyptian legal advices. Another could lie in the "islamo-nationalism" of Palestinian actors, whose national claims disrupt the master narrative of the *umma* voiced in the Egyptian press.

One could hypothesize that the debate staged in and by the Egyptian press over the Saudi fatwa instrumentalized the Palestinian national cause with the aim of serving a specific domestic agenda, while claiming to speak in the name of a transnational Arab opinion. This agenda, no doubt supported by the state to fight off the influence of Islamists on public opinion, relies on the quite novel idea that the 'ulama hold not just the historical middle position between the ruler and the people, but that they author public opinion. The way in which the specialist's opinion (the opinion of a *'alim* co-opted by the state) is coming to stand for and pass as the opinion of the average Egyptian is precisely in staging the debate (1) as a controversy between specialists over the interests of the *umma*, and (2) as the expression of an "Arab opinion" over Palestine. The simultaneous mobilization of the religious and secular registers ultimately serves this doxic substitution. What is being subtly equated with the opinion of an imagined *umma* (about a fantasized Palestine) is claimed to be not Egyptian but "Arab" public opinion.

The Conjunction of Journalism and Islamic Consultation

What the Egyptian press did not question, but indeed built upon, was the way in which the "embarrassing," the "unacceptable," the "depressing" fatwa, and "the fatwa which came from nowhere," was fitted into the Saudi newspaper that published it. What the Egyptian press did not question was the way in which authorized opinion was being reconfigured as public. It missed the distinctive effects of the very conjunction of journalism and Islamic consultation (*sihafa* and *ifta'*). This conjunction represents the mechanism through which the doxic substitution was being effected in the Egyptian public opinion. The journalist who carried out the interview with the Saudi Grand Mufti indulged in the imitation of the rhetoric of *ifta'*: the factual questioning proper to the reporter was replaced by the general enunciation that is integral to the delivering of a fatwa. In other terms, whereas it was expected from the mufti *as a mufti* to answer in very general and non-nominal terms, it was not expected of the journalist *as a journalist* to renounce descriptive and objective questioning and to indulge in sibylline formulations and circumlocutions.

The consequence was that while the mufti remained a mufti in the exercise of his institutional tasks — that is, the frame of the interview did not seem to affect his status — the journalist, quite conversely, adopted the role of the questioner or *mustafti'*: a deferent tone was used in addressing the mufti, and value judgments were passed in the coining of the questions, whereby the journalist *urged* the mufti to make a legal pronouncement. This feature has considerable significance for the way an "Arab public sphere" is being postulated by the Egyptian press when it claims to voice Arab opinion, through naturalizing religious expertise into its agenda and by assuming its universal validity.

The Arab Public Sphere

A recent "interactionist" reassessment of Habermas's concept of the public sphere has resulted in its redefinition as a locus of "shared anticipation" and an ever-widening circle of reciprocity (Eickelman and Salvatore 2004 [2002]: 15–20). Habermas himself described it dynamically as the competition over the definition of the "public interest" and defined it procedurally as "rational-critical discourse" (Habermas 1989 [1962], 1992). It is the mechanism through which private people come out as public and are enabled, as recalled in chapter 1 of this volume, to contest hegemonies. But Habermas encapsulated in his concept a historical development as well as a normative claim. For the sake of argument, let us however assume that the public sphere exists in as "natural" a way as is assumed of Arab public opinion by the Egyptian press. This allows an assessment of the concept's implications vis-à-vis the context at hand, rather than requiring a discussion of its normative and historical articulation. These implications are threefold.

Is a Religious Hegemony Preclusive of a Public Sphere?
The "naturalization" of Islamic consultation (*ifta'*) in and by the press signals that public opinion is hegemonically shaped by concepts pertaining to the religious sphere. This said, it must be stressed that the presence of a hegemonic religious discursive referent does not, in itself, preclude the existence of a public sphere. This hegemonic discourse is the dominant rationality in which debate is carried out, and I have highlighted the fact that the language of the "specialist" was in the process of being appropriated

if not (yet) questioned by the "lay" (as much as the specialist's discourse was being penetrated by extra-jurisprudential concepts and ideas). This is certainly a far cry from Habermas's "critical-rational" discourse where personal opinions are relatively unfettered by considerations of status and rituals of authority. However, as a discourse in the making, as a process, it can hardly be dismissed in the advent of a public sphere. Habermas's public sphere as just recalled, is not only a normative concept but also a narrative about the historical advent of a normative concept. What Habermas has described in his work are moments of the public sphere, stations in time where it was closer or farther away from its ideal state. This said, the inability or refusal of some sectors of Egyptian society to debate within the hegemonic frames of public discourse (the secular nationalist intellectuals and the Islamists) is a problematic feature of this public sphere.

As far as the Islamists are concerned, while their ability to engage in jurisprudential argumentation is not in question (though the legitimacy of their expertise and credentials is been critically scrutinized by their institutional detractors), their political interest would be: as they challenge the legitimacy of the Egyptian regime, it is hard to see how a nationalistic or even a pan-Islamic understanding of public interest (*maslaha 'amma*) could serve their agenda; harder even to see how the Palestinian struggle, which was made into a sort of icon of Arab nationalism (or transnationalism), could serve the political goals they pursue. As to the secular nationalist intellectuals, their inability or refusal to engage in what one could call an "etymological posture"—challenging the religious establishment over their monopoly of *common language*—points to the existence of layers of public discourse that never intersect each other rather than to a dialectic public sphere.

There is no etymological reclaiming and no non-nationalistic political reconstruction of terms like *jihad, shahid,* or even *fard kifaya/fard 'ayn,* and no discussions of their sociological or anthropological implications, engaging secular intellectuals with members of the religious establishment. This absence of etymological engagement together with the impossibility to contest the *raison d'État* are indeed very serious impediments to the Egyptian public sphere.

Structural Impediments to Communicative Action
If the existence of the Egyptian public sphere is problematic, what of the transnational one it postulates in its claims to voice "Arab" opinion? As a construct, "Arab public opinion" is either the product of selection or of integration. Selection was the way of the Egyptian press, which hammered together analogous opinions to fit domestic consensus, as when it canvassed the opinion of the Lebanese Shi'a cleric, rather than that of the Moroccan shaykh, into the Egyptian consensus regarding the legitimacy of suicide attacks. Integration was the way of MEMRI, in its survey of Arab press reactions to the Saudi fatwa:[51] it uprooted specific national opinions from their respective domestic contexts, juxtaposed and consequently

forced them into a transnational narrative without profile, as when it integrated into one framework the opposite opinions of people of two different nationalities, a Palestinian and an Egyptian columnist, instead of making sense of noteworthy de facto consonances across national borders *and* the religious/secular divide.

While selection precludes the possibility of communicative action (because the consensual order projected by the Egyptian press through the eviction of dissent would have neither the need nor the means for calling to action), integration assumes the possibility of action, based in the presumption of the existence of a public arena were this action be deployed. However, the arsenal of legal and less-than-legal state obstructions to such a deployment in Arab societies (whether through the torture of political prisoners, censorship, restricted political participation, invasive monitoring on associations, unions, NGOs, etc.) renders this double assumption problematic and leaves us with an as problematic alternative: choosing to see in violent militancy, as MEMRI does, an Arab-Islamic expression of "communicative action" (a negation, indeed, of the very notion of public sphere), or stating derisorily that the Arab public sphere is to be found in . . . London or Paris.

To come back to the Egyptian context, the minimalism of shared universal categories on the one hand and the constancy of vexed action contribute to carving out a "public sphere" that is not *sui generis* but rather *discreet*, in the mathematical sense of discontinuous—a feature that hardly allows for a historical or genealogical approach to its developments. To put it in empirical terms, nothing is legally secured once and for all and in that sense there is never really an institutional experience of the public sphere on which to build higher grounds: each press debate in Egypt, while sometimes forcefully reminiscent of its predecessors, has to systematically redraw for itself the red lines not to be crossed (cf. chapter 5, this volume, by Dupret and Ferrié).

An exemplary illustration of this predicament of the public sphere in Egypt is the disorientation of contemporary Egyptian intellectuals, who had cultivated in the past a keen sense of self-censorship through the successive and cumulative experiences of British, monarchical, and Nasserist censorships. Faced today with the blurring of the tacit alliances between the nationalist intellectual and the state (Botiveau 1993; Hamzah 2001) brought about by the pressure of Islamic "moral entrepreneurs,"[52] they either abstain from participation or put at risk their livelihoods, freedom (Hamzah 2001), and sometimes their lives.

Deontology and Intentionality

The role of the Egyptian press in conveying false or partial information, in forcing meanings into outrageous subtitles was instrumental to the inflation of the debate. That role has been underscored by the actors themselves in this particular debate. If for the purposes of sociological inquiry, the intentions of the Saudi mufti when he issued his fatwa matter less than the way and the backdrop against which his intentions were construed, the same cannot be said of the role of the press, which sidestepped its commitment to objective and accurate reporting. When the public sphere's main channel of publicity (the media) is structurally flawed, it becomes hard to distinguish communicative action from manipulation and control, notwithstanding the abilities of reading-in-between-the-lines developed by social actors in such political contexts. In this particular debate distortions were so overpowering as to preclude the very conditions of debating.

A more positive role of this dispute has been the circulation of legal opinions that it made possible, though it would be important to locate the actual fatwas in the mass of delivered general opinions, distinguishing between casually expressed opinions and legal opinions, and acknowledging quotations where quotations are due. The fact, for instance, that no reader or commentator ever referred to the real context of the interview, and to the full-blown jurisprudential argumentation of the Saudi mufti made it possible to receive his fatwa at the other end as a clear-cut hostile piece of advice. As it stands, the Saudi fatwa does not belong to the genre of fatwas of condemnations, usually final and nominal, and is not even definite in its formulation.

Action as Icon or the Ultimate Substitution

By allegedly "tarnishing" the legitimacy of a "just cause," by shedding doubt on the "holiness of the Palestinian *jihad*," the Saudi mufti was desecrating the figure of the Palestinian martyr (*shahid*), that is, of what I have tentatively termed a *transnationalist icon*. By this term I mean the appropriation of the Palestinian national struggle by Arab or Islamic community claims, not just by way of action-oriented slogans (the calls for *jihad* notwithstanding), but by plain self-representation. In allegedly casting a shadow over a projection of self, the fatwa was then disrupting processes of identification. But the quasi sacred dimension conferred upon this transnationalist icon, while certainly fuelled by religious sentiment and imagery, is to be equated with its capacity to provide a substitute for action. The Palestinian Intifada did not fail to mobilize the "Arab street," but the "Arab" political action that ensued was inversely proportional to the mobilization of the so-called Arab opinion. As it appeared, it was not exactly because of his strict orthodoxy that the Saudi mufti was criticized. Rather, it was for messing with that symbolic substitute for action, revealing in the process how insubstantial the Intifada is in building hopes of political change. The very possibility of *action* then, communicative, political, that is, the very pillar of the public sphere, was the ultimate stake of the Egyptian debate.

Notes

1. For the Egyptian national press, a list of all the titles consulted is in the References under the entry "CEDEJ." The systematic "Dossier de Presse"

collated by the library staff of that research center in Cairo was of invaluable help in reviewing the Egyptian debate. The London-based international Arab press (mainly: *al-Sharq al-awsat, al-Quds al-'arabi*, and *al-Hayat*) was also used, as it is available in Egypt to readers, columnists, and the general public.

2. The Middle East Media Research Institute (MEMRI) releases reviews, analyses, and translations of all the Middle Eastern press on its Web site. While it relies heavily on the Egyptian press, it also quotes from otherwise inaccessible national papers. Unfortunately, it has been shown to publish translations predominantly of extremist articles, while ignoring articles even from the same edition of a paper that have moderate or progressive positions or none (cf. Juvan Cole's critique of MEMRI on his "Informed Comment" blog, November 23, 2004) makes its use problematic.

3. "Mufti 'amm al-Sa'udiyya li-l-Sharq al-awsat: khatf al-ta'irat wa tarwi' al-aminin muharram shar'an," *al-Sharq al-awsat*, April 21, 2001.

4. "al-Fatwa al-dalla," *al-'Arabi*, April 28, 2001.

5. "al-Fatwa al-qunbula," *al-Ahrar*, April 24, 2001.

6. Muhammad Salim al-'Awwa, "Fi dhikra al-isra' . . . wa murur akthar min 'am 'ala-l-intifada," *al-Akhbar*, October 19, 2000.

7. Cf. the *Agence France Presse* release of December 10, 2001 in Dubai, "Religious scholars at odds over suicide bombings."

8. It was carried out on January 27, 2002 by a Fatah female ambulance worker in Jerusalem.

9. Unlike the binding ruling (*qada*) of the judge (*qadi*), a fatwa is a non-binding legal advice issued by a mufti on request by individuals or authorities (*mustafti*). Its subject matter is as diverse as issues of cult, society, and doctrine, etc. The mufti, who is a *'alim* known for his wide scholarly knowledge as much as for his moral integrity, can also issue fatwas at his own initiative. History attests to such spontaneous "advice," whether meant to advance the genre or for more political purposes, when muftis sought to counsel or warn the ruler. See Hallaq (1997) and Masud et al. (1995).

10. Ibid., where particular stress is laid on the impetus given to fatwa issuance in colonial settings.

11. Umlil (1996: 24–25) sees the characteristics of the fundamentalist (*usuliyya*) versus the traditional (*taqlidiyya*) fatwa as threefold: "first, it does not recognize the official fatwa nor the scientific and institutional or official legitimacy; second, it is a political fatwa or rather its authors take a political stand by it regarding established order and society and this stand is one of absolute opposition and denial; third, it is bent on authority, since it claims to have the last word and to see it enforced."

12. The conjunction in Umlil's definition of "fundamentalist" and "non-official" is problematic as it closely espouses the lineaments of political and ideological categories developed in the 1950s and 1960s, when diverse Arab regimes proceeded to gain control over their time-immemorial transnational religious centers of learning and predication (al-Qarawiyyin, al-Azhar, al-Zaytuna, etc.) by folding them into state institutions. A more scholarly approach considers that there are no "official" or "professional" proficiency assessments of muftis in Islam and that those habilitated for *ifta'* among the 'ulama are those whose degree of learning and integrity is certified by their scholarly reputation and institutional cooptation (Masud et al. 1996).

13. An accusation of impiety grossly analogous to excommunication, *takfir* is a performative act of speech that instantly "criminalizes" the accused, turning him into an apostate.

14. Cf. Eickelman and Piscatori (1996: 360–63), who speak, in relation to this period of protest, of "contestation of sacred authority."

15. Saudi financial input in Palestinian institutions amounted for the first 18 months of the Second Intifada to $400m: *The Economist*, March 23–29, 2002.

16. *Al-Qahira*, May 8, 2001.

17. Hamid al-Maydawi, the khatib of al-Aqsa mosque for one: "if what is being attributed to the Saudi mufti is true, then we disagree with him," *al-Ahram*, April 24, 2001.

18. Ahmad Rif'at, *al-Usbu'*, April 30, 2001, in an article devoted to unraveling the "mystery" surrounding the issuance of such a fatwa.

19. In "al-Fatwa al-dalla," *al-'Arabi*, April 29, 2001. See also al-Akhbar, May 18, 2001: " '*Amaliyyat al-fida'iyyin laysat intihar bal istishhad*."

20. Ibid., *al-Sharq al-awsat*, May 8, 2001: "'Ulama' muslimun yakhtalifun hawla al-hukm al-shar'i li-l-'amaliyyat al-intihariyya," *al-Ahram*, April 26, 2001.

21. *Al-'Arabi*, June 10, 2001: "Mufti al-shi'a: al-intifada aw al-intihar al-jama'i li-l-umma."

22. The first Palestinian daily (*al-Quds*) and the Palestinian Authority-controlled press (*al-Ayyam* and *al-Hayat al-jadida*) in the case of Palestine; *al-Sharq al-awsat* in the case of Saudi Arabia, i.e., the same newspaper that had sparked the controversy in Egypt.

23. *Yanabi'* (*al-Hayat al-jadida*'s supplement), April 24, 2001: "Those Who Support Hamas Must Resign the Leadership to It," translated in MEMRI, *Inquiry and Analysis*, no. 54, May 3, 2001.

24. *Al-Hayat* (London), December 9, 2001, translated in *Courrier International*, December 12, 2001.

25. *Al-Quds*, December 14, 2001.

26. *Courrier International*, December 20, 2001: "Non au suicide collectif d'un peuple!" translated from *al-Nahar* (Beirut), December 2001.

27. *Al-Sharq al-Awsat*, May 8, 2001: "'Ulama' muslimun yakhtalifun hawla al-hukm al-shar'i li-l-'amaliyyat al-intihariyya."

28. Ibid.

29. *Al-Wafd*, May 10, 2001: "Fatawa al-harb . . . wa fatawa al-silm." Translation and commentary in MEMRI, *Inquiry and Analysis*, no. 53, May 2, 2001.

30. In MEMRI, *Inquiry and Analysis*, no. 65, July 26, 2001.

31. Cf. e.g., Muhammad Rushdi, *al-Ahrar*, April 24, 2001: "al-Fatwa al-qunbula."

32. Cf. *al-Sharq-al-awsat*, May 8, 2001: " 'Ulama' muslimun yakhtalifun hawla al-hukm al-shar'i li-l-'amaliyyat al-intihariyya."

33. *Al-Sharq al-awsat*, May 8, 2001.

34. *Al-Ahram*, April 26, 2001.

35. *Al-'Arabi*, April 29, 2001.

36. *Al-Ahrar*, April 24, 2001.

37. *Al-Hayat al-jadida*, April 27, 2001, translated in MEMRI, *Inquiry and Analysis*, no. 54, May 3, 2001.

38. *Ruz al-Yusuf*, April 28, 2001.

39. The four scholars are: Nasr Farid Wasil, the Mufti of the Egyptian Republic; Palestine's shaykh Tahbub; Ibrahim al-'Idwi, professor of Islamic history,

University of Cairo; Ahmad Taha Rayan, professor at al-Azhar. Cf. *al-Ahrar*, August 10, 2001, "Tahwid al-Quds."

40. Al-Qaradawi, on more than one occasion. E.g., *al-Ahram al-'arabi*, February 3, 2001.
41. *Al-Ahrar*, April 24, 2001, "al-Fatwa al-qunbula."
42. Jonathan Kuttab: *al-Hayat*, December 9, 2001; 'Abd al-'Aziz al-Rantisi: www.amin.org, December 26, 2001.
43. This feature is absent from the debate that unfolded in Palestine between the autumn of 2001 and the summer of 2002. Cf. Hamzah and Larzillière (2005).
44. *Al-Raya*, April 25, 2001, quoted and translated in MEMRI, *Inquiry and Analysis*, no. 53, May 2, 2001.
45. *Al-Akhbar*, May 11, 2001: "Kayfa yakhlaqun irhabiyan isra'iliyyan 'aqa'idiyyan?"
46. www.amin.org, Khaled Amayreh, September 6, 2001, "Israeli oppression pushes Palestinians to martyrdom operations."
47. See e.g., *al-Usbu'*, April 23, 2001, "Iftahu al-abwab, fa-l-rabi' qadim—al-tifl al-shahid Ahmad Qawasmi."
48. Khaled Amayreh, www.amin.org, September 6, 2001, "Israeli oppression pushes Palestinians to martyrdom operations." Tawil's Islamist son died in a suicide operation in March 2001.
49. Yusuf Al-Qaradawi, February 3, 2001, *al-Ahram al-'arabi*, translated in MEMRI, *Inquiry and Analysis*, no. 53, May 2, 2001.
50. Shaykh Hamid al-Bitawi, and an official of Hamas in Nablus (*al-Hayat*, April 25, 2001); the Palestinian Authority's mufti, Ikrima Sabri (*Sawt Filastin*, May 25, 2001); the mufti of Jericho, shaykh Muhammad Isma'il al-Jamal (*al-Hayat al-jadida*, April 27, 2001); Yasir Za'atra, chief editor of Hamas's former newspaper, *Filastin al-muslima* (*al-Dustur*, Amman, April 26, 2001); Hamas leader 'Abd al-'Aziz al-Rantisi (*al-Hayat*, April 25, 2001). As one can see, all (but one) reacted within days of the Saudi fatwa.
51. MEMRI, *Inquiry and Analysis*, no. 54, May 3, 2001.
52. Howard Becker's sociological category has been recently revisited in the context of the contemporary Middle East (cf. Dupret and Ferrié 2001; Salvatore 2001).

References

Anderson, Benedict. 1991 [1983]. *Imagined Communities. Reflections on the Origins and Spread of Nationalism*. London: Verso.
Borlandi, Massimo, and Mohamed Cherkaoui, eds. 2000. *Le Suicide: un siècle après Durkheim*. Paris: PUF.
Botiveau, Bernard. 1993. "Penser, dire et interdire: logiques et enjeux de la censure des écrits en Égypte." *Égypte/Monde Arabe* no. 14.
Bourdieu, Pierre. 1971. "Genèse et structure du champ religieux," *Revue Française de Sociologie* 12: 295–334.
Bucaille, Laetitia. 1998. *Gaza: la violence de la paix*. Paris: Presses de Sciences Po.
———. 2003. "L'impossible stratégie palestinienne du martyre: victimisation et attentats suicide." *Critique internationale* no. 20: 117–34.
CEDEJ. 2001. *Dossier de Presse*, section on *Al-Qadiyya al-filistiniyya: Intihar/istishhad* [Press clippings from the Egyptian national press: *al-Ahali, al-Ahram, al-Ahrar, al-Akhbar, al-'Arabi, al-Jumhuriyya, al-Hayat, al-Midan, al-Musawwar, al-Qahira, al-Usbu', al-Wafd, Ruz al-Yusuf, Sawt al-Umma*].

Daisha, Adeed, ed. 1983. *Islam in Foreign Policy*. Cambridge: Cambridge University Press.

Dupret, Baudouin, and Jean-Noël Ferrié. 2001. "The Inner Self and Public Order." In *Muslim Traditions and Modern Techniques of Power*, vol. 3 of *Yearbook of the Sociology of Islam*, ed. Armando Salvatore, Hamburg: Lit; New Brunswick, NJ: Transaction.

Durkheim, Emile. 1960 [1897]. *Le Suicide*, Paris: PUF.

Eickelman, Dale F. 1992. "Mass Higher Education and the Religious Imagination in Contemporary Arab Societies." *American Ethnologist* 19, 4: 643–55.

Eickelman, Dale F., and James Piscatori. 1996. *Muslim Politics*. Princeton: Princeton University Press.

Eickelman, Dale F., and Armando Salvatore. 2004 [2002]. "Muslim Publics." In *Public Islam and the Common Good*, ed. Armando Salvatore and Dale F. Eickelman, Leiden and Boston: Brill, 3–27.

Habermas, Jürgen. 1989 [1962]. *The Structural Transformation of the Public Sphere*, trans. Thomas Burger, Cambridge, MA: MIT Press.

———. 1992. "Further Reflections on the Public Sphere." In *Habermas and the Public Sphere*, ed. Craig Calhoun. Cambridge, MA: MIT Press, 421–62.

Hallaq, Wael. 1997. *A History of Islamic Legal Theories*. Cambridge: Cambridge University Press.

Hamzah, Dyala. 2001. "La censure ou comment la contourner: dire et ne pas dire dans l'Egypte contemporaine." *Egypte/Monde Arabe* no. 3.

Hamzah, Dyala, and Pénélope Larzillère. 2005. "De la lutte nationale à la fondation étatique et retour: les intellectuels palestiniens, d'Oslo I à Intifada II." In *Les nouveaux intellectuels en Islam*, ed. Malika Zeghal and Farhad Khosrokovar, Paris: Balland.

Khosrokovar, Farhad. 1993. "Chiisme mortifère: les nouveaux combattants de la foi." *L' Homme et la Société* no. 107–08: 93–108.

Masud, Muhammad Khalid, Brinkley Messick, and Ahmad Dallal. 1995. "Fatwa," *Oxford Encyclopedia of the Modern Islamic World*, vol. 2, 8–16.

Masud, Muhammad Khalid, Brinkley Messick, and David S. Powers, eds. 1996. *Muftis, Fatwas, and Islamic Legal Interpretation*. Cambridge, MA and London: Harvard University Press.

MEMRI (www.memri.org): *Inquiry and Analysis*, no. 53 (May 2, 2001); no. 54 (May 3, 2001); no. 65 (July 26, 2001); no. 66 (July 27, 2001): "Debating the Religious, Political and Moral Legitimacy of Suicide Bombings," Parts I to IV.

al-Quds al-'arabi, London.

Regional Surveys of the World. 2001. *The Middle-East and North-Africa 2002*, 48th ed., London: Europa Publications.

Rosenthal, Franz. 1946. "On Suicide in Islam." *Journal of the American Oriental Society* 66: 239–59.

———. [1971] 1986. "Intihar," *Encyclopedia of Islam*, vol. 3, 2nd ed.

Salvatore, Armando, 2001. "Mustafa Mahmud: a Paradigm of Public Islamic Entrepreneurship?" In *Muslim Traditions and Modern Techniques of Power*, vol. 3 of *Yearbook of the Sociology of Islam*, ed. Armando Salvatore, Hamburg: Lit; New Brunswick, NJ: Transaction.

Skovgaard-Petersen, Jakob. 1997. *Defining Islam for the Egyptian State, Muftis and Fatwas of the Dar al-Ifta'*. Leiden: Brill.

Tyan, Emile. 1960. *Histoire de l'organisation judiciaire en pays d'Islam*. Leiden: Brill.

Umlil, 'Ali. 1996. *al-Sulta al-thaqafiyya wa-l-sulta al-siyasiyya*. Beirut: Markaz dirasat al-wahda al-'arabiyya.

World Wide Web: www.islamonline.net, www.amin.org, www.mfa.gov.il, www.hrw. org, www.jmcc.org

Willis, John Ralph. 1996. "The fatwas of condemnation." In *Muftis, Fatwas, and Islamic Legal Interpretation*, ed. Muhammad Khalid Masud, Brinkley Messick, and David S. Powers, Cambridge, MA and London: Harvard University Press, 153–61.

CHAPTER 8

COVER STORIES: A GENEALOGY OF THE LEGAL PUBLIC SPHERE IN YEMEN

Brinkley Messick

Introduction

Compared with most countries of the Middle East and North Africa, the background of modern legal change in Yemen is unusual in several key respects. First, is the absence of a period of Western colonial rule, at least for the northern highlands. This meant that legal transformations generally came later and were markedly different than in most other countries. There was no restriction of existing Islamic legal applications to the sphere of personal status law, or family law, which was typical under colonial rule, and there also was no imposition of Western law in such characteristic areas as criminal and commercial law. Caveats to this non-colonial history, however, are the ramifying legal influences of British rule in Aden (1830–1967) and also the nearly 50-year period of Ottoman rule in the highlands around the turn of the 20th century.

Second, prior to the Revolution of 1962, the Yemeni polity was a type of Islamic state ruled by a classical form of ruler, an *imam*, a commander of both "the pen and the sword." These 20th-century imams, like many before them in the 1,000-year history of the imamate in Yemen, but unlike the typical heads of the old Sunni polities (e.g., kings or sultans), were qualified shari'a jurists and acted as the final level of legal authority in their realms. Imam Yahya Hamid al-Din (d. 1948) was noted for reading and supervising appeals, down to underlining questionable formulations in red ink. Imams also read and issued final execution rulings in all homicide cases. The law of the land was the Islamic shari'a, following the official Zaydi school of interpretation. A shari'a court judge of the era heard cases ranging from homicide and injury to conflicts over contracts, marriage, inheritance, and endowments. Third, highland society was agrarian, based largely on settled cultivation of either rain-fed (as an extension of the regular summer monsoon system), or, to a lesser extent, irrigated lands, and the associated property regime was almost exclusively private, or individualized.

The prevailing property regime on the ground thus approximately matched the scheme envisioned in the legal doctrine of the shari'a (that is, in the humanly authored literature known as the *fiqh*). In this respect, Yemen was unlike the greater part of the Ottoman Empire, for example, where the property regime (until the mid-19th century) was mainly based on *miri* landholding, involving tenant leases from the state. In the Ottoman case, this old property regime had to be converted to modern style private ownership and titles, while that in Yemen already approximated these modern forms.

If such general features roughly describe the distinctive character of the background of modern legal change in Yemen, that of the foreground, that is, the character of the current legal situation in Yemen, may be approached through the pages of a new Yemeni monthly journal, or magazine, *al-Qistas*, "The Scales [of Justice]" or "The Balance," which commenced publication in 1998.[1] On its masthead page *al-Qistas* characterizes itself as comprising "A program of legal culturation (*barnamaj al-tathqif al-qanuni*) of the Forum for Civil Society (*multaqa al-mujtama' al-madani*)." On the same masthead page, this forum is described as,

> an organization that is non-governmental, non-party (based), and non-profit, concerned with the development of democracy, the support of elections, strengthening civil society and participation in programs of legal development.

Entirely in Arabic and at a standard 48 pages per issue, but with the articles mostly one page and, at most, three to four pages long, *al-Qistas* is a new type of professional publication in Yemen and a complicated phenomenon. A great number and variety of topics are touched upon in each volume, all apparently with "legal" (*qanuni*) relevance. The publication's covers are in full color, with "al-Qistas" written at the front top in a large and elaborate semi-Kufic script under an image of scales. Inside the body of this title script is a Qur'anic text that employs the word in question ("*wazanu bi-l-qistas al-mustaqim*"). Underneath the title on the cover, preceding the volume number, the date, and the (accessible) issue price (50 *riyals*), the publication is identified with the phrase, "The only legal journal/magazine (*majalla qanuniyya*) in Yemen." On the masthead page, under the Basmallah and then the title, is a further identifier, "legal monthly" (*shahriyya-qanuniyya*). *Al-Qistas* is obviously about the "legal" (*qanuni*) domain, that of state law or *qanun*, but what does this domain consist of in contemporary Yemen? What are the positions and attitudes of *al-Qistas* with respect to this domain of the "legal"?

There is a regular cover story for each issue, typically introduced with a dramatic color photo on the cover and with an accompanying headline at the foot of the page. A series of smaller headlines announcing other lead items runs up the right side of the cover page. The back cover, also in full color, typically is a full-page advertisement, for a company such as Pizza Hut. Ads are also placed on the inside covers, but only rarely elsewhere in the body of an issue. In addition to its cover price, the publication's financing is further explained on the masthead page where it is stated that support is provided by "establishments," presumably commercial companies such as Pizza Hut, "and the Embassy of Holland." Later issues also give annual subscription information for three categories of subscribers: individuals, establishments, and foreign.

Al-Qistas is serious in purpose and modern and communicative in design, attracting its readers more in the manner of an accessible popular magazine than a dry, lawyer's journal. Its editors also are fully conversant with Internet technology, with its masthead providing both e-mail contact information and reference to a Web site associated with the Forum for Civil Society (www.transparencyyemen.org.ye). How strikingly different *al-Qistas* is in comparison with, for example, the monochromatic and scholarly, and also relatively specialized and inaccessible *al-Muhami* ("The Lawyer"), the Moroccan journal of the Marrakesh Lawyer's Association? Yet, if *al-Qistas* nevertheless shares an important family resemblance with such civil society publications, it may also be compared to new types of legal publications that are being issued by state organs. An example is the journal known as *Mimbar Hukum*, issued six times a year by the Directorate of Religious Justice in the Ministry of Religion in contemporary Indonesia (Bowen 1999). Where *al-Qistas* derives from a nongovermental nexus, *Mimbar Hukum* is explicitly governmental. From very different, even opposed structural positions, both publications are concerned with advancing the proper institutionalization of modern state law, *qanun* in Yemen and *hukum* in Indonesia. In both settings, the work of constructing positive state law must occur against the backdrop and framework of Islamic law, specifically with reference to the extant legal corpus of the *fiqh*. Although *Mimbar Hukum* is a vehicle for conveying official views, it is also designed as a "*fiqh* watchdog" for the review of problematic court decisions, and in Bowen's analysis, the fact of publication itself has fundamentally transformed public discourse on "law."

Who are the readers of *al-Qistas*? When I e-mailed the editor about his publication's press run he replied that it ranged from 5,000 to 7,000 copies a month. What evidence is there for how a targeted readership, a specialized reading public, is constructed and addressed? How may this "legal" publication be located with respect to the history of print culture in Yemen and to the surround of other modern media? How does the *al-Qistas* project and its reading legal public relate to other institutional elaborations of specifically legal dimensions of the "public" realm? I propose to read selectively some issues of *al-Qistas* and my aims are to sketch the antecedent and contemporary conditions for the emergence of such a publication and also to assess its character and agenda as the recently emerged voice of the maturing legal profession in Yemen. In the pages of *al-Qistas*, a new community of legally trained specialists in Yemen exhibits a novel and complex self-awareness, an awareness that is mobilized in a thoroughgoing, and also quite new project, public legal criticism. Where traces of debate

and dissent among *fiqh* scholars are to be found in the Indonesian governmental publication studied by Bowen, debate and dissent by modern
lawyers are the main project of *al-Qistas*.

Shari'a and *Qanun*

In this new emphasis on *qanun* what has happened to the old shari'a?
Again, the key rubric in the language of *al-Qistas*, is *qanuni*, "legal" in the
sense of state law, or legislated law.[2] As I observed at the outset, prior to the
Revolution of 1962 the imam-led Islamic state of highland Yemen knew
one of the most complete realizations of the theory and practice, ideology
and application, of a shari'a regime. As I also noted earlier, the initial impetus to legal change in Yemen was not the wholesale replacement of major
sectors of the law with Western forms under colonial auspices, or the sort
of large-scale reception of Swiss law and formal abandonment of the
shari'a that occurred in 1926 in the new Turkish Republic. In Yemen,
according to the ideologies of the respective 20th-century states, the imamate (1918–1962) and the republic (1962–), there was a shari'a system
before, and a shari'a system after the Revolution. According to the 1970
Constitution of the first northern state, the Yemen Arab Republic, the
shari'a is "the source of all laws" (Art. 3). By the time of the second
Constitution (1991), that of the unified Republic of Yemen, in an effort to
accommodate the very different legal history of the southern state (the
People's Democratic Republic of Yemen), which had drawn heavily on
socialist models of states such as East Germany, this key statement was
revised to "the primary source of all laws." By later amendment, however,
Art. 3 once again became, "The Islamic shari'a is the source of all laws."

Differentiating Yemeni "shari'a systems" before and after the
Revolution of 1962 involves moving analytically beyond such lexemic continuities. The historical legal rupture that occurred in Yemen is partially
concealed by the ideological continuity of the shari'a idiom, a continuity,
again, facilitated by the absence in the highlands context of the sorts of
explicit discontinuities associated with a colonial period and by the historical nature of the highland property regime. Regarding property, one of
many other striking lexemic continuities, significant both in the doctrine
and on the ground, is that of the shari'a-based individual property form
known as *milk*. The 1,000-year-old category of *milk* property, the central
form in the older Yemeni shari'a capitalism of the agrarian era, remained
central to the commercialized relations of the developing Yemeni state of
the last half of the 20th century.

To the extent that it was relevant and applicable in a given setting—that
historically was quite variable—the shari'a depended on attaching itself to
a particular context. However exhaustively elaborated shari'a doctrine
might at times appear, it remained intrinsically incomplete. All historical
shari'a regimes thus entailed a specific relationship with the varieties of
local custom (*'urf*). The comparatively comprehensive realization of the

shari'a presided over by the ruling *imam*s of Yemen involved an intimate attachment to customary forms, substantive and procedural. If the persistent generality of the framework of shari'a rules always necessitated a fleshing out in local detail, the guiding principle of this shari'a-custom relation (from the shari'a side) was that accepted custom not be in violation of shari'a principle. In Yemen, a significant segment of custom was, and is, associated with the structures of tribal relations, and this was true not only beyond the pale of the state but at its urban heart as well where certain types of conflicts, notably those entailing "honor" issues, were handled by means of customary resolutions, such as sacrificing a bull at the door of the offended family. In these and many other types of cases that had out-of-court settlements, involving mediation or arbitration and blends of shari'a and custom were, and remain very common.

As I have discussed elsewhere (Messick 1993: 68), much of what was produced by the modern republican legislators was not shari'a-based but instead involved state regulations and legislation of many types unknown to the shari'a, including also such legal forms as related to corporations, trademarks, and banking. For some specific bodies of legislation, however, notably the new Civil Law (1979), *al-qanun al-madani*, the shari'a was the model (Messick 1993: 69). The new legislated law was, as it states, "taken from Islamic shari'a principles" and the old doctrine continued to have relevance as a "source." Article 1 states, "If a specific text is not found in this law (*qanun*) it is possible to proceed by means of reference to the principles of the Islamic shari'a from which this law is taken." Article 20 further specifies "the authoritative reference for the explication of the texts of shari'a legislation and their application is Islamic jurisprudence (*fiqh*)." In this process, however, the "shari'a" was separated from its old doctrinal referent, namely the *fiqh*, but continued to be used to broadly characterize the law of the successive republics. With *fiqh* repositioned as a background "source," the legislation itself, the new body of *qanun*, emerged, at least ideally, as the law. If the coming of the 1962 Revolution marked the end of many centuries of scholarly production of *fiqh* texts, it also marked the beginning of nation-state legislative production of the modern law known as *qanun*.[3]

In the old shari'a system prior to the revolution, court judges typically were appointed to hear the range of cases that came before them in their level of administrative district. At the time, there was no distinction between "criminal" and "civil" cases, nor were there specialized courts for "personal status" or "commercial" matters. Above the judges in administrative districts was an appeal court, an innovation introduced in Yemen by the Ottomans, and at the pinnacle of the system was the imam. After the revolution, the first innovation was to institute panels of judges in the various courts, but these later were abolished and the court system returned to the single judge format. Modern Yemeni courts continue to be described as "shari'a courts," although they are quite different from their predecessors in their topical specializations ("criminal," etc.), in their new patterns of interrogatories (by lawyers, prosecutors, and judges), and in the fact that the ideally guiding law for their procedures and their judgments became legislated *qanun*. Where, in the old imamic state, the imam was simultaneously the temporal ruler and the spiritual leader, the ultimate interpreter of the law, in the nation-state most of the presidents (with the important exception of 'Abd al-Rahman al-Iryani, president 1967–1974) have been military men. Under the nation-state, legal authority passed not only from the leadership of an imam to a president but also from interpretive authority of old-style independent legal scholars, the 'ulama, to civil servants such as bureaucrats and elected legislators.

Legal education changed as well. As I have described elsewhere (Messick 1993), the centerpiece of instruction in the old *madrasa* (school) was shari'a law, beginning with the basic manuals of *fiqh* that pertained to the Zaydi or (in Lower Yemen) Shafi'i schools. Opened in 1926, Imam Yahya's hybrid academy for the training of jurists produced many of the court judges of that era and also of the early years of the republic. After the Revolution, this and the remaining other old *madrasa*s ceased to function, and, in 1965, the Yemeni university opened. Shari'a instruction was displaced from the centerpiece of instruction to a position as one of several subjects of higher education. At the new university, one of the main programs was the study of "shari'a and *qanun*," the dual subjects of the formation of the modern Yemeni lawyer. The change on the shari'a side of the program was that students now studied a spectrum of schools of *fiqh* interpretation rather superficially, instead of the single school of their local tradition in depth.

There were no lawyers in the old shari'a system. That is, there were only *wakil*s, legal representatives, whose main skills, beyond whatever instruction they may have acquired at a *madrasa*, were their court experience and their facility in expressing themselves in speech and in writing. By the early days of the Revolution, these representatives were generally portrayed as unscrupulous and the stage was set for the training of the first classes of university-trained lawyers, professionals certified not only by standardized state diplomas (rather than the individualized *ijaza*) but also by membership in their professional association. Their specialization no longer concerned the shari'a in the narrow sense of a particular school of *fiqh*, but rather, broadly, the "law," the corpus of Yemeni *qanun*, which, again, referenced *fiqh* works as a background "source." Although in comparison to many other Middle Eastern states (e.g., Ziadeh 1968, on Egypt) they were very late in appearing on the scene, lawyers in modern Yemen are now the existing legal specialists in the law currently on the books.

At contemporary Yemeni shari'a courts, before robed and turbaned judges, two types of suit-wearing lawyers now commonly appear: the *muhami*, or private lawyer, a graduate of a law school and perhaps a member of the bar association, and, mainly in criminal cases, the *na'ib*, the legally trained prosecutor representing the state, a member of the administration known as *al-niyaba al-'amma*, instituted in 1977 and functioning at the provincial level by 1979 (Messick 1983). According to Art. 17 of the

Law of 1977, a prosecutor was to be the "recipient of a degree in shari'a and *qanun* from San'a' University, or a degree in law from a recognized university with the Islamic shari'a as the major subject" (cited in Messick 1983: 515). A third new figure on the legal scene is the law professor, the instructor in the university system that now produces the practicing lawyers and prosecutors, and a fourth is the modern shari'a court judge. These four new figures also account for the main types of authors whose writings appear in the pages of *al-Qistas*.

As part of a new mandate, the Niyaba Law of 1977 also set forth a responsibility over an extended "public" legal terrain. The Niyaba created in Yemen was modeled on a similar institution that had existed in Egypt since 1876, which, in turn, was modeled on the French public prosecution institution known as the *ministère public* (or *parquet*). By contrast, the old shari'a system had no prosecution office (Schacht 1964: 189), except for what was entailed in the classical institution of *hisba* (based on the injunction to command good and to prohibit evil) and the associated office, or role, of the *muhtasib*. Also, in prerevolutionary Yemen, prior to either the advent of the "criminal" as a category of public legal matters or the existence of a state prosecutor, cases concerning homicide or injuries were brought by private individuals. In a 1960 case I have studied (Messick 1998a), for example, the court claim was presented by the mother and father of the murdered man.

The new "public" responsibilities of the Yemeni Niyaba begin with investigation and bringing criminal cases, together with the responsibility for the oversight of prisons, although the relevant Penal Code would first appear in draft form in 1979. In contemporary Yemen, it is state prosecutors rather than parents or other relatives who raise criminal claims in court. There also are noncriminal dimensions of the Niyaba's responsibility that are similar to responsibilities of the old-style shari'a judge, such as concerning minors without parental protection. Grafting the old upon the new, the quasi-public claims of *hisba* were explicitly made part of the Niyaba's mandate. Art. 8 of the 1977 Niyaba Law associates *hisba* claims and general "public claims." Not all of this new "public" responsibility is *hisba*-related, however. Art. 7 speaks simply of a "public right" and of rights without upholders, and Art. 9 of "claims connected with public order and morals."

Procedures in the shari'a courts of the Republic of Yemen are different in a number of respects from the shari'a courts of the preceding imamic period. Where the former judge was relatively passive, mainly a listener who heard testimony or managed the receipt of written evidential documents, the modern judge is an active questioner (Law 90 of 1976). In prerevolutionary litigation, testimony was simply given as a whole, without interruption and witness integrity later could be challenged or supported by other witnesses (see Messick 2002) or it could be contested in statements made by the opposing litigant. In contrast to the situation that obtains now, there was no investigation or interrogation by a judge, and there was no questioning by figures such as lawyers or prosecutors.

According to the old authoritative text of the Zaydi school of interpretation (cf. al-'Ansi 1993 [1938]: 184–206), a court judge had to meet six conditions. He had to be male, of full adult capacity, neither blind nor mute, capable of independent legal interpretation (*ijtihad*), of verified justness, and appointed. The modern Law of Judicial Authority (Republic of Yemen Law 1 of 1991: 10–11) reformulates the concerns of these six old conditions. As its first requirement for a judge, the modern law introduces the characteristic nation-state marker of citizenship in the Republic of Yemen. The second, also new, is a minimum age of 30 for the judge. The judge is constituted as a functionary, as a "public employee" who renders "service" and who can benefit from "promotion" through specified levels of appointment and who gains "seniority." The judge's professional age also acquires a terminus, which is 65, and the new official lifetime category of "retirement" is created by Law 1 of 1991 (Arts. 75–78). By contrast, imamic-era judges used to die in their judgeships. Prior training and experience, which are not mentioned in the old *fiqh* texts, also become a formal requirement in the modern law. In the 1970s, it was still common for judges' sons to be present at their fathers' litigation sessions and for them to begin handling the resolution of certain disputes passed along to them. The modern judge, however, must in theory pass through at least two years of prior training in the judicial sphere before assuming a regular post. As for the two key old requirements, the capacity for interpretation and "verified justness," the first is replaced by requirements generally expressed as "full qualification" and, more specifically, as holding an advanced degree from the High Judicial Institute following an undergraduate degree in "shari'a and *qanun*." The second is replaced by a combination of "good reputation" and "praiseworthy behavior and deportment," on the one hand, and, on the other, and more technically, not having been convicted of a crime (*jarima*, itself a modern category) involving the violation of honor or trust.

In the mid-1970s, the first judges to carry briefcases were appointed, and in vol. 30 (January 2001) of *al-Qistas*, one finds an interview with one such judge, al-Qadi al-Wushali, now the head of the provincial appeal court in Ibb. As in Judge al-Wushali's jurisdiction, in most urban settings a specially constructed and furnished public court building has replaced a "court" that, in the imamic era, was held in front of the judge's house and, after the revolution, in an unspecialized rental space. In the former era shari'a proceedings were "public" in that they were held in the space or courtyard before the judge's house, which was open to the passing alleyway. The publicness of the proceeding was not stipulated in the *fiqh* except insofar as there was an emphasis on the required presences of both of the litigants or their representatives. In the modern court, by contrast, rulings must be pronounced in a public session (Art. 5b).

The term for this "public," or "publicized" quality (*'alaniyya*), now mandated in the law for the court session, also was used by some of the early Muslim jurists, who were concerned, for example, that a marriage contract be properly "publicized." In the contemporary world of *al-Qistas*, there is both the mandated "public" nature of the court process and, in a closely related usage, there is "publicity" in the sense of the private advertisement (*'ilan*)—Pizza Hut again. Collective public announcements in the old regime mainly were confined to the limited circulation imamic newspaper, or worked through "word of mouth." An announcement at the local level was made by physically assembling the populace, using a town-crier, or through posting a notice on the door of the Great Mosque or on the main gate to the town. An example of this last from Ibb town was the annual posting of the "announcement of the timing of the harvest" that informed landowners about the order in which the harvest would be carried out (and the limited migrant harvest labor distributed) in the cultivated areas around the town.

Modern legal identities are based on modern personal papers. Associated with the rise of the citizen of the nation-state in Yemen, personal papers, passports, folders, and files came into use as well. While they might have had handwritten property documents of various types, the subjects of the former imamic state had no printed or typed identity cards or papers in the modern sense, that is, official state documents bearing new style family names and new identifying numbers—street addresses, telephone numbers, license numbers, and so on. This documentation now is produced, with photos and in multiple copies, by the ubiquitous technology available at local photo and photocopying studios. Mechanical reproduction gradually replaced the manual reproduction of copies (Messick 1993: 240). A parallel event was the print-era transformation of Yemeni literature, notably including the appearance of novels, first in the postcolonial south and then later in the northern highlands, and, more importantly, the advent of the Yemeni short story (Messick 1998b). Although most court judgment records continued to be handwritten after the Revolution, now they were entered on printed forms. The Commercial Courts, which existed separately for a short time, innovated by producing typed court records. Across the varieties of genres, from the mundane state document to the literary and the legal, a new manner of reading was constituted.

For important written instruments, such as marriage contracts, wills, leases, and property sale documents, there was no state repository or registry organ, except for the optional placing of a copy in a designated court register. In British Aden, a public registry of title deeds was established in 1871, but in the highlands most documents were kept by private individuals. One of the new Yemeni institutions of the 1980s was the first state *arshif*, a new form of public archive for historical documents, manuscripts, and such items as the full run of the imamic period newspaper, *al-Iman*. Prior to this, the only sort of archive was actually a library, located at the Great Mosque of San'a' (see Messick 1993: 119–22).

Printed Law

Habermas (1989: 16) writes of the newly emergent public sphere in Europe that its "decisive mark was the published word." In Yemen, the local history of the rise of printed legal materials is simultaneous with the beginning of print culture (Messick 1993: 115–31). Unlike some other Muslim settings (such as North Africa and the Indian subcontinent) where lithography was preferred, in Yemen moveable type was the technology utilized (Messick 1997b). Some of the earliest Yemeni books published outside of Yemen in the 1920s were either works of Zaydi school *fiqh* or biographical histories, which are overwhelmingly concerned with the lives of jurists. In the month of Ramadan, 1352 [1934], in the ninth year of its publication, the imamic newspaper *al-Iman* devoted nearly an entire issue to a report on a single case of great political significance. The unusual case concerned a Ford car agency contract and a purported mineral concession both of which had cast a shadow on the reputation of one of the Imam's sons.

This case appeared in print due to its unusual significance, but no other judgments would be discussed in the remaining decades of *al-Iman*. In 1938, the first of four volumes of *The Gilded Crown*, by al-'Ansi, a legal commentary (on the authoritative 15th-century work, *The Book of Flowers*) was published (al-'Ansi 1993 [1938]). This was the first such work to be written for print and it appeared with text innovations of many kinds, including footnotes. Although there also were printed editions of some of the other manuscript-era classics of Zaydi *fiqh*, most students could not afford them and continued in their old practice of manually copying out their own personal texts in the course of their lessons.

As I have described, with the Revolution of 1962, nation-state constitution-making and legislation began and the Zaydi and Shafi'i *fiqh* works suddenly were repositioned as "sources." The ever-expanding corpus of modern legislation has been issued by the government in a new public printed genre, the *Official Gazette (al-jarida al-rasmiyya)*. Starting in 1965, this gazette was available for purchase from a government office. Although it had a very limited readership, it was the primary means for the reporting and the circulation of new laws. Under republican rule, while major new works were not being written, a number of older *fiqh* works were being printed, continuing efforts begun decades earlier under Imam Yahya. The Ministry of Justice and the Supreme Court, for example, issued the first printed edition of al-Jalal's *Light of Day*, an important 17th-century commentary on the *Book of Flowers*. In 1980, also under official auspices, this time under that of the High Judicial Institute, a legal codification project carried out in the 1950s during the last decade of imamic rule finally appeared in print. In the republican decades many private presses and bookstores took up printing older legal works, including many never before published. At the same time, mainly from foreign press, the works of other legal schools and of jurists not indigenous to Yemen became widely available in Yemeni bookstores.

Local legal scholars also began to rework the relations of authorship and reading, rethinking the constraints of legal genre much as other Yemeni writers were innovating in fiction and poetry. In contrast to the former requirement, under the old school system, that instruction in matters such as *fiqh* and *hadith* (traditions of the Prophet) be mediated by a teacher, two authors of the 1990s, men of the old school who were educated before the Revolution, issued books of a new type. Muhammad Yahya Mutahhar (1985) wrote on personal status law (*al-ahwal al-shakhsiyya*), itself a new, modern legal category unknown to the old *fiqh*, and Muhammad ʿAli al-Ghurbani (n.d.) a student guide on the theory of *hadith*. Both explained to me that their books were different in that they were designed to be read and studied directly. In exactly the same formulation, each man stated that his book "did not need a teacher."

Legal case materials are a separate matter. Publication of Yemeni court judgments first occurred under the official auspices of the state Legal Office in a publication titled, *al-Majallah al-qadaʾiyya*, vol. 1 of which was issued in 1979. This first (and, to my knowledge, last) issue of this publication comprised "Judgments of the Appeals Court, Commercial Section, 1977–8" (in Arabic). This is a remarkable, 129-page work, covering in detail some 96 cases, broken down into a classification consisting of 13 categories. As noted earlier, the Commercial Courts were ahead of the other sections of the republican court system, not merely in having converted their issued texts to typewriting but also, generally, in their application of international juristic standards in their rulings. However, theirs also was the segment of law least bound by shariʿa principles, or where shariʿa forms (of contract, property, etc.) fit comfortably with international legal forms.

According to the Preface to the volume (p. 3, by the Head of the Legal Office, Husayn al-Hubayshi) the separate *qanun*s referenced in this publication of case materials included the recent law of the seas, banking law, companies law, general commercial law, procedural law, and the shariʿa evidence law. The Preface also notes that "publication of these judgments and placing them within reach of everyone (*al-jamiʿ*) will provide readers the opportunity for acquaintance with the laws and for the avoidance of the danger of errors in their interpretation." This "everyone" refers to, or seeks, a newly informed and interested readership. The Preface continues that the publication "will make easier the task of the men of the law, including lawyers and judges, when they handle or decide similar cases." Finally, the volume is said to represent a contribution to general "legal culture" (*thaqafa qanuniyya*), the first local use (to my knowledge) of a notion that would later figure centrally in the editorial rationale of *al-Qistas*.

In general, however, shariʿa court judgments were not written or designed for any form of subsequent publication or citation. A shariʿa court judgment was not intended to create law. As distinct from Anglo-American law, there is in the classical shariʿa system neither a rule of precedent nor an associated legal reporting tradition. As a result, there were only rare examples of classical shariʿa court cases being reported. In modern times, shariʿa court cases have been published either under colonial auspices (e.g., Moroccan Appeal Court cases) or in hybrid jurisdictions, such as in Anglo-Muhammadan law jurisdictions of the Indian subcontinent.

In Yemen, the model of case reporting, involving English judges and mixed foreign and Islamic law matters, was established by the British in the mid-20th-century *Law Reports of Aden*.

An entirely distinct phenomenon was the advent of published works *about* law and legal matters, as opposed to the various just discussed printings of legislation, works of law, and judgments, that is, of the law per se. The main example of this sort of publication is one that used the same title as the previously mentioned work, *al-Majallah al-qada'iyya*. This was issued by a different branch of government, the Ministry of Justice (YAR), and began with vol. 1, 1982. This journal contains sections on "Research and Studies" (including "Judgment in Islam," "Structure of the Commercial Courts in the Y.A.R.," "Principles of Equality in Islam," etc.); on judging in the YAR ("Achievements of the Ministry over Twenty Years," including reprints of some short laws); on judicial history ("Famous Judges: al-Imam 'Ali bin Abi Talib"); an interview section (with the Minister of Justice and another official), and, finally, a section of judicial statistics. The same volume also includes a very brief section (pp. 69–72), under the heading "Principles of Judgment," with sketches of three High Court cases, one on personal status (again, a modern category of law), involving inheritance, a will, a sale, and a settlement; one in the "civil" (*madani*, also a new legal category) category, specifically, a conflict over a sewer; and one, in the commercial section, concerning appeal rights. This last was authored by an Egyptian (from the Court of Cassation) who was acting as an advisor to the Yemeni High Court. Among the articles in the "Research and Studies" section one was written by an Egyptian Dean of the College of Shari'a and Qanun at San'a' University and former university president; still another is by an Egyptian law professor jointly appointed at the University of Alexandria and at San'a' University. Although Yemeni officials and jurists also were involved in the publication, the role of foreign advisors is significant.

An Egyptian advisor likewise played a key role in another new judicial publication issued by the High Judicial Institute, the *Majallat al-buhuth wa-l-ahkam al-qada'iyya al-yamaniyya*, vol. 2 of which appeared in March 1982. Vol. 1 (ca. 1980) contains an analysis of legal materials called *ikhtiyarat*, literally, "choices." The issuance of such "choices," which concern issues of *fiqh*, was a characteristic feature of rule of Zaydi imams, some of whom, including both premodern imams and Imam Yahya and his son, Imam Ahmad, in the 20th century, issued personal "choices." Typically involving a one-line statement of a rule, "choices" were made with respect to the Zaydi *fiqh* literature and entailed a position selected among alternative rules. Such "choices" were intended to guide court judges of the realm in the handling of relevant cases. They tended to be issued in difficult areas of the applied law, such as the judicial dissolution of marriage (*faskh*) or sale preemption (*shuf'a*), and they also addressed related areas of prevailing customs. In Imam Yahya's era, a handwritten list of his 13 original "choices" was posted for reference at the Supreme Court. A handwritten copy of this list is reproduced in Rashad Muhammad al-'Alimi's modern-style study of law in Yemen, *al-Taqlidiyya wa-l-hadatha fi-nizam al-qanuni al-yamani* (1989: 258–59).

In 1937, Imam Yahya's "choices" were published in a versified version and an extended commentary by 'Abd Allah al-Shamahi (1937), but Imam Ahmad's list circulated in the 1950s in handwriting only. Practicing jurists often made their own copies of the ruling imam's "choices." In the following republican era, for political reasons, the notion of an imamic origin to specific "choices" went unmentioned as new lists were published. The first republican publication of such *ikhtiyarat* occurred in a booklet issued in 1971, prior to most of the modern legislation. This booklet contains 68 concise "rulings" (*qararat*) of the Ministry of Justice: it was now the ministry that made the "choices." Although the booklet claims that new types of cases now called for "new rulings" (*ahkam jadida*) and necessitated "interpretation anew" (*ijtihad min jadid*), most of the rulings were actually old imamic *ikhtiyarat*. The next publication of these same materials came in vol. I of *Majallat al-buhuth*, which, again, makes no mention of the pre-revolutionary imams.

The opening statement in the *Majalla*, written by the Minister of Justice, portrays a movement from former obscurity and disorder to present clarity and order. He writes that the relevant texts were extracted from "the old registers and archives at the High Court."

> The "choices" were scattered about in the pages of registers and in folders, which lacked indexes or tables or contents, making it difficult for the student to gain access to what he was looking for.... But now they are before you, in a single volume, distinct and clear in method and meaning, divided in chapters and indexed.

The aim of publication was a modern one, to put law materials "before you": the law is placed in a public domain, "before" the addressed "you," the reader, the modern Yemeni citizen. Aside from physically finding the "choices," the main analytic work of the Egyptian advisor was to connect these concise principles to existing legislation. In an entirely novel ordered form, the presentation of each of the 52 entries provides a summary gloss, a quoted principle, and a section of explanatory remarks. A couple of years later, Muhammad al-'Amrani (b. 1922), a jurist who had been an imamic-era teacher in the "shari'a sciences" and who later, in the 1990s, acted as a "media mufti" (Messick 1996), published a book on the Yemeni legal system in which he presented 23 "choices," again unidentified as to their imamic sources, in his own system of classification (al-'Amrani 1984: 227–32).

At this juncture, having recapitulated the major steps in government-issued publications of law and about law, and having mentioned in passing the two important general scholarly books on the Yemeni legal system by Yemenis, by al-'Amrani and al-'Alimi, we arrive at the place and moment of *al-Qistas*, which, unlike all its predecessors among the just discussed legal journals, is a nongovernmental publication.

Cover Stories

As noted, issues of *al-Qistas* commonly present a "cover story" (*mawdu' al-ghilaf*). A mundane feature of modern magazine publishing, the "cover story" is a relatively recent phenomenon in Yemen, although the use of headlines goes back to the imamic newspaper *al-Iman*, and likely also to preceding publications in the old Ottoman Province of Yemen. Use of the international publishing convention of the "cover story," however, indexes a systematic appropriation of the forms of the modern magazine. Such appropriations are integral to new levels of editorial expertise and mission as well as to the expectations of a newly constituted modern professional readership. Behind all such formal possibilities, of course, lies the technical power of desktop publishing. Placed at the front, on the cover, and thus emphasized by the editors for their readers and also highlighted with a color photo and the largest headline, the "cover story" formula frames and promotes *al-Qistas*'s innovative mission, public legal criticism.

Based on a Saudi example, Talal Asad (1993: 200–36) has written an important comparative account of the public contours of Muslim "religious criticism," specifically in the genre of *nasiha*. Criticism also has a history in Yemen that I want to briefly sketch before continuing. Prior to the Revolution of 1962, even before the Coup of 1948, discussions critical of the regime and its institutions famously occurred in certain mosque lesson circles and, among other literati, in certain afternoon, qat-chewing gatherings in the major towns. Some of these, such as the lesson circles at the Fulayhi Mosque in San'a' and the discussion group led by the "philosopher" al-Du'ais in Ibb, jelled into opposition groups. The outcome of this activity was essentially the elite dimension of (northern) Yemeni political history up to 1948. Other forms of critique were popularly rooted, such as the reversal skits put on in the countryside near Ibb, and probably in other places as well, which portrayed venal judges in dastardly acts. The tradition of the critical skit continued after the revolution, as is illustrated by two examples I have translated that deal with the Quranic school and with corrupt practices in shari'a courts (Messick 1993: 99–100, 197–200). These urban skits have written (but unpublished) scripts and were performed on such official and public occasions as school awards days and national holiday celebrations. Perhaps the greatest medium of critique in Yemen is poetry, including a spectrum ranging from oral tribal declamations to formal urban compositions. In one standard "public" venue, critical poems are read out at the occasions that punctuate the annual republican calendar. In their study of Islamist movements and discourses in Yemen Paul Dresch and Bernard Haykel (1995) cite many examples of political poems, including tribal ones uttered at political gatherings in rural districts and others published in Yemeni newspapers of various political stripes. In recent years, especially just after national unification on May 22, 1990, the Yemeni press has been vigorous and critical, although the government also is known to crack down. There is an independent English language weekly, *The Yemen Times*, which, like a number of other newspapers, mainly including the principal "government" papers, also has an online edition. A cover story in *al-Qistas* exists in a local (and international) print media world that consists of government and private newspapers and a range of other magazines and journals and, as a consequence, of many modalities of public discourse and criticism. Radio and TV, however, remain exclusively Yemeni state services that are characteristically muffled in their capacity for criticism, yet dishes bring in the broadcasts of CNN and al-Jazeera.

On the *al-Qistas* masthead page an overview is provided of the issue's contents. It is worth repeating that such, to us, routine metatexts (covers, masthead pages, tables of contents, forewords, prefaces, acknowledgments, indexes, etc.) and also such supporting texts as footnotes and bibliographies were not common in prerevolutionary legal writings, although there were a few exceptions, such as the footnotes that appear in the previously mentioned Zaydi legal work written for print publication, *The Gilded Crown* (al-'Ansi 1993 [1938]). In the body of the monthly issues there typically are a number of articles that appear under subheads. In vol. 19 (January 2000), for example, located just after the masthead page, there is the regular subhead, "Follow-up," which announces a multiple-page section that contains a large number of short (much less than a page) stories and several longer articles, some bringing the reader up to date on stories from earlier issues. In most issues there is a separate subhead, "Case" (*qadiyya*), in vol. 19 concerned with a ten-year-long conflict that is called, "the Chicken of Sa'ada [a town in the far North]." Cases addressed in other issues include matters of check fraud, house seizure, arrest in one jurisdiction and prosecution in another, an injury by burning (a cover story, see below) and a 20-year-old case. The "cover story" of vol. 19, on "Private and Illegal Prisons," also involves case details. Unlike the commercial appeal records published in 1979, however, cases published in *al-Qistas* are not presented in the form of verbatim or excerpted records, but rather as narratives.

Other subheads in vol. 19 are: "News of the Forum"; that is, the Forum for Civil Society; "From the Internet," mostly unusual, even outrageous legal items from jurisdictions in the United States—a drunk judge in California, an error in a jail sentence, a ruling on whether a teacher must wear a tie, and so on; "Round Table"; "Research"; "Investigation"; "Legal Culture" (*thaqafa qanuniyya*); "Studies"; "Letters from Readers"; and "Complaints Section" (*diwan al-mazhalim*). In addition to what appears under these named subheads there are 13 other major articles in the issue, not counting the very brief articles in the first pages of the "Follow-up" section. A complimenting register of visual commentary and criticism is provided by another regular feature: cartoons. In every issue there are numerous illustrating cartoons, drawn by a regular staff cartoonist who signs and dates his work.

Following the cover story in vol. 19 on "Private and Illegal Jails," which is introduced with a color cover photo of a seated man in ankle chains, cover stories in later issues include: "Take Your Hands Off the Bar Association" (vol. 20); "Success of the Conference [of the Bar Association] . . . Will the Council Succeed?" (vol. 21); "Don't Play with Fire," with a photo of a former administrator and his burned face (vol. 28); "Escaped From Justice . . . but He is in Jail," with a picture of a man behind bars (vol. 29); "Towards World Criminal Justice" (vol. 30); "Arms Kill More than Two Thousand Citizens a Year," with a photo of numerous pistols and Kalashnikovs (vol. 31); "The Greatest Criminal . . . Accused of Taking Sixty Riyals [less than one US$]," with a man's photo (vol. 34).

Al-Qistas also has international interests, a wider frame of reference in which the editors seek, implicitly and explicitly, to locate Yemen. There are articles, for example, on the claim that there are no political prisoners in Kuwait (vol. 21) and on new legal divorce rights for women in Egypt (vol. 22). The same two issues also have articles on international "human rights" and on the finding by an international organization that women are less likely than men to be involved in corruption. Elsewhere (vol. 20), one can read about the impact of DNA research on "shariʿa medicine," the expertise of the medical examiner in criminal cases. Vol. 19 contains articles on the Durban conference that, as is noted, included among its signatories the editor of *al-Qistas*; on the Rabat Conference on Human Rights, also attended by the editor; and on conditions of corruption in regions and countries of the world. This last article comprises a chart that ranks countries (in 1999) according to their incidence of corruption (*rashwa*), from Denmark to Cameroon, with Tunisia, Jordan, Morocco, Turkey, Egypt, and Pakistan included in the rankings. While Yemen (among other countries) is not specifically mentioned, publication of the list implicitly reframes a local problem with respect to a worldwide issue. However, in a later issue (vol. 30: 24), following a lengthy article on the international court of criminal justice, there is a list of countries that have either signed or concurred with "The Basic Organization for the Creation of an International Criminal Court." Once again, that is, in the pages of *al-Qistas*, Yemen takes its place in an international legal initiative: the country name appears in a list of countries, Yemen having signed, as is noted, on December 28, 2000.

Among the diverse locally oriented think pieces in *al-Qistas* are articles on apostasy and the freedom of religious beliefs, the technical aspects of acknowledgment and evidence, the issue of revenge (*thaʾr*), magic, forgery, the condition of the jailed during Ramadan, election monitoring, and criminal justice for women. Women's issues are regular features in *al-Qistas*, such as the article on women prisoners in vol. 31, or "The Wife Between the Law and the Judge" in the same issue. Female lawyers occasionally also appear as authors of articles (e.g., vol. 30: 4–5, with a photo of the unveiled Adeni lawyer-author, a member of the Bar Association Council, who also is interviewed in vol. 29: 3) or, in the "Round Table" of vol. 19, as a participant in discussions (with a photo of a veiled woman at the table, p. 19, and, in a side bar, another photo, her name and a quoted statement, p. 20). As an indicator of the tenor of related issues, however, an article in vol. 19 (p. 4) discusses protests against a recent order for the closure of the San'a' University Center for Applied Research and Women's Studies. The article states that

> Protests came from all forces backing freedom of thought and scholarly research, and [from] the institutions of civil society, the unions and the associations, and legal and informational agencies, and human rights organizations, and national figures and journalists and members of committees of instruction.

Most issues of *al-Qistas* have news and other items on two key organizations, the Forum for Civil Society and the Yemeni Bar Association, the principal ongoing preoccupation being the structure and the "independence" of the latter. Although they are, like the old shari'a *wakils*, private entrepreneurs, Yemeni lawyers perform their work with government agency oversight and according to state laws, the most recent of which is the "Law of the Organization of the Profession of Lawyer" (No. 30 of 1999). They await, however, a delayed new basic law of the Bar Association. Articles also refer to relations between the Yemeni association and such international organizations as the Union of Arab Lawyers. In vol. 20 (pp. 6–11), there is a list of the names of all member lawyers in the Yemeni Bar Association together with their specific court attachments, by level (High, Appeal, First Instance) and town (San'a', Aden, Ta'izz, Ibb, al-Hudayda), also indicating which have paid their dues and thus are eligible to attend the upcoming Third General Conference. It is noted that publication of this list of lawyers' names occurs simultaneously in *al-Qistas* and in "some newspapers." As an example of the distribution of numbers involved, there are 148 lawyers (including at least one woman) attached to the High Court in San'a', 70 (including at least two women) to that in Aden, 28 in Ta'izz, 8 in Ibb, and 9 in al-Hudayda. For the San'a' First Instance Court, there are 253 lawyers listed as attached to the court. By my count, the total of names at all levels and in all towns is 1,132 lawyers, which also provides an approximation of at least one part of the readership of *al-Qistas*.

Private Jails

Returning to the cover story of vol. 19 (January 2000), on illegal jails, I want to have a closer look at one specific example of legal criticism in *al-Qistas*. This cover story is illustrated on the masthead (p. 1) and inside the issue (p. 13) with the same photo (without a caption) of two standing men wearing ankle chains. The internal title to the article is "Following the

Campaign Against Private Jails: When Will We Close Illegal Jails?" The article is unsigned, which is not often the case in *al-Qistas*. I was surprised to find the discussion referred by name to a man I know from a rural subdistrict in Ibb Province, just west of Ibb town. It seems there had been an armed confrontation, involving two deaths, the previous October (1999) in the subdistrict of al-'Udayn between government forces and tribal forces of two shaykhs, one my acquaintance. In the aftermath, the article continues, the question of "people of influence" having private jails was posed, although the local authorities denied the existence of such jails.

The article states, "The press concerned itself with the•matter and many demanded the opening of the 'folder' of private jails associated with tribal shaykhs in the provinces of the republic." *Al-Qistas* then uses the rhetorical technique of recapitulating some of the press coverage, naming specific newspapers. A government paper, *al-Wahda*, mentioned that the president, who had received a report from a special parliamentary investigative committee, issued an order for the closing of private jails wherever found and for the arrest of the two shaykhs' criminal supporters; the international newspaper, *al-Hayat*, published in London, however, reported that the president released the accused son of Shaykh Basha, my acquaintance, and also the son of the other shaykh; and a Yemeni opposition paper, *al-Thawri*, stated that Shaykh Basha was considering bringing a legal case against the military leadership of Ibb Province. Newspaper citations not only serve to document the story but also, at a more strategic level, tie *al-Qistas* to journalist allies in the print media.

To take on a powerful tribal figure such as Shaykh Basha is a serious matter indeed. One of many sons of 'Ali Muhsin Basha (Arabic for the Turkish "Pasha," such family name dates from Ottoman period titles recognizing rural leaders), Shaykh Sadiq Basha emerged after the death of his formidable father as the new paramount shaykh. In the style of shaykhs in Lower Yemen, Shaykh Basha is a large-scale landowner who also entered regular politics through service in the national assembly. The whole ambiguous phenomenon of the relation of the Yemeni state to the tribes is best posed by the dual roles of Shaykh al-Ahmar, simultaneously the paramount Hashid Confederation leader and the head of the national Parliament. Shaykh Basha characteristically arrives in Ibb town in Land Cruisers, accompanied by swaggering young men in colorful men's skirts and jaunty turbans, with AK-47s slung over their shoulders. Shaykh Basha is an individual whose armed men could clash with government troops and who could subsequently think of raising a legal claim against the provincial authorities. A cartoon in a later article in the same issue of *al-Qistas* (p. 30) shows a man threatening a judge with a rifle and saying, "I am a shaykh, son of a shaykh, a political authority and a prosecutor, watch how you approach."

As a further strategy of its presentation, the *al-Qistas* article goes on to summarize the points of the parliamentary commission's recommendations. Set off with bullets in the text, these include: that the government immediately see to the carrying out of legal processes against those accused by the provincial police commission; concerning other citizens' claims against the two shaykhs, that these cases be transferred to the local Niyaba for urgent prosecutorial decision; concerning private jails, that the government see to the implementation of the Law of Prison Organization and forbid any type of jail other than those legally specified; finally, concerning the destruction of several buildings owned by the two shaykhs, dated minutes of the provincial police investigation are cited concerning the legality, or not, of these actions. Revealing the publication's own investigative journalism, the article then states that, "based on a memorandum of the police authority in al-ʿUdayn, of which *al-Qistas* obtained a copy," there were 28 individuals, followers of the two shaykhs, who were accused of police infractions.

The legal ramifications of all this, according to the *al-Qistas* article, are many-leveled. The accusations against the tribal followers of the shaykhs involve "assault, highway robbery, kidnaping and inciting tribal strife." Such acts are framed as "violations of human rights and attacks on public security." The article continues, generalizing, "the matter does not end with the opposition to private jails" in these specific locales, "but rather the correct legal situation is . . . the closing of any private jails in any region of Yemen." According to the article, the situation is that there are many such private jails, associated with such influential persons as Shaykh Basha, which neither the Prison Administration nor the Niyaba can have access to or supervise. Furthermore, there are governmental jails not in compliance with the prison law that also must be brought into compliance and given proper oversight.

Conclusion

Al-Qistas represents a new level, range and pattern of circulation in Yemen of both legal awareness and engaged legal criticism. It may also represent something relatively unique in the Arab world. The other question I put on e-mail to the editor concerned models that may have been in the minds of the founding group. He responded as follows:

> When we created it, there were not other examples in the Arab countries. However, we got many ideas from the IBA publications [International Bar Association, www.ibanet.org, which also has an interest group, the Arab Regional Forum]. Still today, there are no similar examples in the region.

I have attempted here to join a genealogical treatment of the background of the *al-Qistas* phenomenon with detailed foreground materials on the rise of a legal-public domain and of forms of legal publicity. However familiar to us, from a Pizza Hut advertisement to a bar association and a lawyers' publication, what has taken place in Yemen does not simply represent an implanting in the highlands of outside conceptions and institutions.

Rather, these admittedly international institutions and forms have been grafted onto, among many other features, certain already existing "capitalist" features in Yemen, from the indigenous form of private or individual property to an old legal notion of the "public." The result is a legal situation that is both similar to many others in the world, especially in the Muslim world, and yet also resolutely particular to Yemen.

Analysis must attend to the detailed local history of this grafting. Even if such Habermasian categories as "public sphere" and "civil society" cannot be unproblematically applied in understanding a situation such as obtains in contemporary Yemen, versions of such categories are in global circulation and, even more significant, local people, such as the writers and editors of *al-Qistas* consciously employ them in their political agendas. If Habermas's categories cannot be directly transferred to such non-Western cases, a genealogical account of the history of the present grafting nevertheless may be inspired by his rich historical and social analyses of the Western case, including his emphasis on the transformative role of the press and the print media generally.

The vantage point of *al-Qistas* is that of the "law," specifically in the sense of the modern *qanun*. Just as the *qanun* has displaced the shari'a, represented by *fiqh* doctrine, from the practical focus of legal initiatives in the Yemeni nation state, so *al-Qistas* views the shari'a at a certain respectful distance. Perhaps it should not be a surprise that a legally oriented old Yemeni elite has given way to a new orientation, also legal but with a hybrid connotation, among the newly emerged community of professional lawyers, although the place of modern lawyers in Yemen remains to be understood. The *al-Qistas* vantage point also is decidedly different from that of contemporary Yemeni Islamists, whose very local characteristics, including their important tribal connections and their national political party, have been analyzed by Dresch and Haykel (1995). What the shari'a has become for Islamists, in Yemen and elsewhere, is an open question, but the emphasis seems to be on a "new shari'a" emptied of most of its old doctrinal content of *fiqh*. Whereas the formerly central *fiqh* "does not dominate society as it once did," Norman Calder (1996: 995–96) argues, "the inspirational power of *Shari'a*, a concept devoid of detail or specificity, has increased."

The seemingly secure sense, early in my account, of the inevitable directions and the predictable course of specific legal developments finally is disrupted by a close look at specific critical interventions in *al-Qistas*. Much of the movement of the modern in Yemen, including legal change in particular, is shown to be inhabited by that which was to be replaced or surpassed. Thus, in the example just presented, the rule of state law in such a specific domain as prison administration is frustrated by enduring tribal authorities of powerful shaykhs. Located at a distinct angle from state institutions and from the "law on the books" it would support, that is, as an institution of an emergent civil society in Yemen, *al-Qistas* is engaged in its own struggle with the country's recalcitrant legal and political realities, which include the realities of state institutions. In its detailed, reasoned, legally based criticism *al-Qistas* engages directly in cultivating the views and understandings of the "legal" in its readers, the private professional lawyers, law professors, and members of the judiciary and prosecution. At the conclusion of his interview with *al-Qistas* (vol. 30: 26–29), Ibb Judge al-Wushali is quoted as saying,

> Thank you to *al-Qistas* magazine, which is like its name ["the balance"]. It is a judicial and legal magazine which is benefited from more than is benefited from others, due to its detailed examinations of realities (*haqa'iq*) and [its] dissemination/publication (*nashr*) of judicial and legal awareness (*wa'i*) and [its] asking of information from its sources. I wish for its continuing development and success.

Notes

The original version of this essay was prepared for Workshop IV, "Islamic Movements and Discourses within Local, National and Transnational Public Spheres," held March 20–24, 2002, in the Third Mediterranean Social and Political Research Meeting, Montecatini, Italy. I am grateful to the dynamic workshop organizers, Armando Salvatore and Amr Hamzawy, for their careful and insightful stewardship, and to all the participants for an exceptionally high level of interchange. Key texts by Salvatore (1997, 2001) provided significant conceptual background for the workshop and for my essay. I appreciate also his comments and those of an anonymous reviewer on this last version.

1. I have had access to nine issues, vols. 19–22, 28–31, and 34, covering the period January 2000 to May 2001. My thanks to Anna Würth for providing me these issues to photocopy. See also her important work on court cases in contemporary Yemen (Würth 1995, 2000). The role of the Dutch Embassy in funding and otherwise supporting the launch and continuing production of *al-Qistas* should not be underestimated. In this connection I appreciate the insightful comments and assistance of Laila al-Zwaini, of ISIM, Leiden. Another journal, *Huquqna*, which appeared in March 1999, is partly in English and is supported by the Danish Embassy. I have seen only one issue of this publication.
2. In an older sense, in the Ottoman Empire, *qanun* was a law parallel to but not in conflict with the shari'a, and, as such, was promulgated by Ottoman sultans.
3. Antecedents of nation-state legislation in Yemen date to the late-19th-century Ottoman *majalla*, the streamlined *fiqh* commentary by Ahmad al-'Ansi, the first volume of which was published in 1938, and the codified corpus of *fiqh* rules developed in the 1950s (but not published until 1980).

References

al-'Alimi, Rashad Muhammad. 1989. *Al-Taqlidiyya wa-l-hadatha fi-nizam al-qanuni al-yamani*. San'a': Dar al-kalima.
al-'Amrani, Muhammad Isma'il. 1984. *Nizam al-qada' fi-l-islam*. Damascus: Matba'at al-katib al-'arabi.

al-'Ansi, Ahmad b. Qasim. 1993 [1938]. *Al-Taj al-mudhhab li-ahkam al-madhhab*, 4 vols., San'a': Dar al-hikma al-yamaniyya.

Asad, Talal. 1993. *Genealogies of Religion*. Baltimore: Johns Hopkins University Press.

Bowen, John R. 1999. "Legal Reasoning and Public Discourse in Indonesian Islam." In *New Media in the Muslim World*. ed. Dale F. Eickelman and Jon W. Anderson, Bloomington, IN: Indiana University Press, 80–105.

Calder, Norman. 1996. "Law." In *History of Islamic Philosophy*, ed. Seyyed Hossein Nasr and Oliver Leaman, London and New York: Routledge, 979–98.

Dresch, Paul, and Bernard Haykel. 1995. "Stereotypes and Political Styles: Islamists and Tribesfolk in Yemen." *International Journal of Middle East Studies* 27, 4: 405–31.

al-Ghurbani, Muhammad 'Ali. n.d. *'Ilm usul al-hadith*, unpublished manuscript.

Habermas, Jürgen. 1989 [1962]. *The Structural Transformation of the Public Sphere*, trans. Thomas Burger, Cambridge, MA: MIT Press.

Messick, Brinkley. 1983. "Prosecution in Yemen: The Introduction of the *Niyaba*." *International Journal of Middle East Studies* 15: 507–18.

———. 1993. *The Calligraphic State: Textual Domination and History in a Muslim Society*. Berkeley: University of California Press.

———. 1996. "Media Muftis: Radio Fatwas in Yemen." In *Islamic Legal Interpretation: Muftis and Their Fatwas*, ed. Muhammad Khalid Masud, Brinkley Messick, and David Powers, Cambridge: Harvard University Press, 310–20.

———. 1997a. "Genealogies of Reading and the Scholarly Cultures of Islam." In *Cultures of Scholarship*, ed. Sally C. Humpheys, Ann Arbor: University of Michigan Press, 387–412.

———. 1997b. "On the Question of Lithography," *Culture and History* (Copenhagen) 18: 158–76.

———. 1998a. "L' écriture en procès: les récits d'un meurtre devant un tribunal shari'a." special section of *Droit et Société*, ed. Baudouin Dupret, 39: 237–56.

———. 1998b. "Written Identities: Legal Subjects in an Islamic State." *History of Religions* 38, 1: 25–51.

———. 2002. "Evidence: From Memory to Archive." *Islamic Law and Society* 9, 2: 231–70.

Mutahhar, Muhammad Yahya. 1985. *Ahkam al-ahwal al-shakhsiya*. 2 vols., Cairo and Beirut: Dar al-kutub al-islamiyya.

Salvatore, Armando. 1997. *Islam and the Political Discourse of Modernity*. Reading, UK: Ithaca Press.

———. 2001. "After the State: Islamic Reform and the 'Implosion' of *shari'a*." In *Muslim Traditions and Modern Techniques of Power*, vol. 3 of *Yearbook of Sociology of Islam*, ed. Armando Salvatore, Hamburg: Lit; New Brunswick: Transaction.

Schacht, Joseph. 1964. *An Introduction to Islamic Law*. Oxford: The Clarendon Press.

al-Shamahi, 'Abdallah. 1937. *Sirat al-'arifin ila idrak ikhtiyarat amir al-mu'minin*. San'a': Matba'at al-ma'arif.

Würth, Anna. 1995. "A Sana'a Court: The Family and the Ability to Negotiate." *Islamic Law and Society* 2, 3: 320–40.

———. 2000. *Ash-Shariʿa fi Bab al-Yaman. Recht, Richter und Rechtspraxis an der familienrechtlichen Kammer des Gerichts Süd-Sanaa, (Republik Jemen) 1983–1995.* Berlin: Duncker & Humblot.

Ziadeh, Farhat. 1968. *Lawyers, the Rule of Law, and Liberalism in Modern Egypt.* Palo Alto, CA: Stanford University Press.

CONCLUSION

PUBLIC SPHERES TRANSNATIONALIZED: COMPARISONS WITHIN AND BEYOND MUSLIM MAJORITY SOCIETIES

Cecelia Lynch

In this chapter, I explore the implications of the findings in this volume for the globalized academic discourse on the concepts of *public sphere* and *civil society*. I first summarize and analyze a number of the rich empirical and theoretical insights generated in the volume. These insights point to both differences and similarities in Muslim majority societies, and confirm the necessity of understanding context and contingency in drawing conclusions about Islam and the public sphere. I then examine the stakes involved in distinguishing the concepts of "public sphere" and "civil society" (while privileging the former), as is done by LeVine and Salvatore in chapter 1, versus considering them as inseparably related components (conceptually and substantively) of the task of breaking down the secularist/modernist assumptions so ingrained in international relations and democratic theory. In so doing, I discuss how the empirical and conceptual contributions in this volume relate to understandings of public spheres and civil societies elsewhere in the world. Finally, I look at the relationship between the notions of "common sense" and "common good" as articulated by Salvatore and LeVine and the theological discourse on "casuistry" (i.e., the process of ethical reasoning that pays close "attention to the specific details of particular moral cases and circumstances": Jonsen and Toulmin 1988: 2). What do these bodies of work tell us about the necessity of examining the casuistic interstices of daily practices, tradition, and common good, for understanding the constitutive character of religious ethics in the world?

Substantive Insights

Analyzing the public sphere in Muslim majority societies can tell us much about the role of religion in politics historically as well as today.

The contributions to this volume both broaden the notion of public sphere and make it more specific in particular contexts. For example, most of the chapters concern nationally and locally situated public spheres, in Yemen, Egypt, Lebanon, Pakistan, and Iran. They grapple with the definition and construction of the public sphere in these contexts, describe and analyze the relationship between conceptualizations of the common good and social justice in Islam, address polarizing issues such as the representation of suicide bombers in public debate, and employ methods that, to varying degrees, situate local practices within broader historical and geographic trends.

Raymond Baker and Dyala Hamzah, for example, explore these questions in relation to Egypt. Baker documents the genealogy of Islamist arguments about the common good in Egypt, focusing on the "progressive" nature of the Egyptian New Islamist movement since 1970, while Hamzah deals with the alleged relationship between Egyptian elite views and the broader "Arab" public sphere. For Baker, the "centrist intellectuals" of the New Islamist movement represent a significant, yet underappreciated, counterpoint to the stereotypical portraits of Islamist militant movements so prevalent in the West. The New Islamists' message ties the common good to peace and pluralism. This movement, Baker argues, has successfully transformed itself from an elite to a mass phenomenon.

Yet, the New Islamist School also represents one of a number of "diverse networks that are all undergoing rapid and unpredictable changes" (Baker, this volume: 15). While the New Islamists have deftly negotiated this fluid terrain in the post- Nasser years and are likely to remain significant players in the future of the Egyptian public, the underlying condition of fluidity also means that future network constellations are unpredictable.

Such fluidity and unpredictability may also characterize the more generalized Arab public sphere, but Hamzah argues that the Egyptian press actually closes off public debate by presenting only a narrow subset of opinion while claiming to represent a much broader transnational constituency. Hamzah examines the views of prominent Egyptian clerics who criticized a fatwa against Palestinian suicide bombings articulated by Saudi Arabia's Grand Mufti. She argues that the Egyptian press presented a limited range of views critical of the fatwa, and none supporting it, though many Palestinians themselves agreed with the Saudi cleric. It is also interesting that some of the critical opinions came from members of Baker's New Islamist School, including shaykh Yusuf al-Qaradawi and Muhammad Salim al 'Awwa. Hamzah argues that this limitation of the debate distorts the function of the public sphere and disallows genuine communicative action. Moreover, she argues that the distortion is all the more troubling given that the Egyptian press self-consciously presents itself as the "recipient, and amplifier, of an 'Arab voice,'" employing the cover of 'Arab' opinion to advocate Egypt's national points of view (Hamzah, this volume: 181).

Lara Deeb also contextualizes the politicized nature of nationalist public debate, bringing in issues of gender to focus on women's Islamist trends in Lebanon. Deeb examines the participation of women's groups in defining the common good through reconfiguring religious rituals. She charts the changing practices of Lebanese Shi'a women, who, by engaging in new types of commemorations of the 'Ashura story (the martyrdom of Imam Husayn, and the role played by his sister, Sayyida Zaynab), have legitimized a particular type of women's participation, focusing on social justice, in the public sphere. These changing practices represent a shift, from a "traditional" 'Ashura to an "authenticated" one. The former had sunk into a relatively apolitical, emotive exercise, including self-flagellation and exaggerations of the story designed for emotional catharsis, while the newer, authenticated practices tend to be more restrained emotionally, hew more closely to historical and sacred texts, and in so doing represent a more politicized understanding of the connections between past and present.

Whereas Hamzah's Egyptian press represents itself as speaking for a much broader, even transnational, public, Deeb concludes that women's 'Ashura commemorations in Lebanon essentially represent one of many interrelated public spheres. These spheres are gendered in ways that, we can infer, may leave little room for unity. The nexus of gender, religion, and nationalism can thus produce different types of action. Deeb and Hamzah also have different, contextualized, answers to the question of the relationship between the "public" and the "nation." While the question is interesting for Deeb's analysis (especially if Hizbullah and the increased politicization of ritual are linked to nationalism), it takes on new meaning for Hamzah's argument about the way in which the Egyptian elite conspires to create a transnational public to be used for nationalist ends. Similarly, Setrag Manoukian argues that the 20th-century Iranian context has been marked by consistent appeals to "the people." By interpreting three public artifacts from different periods, 1917, the 1950s, and 1979, and situating each of them in the context of an identity that has long appealed to its linguistic particularity, Manoukian demonstrates the strength and persistence of the idealization and construction of "the people." He also shows that the religious dimension of life in Iran cannot be ascribed any particular role over time, but is rather shaped by the nexus of power dynamics in given contexts. Religion is contingent, not fixed, and interacts with various other "encroaching trajectories" (such as the state, the British, the economy, education, and natural resources) to influence the relationship between the people and Islam. Debates about the content of the common good are constructed first according to actors' assertions about the people's needs and wants. Religion resonates when it is framed in terms of the common good characterized as "the nation" or "the people."

For Manoukian, therefore, the state is central to the analysis of the public. Muhammad Khalid Masud, however, refocuses our attention on religion, putting at the center of his analysis the question of whether or not shari'a and the public sphere can coexist. Masud's answer is that shari'a and the public sphere do indeed coexist in Pakistan, and that shari'a is a socially constructed phenomenon, that is, constructed in the public sphere. Masud's focus concerns the shift from the colonial marginalization of shari'a to its growing postcolonial dominance in Pakistan. Masud shows how the roots of the social construction of shari'a in Pakistan go back to the 13th century, and traces the influence of *madrasas*, or schools, in promoting a variety of legal doctrines based on sources including custom, the Qur'an, and the teachings and practices of the Prophet (the *sunna*). These doctrines, or *fiqh*, differed both from each other and from *qanun*, the laws enacted by rulers. Initially, shari'a was seen as separate from *fiqh*, but over time, the two were increasingly viewed as symbiotically related in an effort to distinguish them from *qanun*. Colonial agents then reconstructed shari'a to be limited to the private sphere, although they did so abetted by the agency of Islamic traditionalists, who espoused legal pluralism. The contemporary period is marked by a debate between the revival of shari'a, promoted by religious political parties, and the reform of Islamic law, fostered by liberals and modernists.

Masud also traces the identification of the purpose of Islamic law with the promotion of the (human) common good to 14th-century jurisprudential writings. But Masud goes further by insisting on the acceptability of shari'a. This is because social actors do not merely receive legal precepts; they are also active in legitimizing them. At the same time, however, when Masud traces the evolution of shari'a in Pakistan over the past 40 years, we see that in two periods, under Zulfiqar Ali Bhutto and Ziaul Haq, such legitimizing public sphere practices were lacking. Under Bhutto, reformism reigned, but modernists promulgated top-down change that did not include the participation or views of populist *madrasas* and mosques. Religious political parties reacted, delegitimized the Bhutto regime, and helped to bring Ziaul Haq to power. The formal aspects of the public sphere broadened under Ziaul Haq, with a huge increase in the number of *madrasas*, the development of rival student forces in each school, and the creation of hundreds of new religious publications. Yet, despite these formal attributes, the public sphere was impoverished, with each religious entity speaking to its own factionalized audience. Thus, Masud finds that the Habermasian construct of communicative action illustrates a necessary condition of meaningful participation in the public sphere.

While Masud analyzes the impact on shari'a of processes of colonization and decolonization, Brinkley Messick highlights the changes in perceptions and definitions of shari'a in a context lacking a background of colonization. Messick articulates the meaning of contemporary legal change in Yemen, focusing on an analysis of a prominent legal magazine/journal. Messick points out that the lack of colonial rule in much of Yemen resulted in more recent legal evolutions than those in many other countries of the region. Change in Yemen has occurred against a background that includes a traditional agrarian economic ethic based on private property rights, and shari'a legal doctrines based on the "humanly authored literature known as the *fiqh*." Given that shari'a was never shunted to a so-called private sphere by colonial authorities and that private property and Islamic law are not seen as contradictory, contemporary legal changes in Yemen have resulted in a unique form of modernism. In this case, the definition of shari'a is changing rapidly (and is currently indeterminate), and legal professionals emphasize *qanun* (legislated law) over *fiqh* doctrine. Shari'a is by no means absent in this new context, but it has been loosened from its former, "traditional" doctrinal moorings. Private property still anchors the economy, but in a broader variety of forms.

Thus, we see the intertwining of localized experiences (i.e., traditions) with broader transnational processes. The legal professionals who publish *Al Qistas*, the journal examined by Messick, appeal frequently and openly to civil society discourses. They also employ sophisticated technology and design to draw popular appeal to their magazine/journal, and hence, to legal issues and political change in Yemen. Moreover, Messick and Masud demonstrate the praxiological (as opposed to doctrinal) nature of the development of shari'a, and the symbiotic relationship between law and popular modes of interpretation, in these very different contexts. In the West, shari'a is often viewed as rigid and unchanging dogma, but Messick and Masud demonstrate that its development relies on popular legitimization, which in turn requires local appeal as well as ongoing debate about its content.

Thus, religion, even in its most rule-bound forms, must be seen as contingent. It is also worth noting that contextual methods are especially necessary when analyzing the nexus between religious belief and politicization. Deeb, for example, highlights the "emotional restraint" that is associated with the politicization of the 'Ashura ritual in Lebanon. Likewise, for many of the contributors, authenticated hermeneutics, that is, adhering closely to accepted textual sources (of stories, law, etc., in Islam) is associated with politicization. However, the type of politicization produced by such textual adherence is indeterminate and must be contextualized. In Lebanon, the emotional restraint of authenticated 'Ashura aligns with the increasing political importance of Hizbullah, whereas in Egypt, according to Baker, textual fidelity can help produce political centrism.

Conceptual Tensions

Public spheres, therefore, can be radical, centrist, or (at first glance) apolitical. In most of the above contexts, however, the public sphere at issue is nationally bounded. Yet, situating a public sphere within a nation-state is both a natural and problematic analytical move. The term's conceptual history, its use by area-studies specialists, and the identification of the public with nationalism in some contexts make situating it within state boundaries appear natural. Yet given the transnational and global phenomena also noted by the contributors, including ideas about and processes of democratization, communications technology, and market economics, such conceptual and geographic limitations are also problematic. This brings us to the definition of the public sphere, as well as its relationship to the state, civil society, democracy, and transnational practices and processes.

The definition of public sphere used by Salvatore and LeVine in this book is from Eickelman and Salvatore 2004 [2002], 5: "the site where contests take place over the definition of the obligations, rights and especially notions of justice that members of society require for the common good to be realized." LeVine and Salvatore have "a broad, transcultural understanding of the public sphere as the communicative and legitimizing basis of potentially democratic political systems" wherein "religious reformers and the public mobilization of religion have long played an important role (LeVine and Salvatore, this volume: 30)." They broaden the liberal notion of public sphere to focus on its role as the site of debates about issues of the common good, rather than limiting it to a tight relationship with the mechanisms of a voluntarist civil society.

Many of the volume's contributors also conceptualize the public sphere in spatial terms. For example, for Masud, the public sphere is a space, created in part by new media and mass education, where debates on "issues of common concern" occur. Masud also highlights additional features of the concept, including "two characteristics of publicness: a plurality of voices and a fragmentation of traditional authority" (Masud, this volume: 155). Thus, the public sphere in this connotation is a site for debate that is not restricted to specialists, either religious or secular. The contributions to this volume demonstrate that the popularization of the public sphere does not inevitably translate into liberal pluralism.

This conceptualization of the public sphere in the context of Muslim majority societies thus provides a substantive counterpoint to Western liberal notions. Nevertheless, the spatial conceptualization still begs the question of how we refer to those sites that are not public. More specifically, to what degree does the concept of the public sphere rest on the binary public/private distinction? Most of the contributors to this volume, including Deeb, Levine and Salvatore, and Messick, explicitly reject the distinction between public and private that characterizes Western liberal conceptions of participation, arguing that such a distinction does not make sense in the contexts at issue. Yet, some of the contributors go further, rejecting any spatial connotation to the concept. For Manoukian, the relevant opposite of publicness is secrecy (instead of privacy). His conception of the public refers to an "abstract quality of wholeness, openness and availability" (Manoukian, this volume: 59) rather than to a space for the enactment of debate. Dupret and Ferrié, while taking Levine and Salvatore's conception of the public as a point of departure, also take a distance from the latter's notion of the public sphere as a site, insisting that the category of the public "has no social reality outside its instantiation" in particular circumstances constructed and imagined as public. They argue, therefore, that their conceptualization "is radically situational, contextual, and bound to people's manifest action and understanding" (Dupret and

Ferrié, this volume: 135–36); thus for them the term merely describes people's understandings of a particular situation. Dupret and Ferrié provide a number of examples that illustrate the problem of boundaries for spatial conceptualizations of publicness. The Moroccan wedding scenario, in which a former prostitute who is now respectably settled but is asked by a friend to fill a gap in a ritualized dance, thereby highlighting her former identity, is a case in point, since virtually none of the aspects of the case can be characterized as an exclusively private or public concern. Deeb's work also underscores the feminist maxim that such distinctions always shift uneasily between artificially constructed boundaries.

Whether or not the public sphere needs a private opposite is also important for conceptual distinctions between the public sphere and civil society. Salvatore and LeVine argue that "the idea of the public sphere is thus a wider and at the same time more specific notion than that of civil society" (Salvatore and LeVine, this volume: 6). Yet, we might ask how useful the analytical construct of the public sphere is as opposed to others such as "democratic participation," or "civil society" in describing the nexus between religiously motivated action and state or transnational politics. We must also address the well-trodden, but still thorny, issue of the degree to which analytical concepts can travel successfully across cultural and religious spaces, especially from "the West" to the rest of the world.

In explaining their position, Salvatore and LeVine quote N. Shmuel Eisenstadt:

> Civil society entails a public sphere, but not every public sphere entails a civil society, whether of the economic or political variety, as defined in the contemporary discourse, or as it has developed in early modern Europe through direct participation in the political process of corporate bodies or a more or less restricted body of citizens in which private interests play a very important role. (Eisenstadt 2002: 141)

The assumption here is clearly that civil society requires the existence of private interests as developed in early modern Europe, while the public sphere is more adaptable to varying contexts.

Working through either concept, however, requires figuring out the relationships between the state/political society, economic society (which might be subsumed under either the market or the state), and possibly elites, masses, and culture more generally. Both the notions of civil society and public sphere connote participation in decision making by nonelites. But whether these non-elites are conceptualized as private individuals (as in the liberal reading), group entities, or some other construct is important for determining what, if anything, constitutes the opposite of publicness.

Simone Chambers, using Habermas, provides a classic and influential reading of the relationship between civil society and the public sphere, treating the latter as one of the important institutions of civil society (Chambers 2002: 92). In this reading, the public sphere provides a broad arena for action, while civil society provides the more pertinent "site of resistance and emancipation." The public sphere, therefore, "is an important extension of civil society," as the place "where the ideas, interests, values, and ideologies formed within the relations of civil society are voiced and made politically efficacious." Such conceptualizations require the democratic participation of "private citizens interacting in the public sphere" (Habermas 1989 [1962]; quoted in Chambers 2002: 96).

But what is a private citizen in a context in which one's social (here, religious) identity is important? Given this problem, the concept of public sphere certainly has analytical advantages over the concept of civil society. Definitions of civil society still manage to insist on its voluntarist character, or on the symbiotic relationship between conditions of private and public autonomy. The notion of the public sphere, in contrast, can incorporate multiple definitions of autonomy as well as relations of hierarchy, and thus is more congenial to including religious, as well as other, motives for debate and action. Thus, it may well be that, while the concept of civil society is in the end too tainted by Western liberalism to apply to the rest of the world without conceptual gymnastic feats that cause it to lose its originality, the concept of public sphere still makes sense in multiple contexts.

Certainly, the editors of this volume make a strong case for such a conclusion, and the work of the authors in this volume demonstrates the intellectual and substantive strength of their argument. Yet, we should not cast out the concept of civil society prematurely, either, for two reasons. First, a large number of contributions on civil society over the past decade by scholars in non-Western areas of the world has deepened the debate about civil society's necessary contents and limits, and broadened our understanding of politics in the non-Western world (Haynes 1997; Kalipeni and Zeleza 1999; Sajoo 2002; Schak and Hudson 2003). For some of these scholars, as Jean and John Comaroff point out, the concept of civil society is no more ethnocentric or rigidly modernist than the concept of "democracy" or a number of others that emanate from Western philosophy and social theory (Comaroff and Comaroff 1999). As long as the concept allows for hybrid forms, it can remain useful.

Despite the profusion of literature relating the concept to non-Western areas of the world, however, the concept of civil society remains fraught with internal contradictions. Foremost is that "the autonomy of civil society from the state, the very autonomy on which the Idea is predicated, is entirely chimerical. It, too, rests on a series of idealized separations, starting with that of political authority from private property" (Comaroff and Comaroff 1999: 24). This is the case not only in Africa, Asia, and the Middle East, but also in Western Europe and North America. Thus, there exists no pure form of civil society from which to assess other forms, but only a series of hybrids.

Second, it is unclear whether the concept of public sphere can escape at least some of the internal contradictions that beset civil society. Indeed, the contributions in this volume indicate that the debate has been joined.

While many of the contributors find the conception congenial to their analyses, and Masud even suggests that the Habermasian conceptualization of communicative action is useful in analyzing the workings of the public sphere in Pakistan, a few are skeptical. In particular, Messick contends that neither civil society nor the public sphere are unproblematic categories for Muslim societies. Dupret and Ferrié insist, moreover, that "the quest for any private instance floating in a vacuum, outside the public realm, is a quest for chimera and ignores the important fact that the procedures used to describe any such private instance must be totally embedded in language" (Dupret and Ferrié, this volume: 139).

At the same time, as we have already noted, still other scholars make use of the notion of publicness while at the same time alienating it from any opposition to the private. Thus, the question of how we should differentiate the public sphere from other sphere(s) of action, or whether any other spheres of action exist, remains. Are there multiple and interlocking public spheres, as Deeb suggests, and if so, how do we evaluate them? Finally, when we transnationalize or globalize these concepts, we need to consider how such a spatial enlargement affects all of these interlocking relationships.

Conclusion: The Common Good, Justice, Tradition, and Casuistic Moral Reasoning

The connections between the transnational (if not the global) and the local are also critical when we consider the notion of the common good. Salvatore and LeVine's guiding hypothesis is that, "Islamists relate to their societies as an extension of their own discourses of justice." Can the discourse of justice be more central than the desire to take over, appropriate, and reshape state power? Religious movements, for example, can either support or undermine the state. Salvatore and LeVine point out that local Islamist charities are woven into global Islamist networks, and that "charity work, and the funding it secures, has been inseparable from resistance" (LeVine and Salvatore, this volume: 31), though such networks can also strengthen mechanisms of state power.

But what about the content of the common good, and how is it determined? This problem is precisely what makes the debate about the morality of suicide bombing (versus martyrdom) so potent. Here, Salvatore and Levine appeal to MacIntyre and Asad's reevaluations of the notion of tradition, highlighting the fact that traditions both define some social and transcendant goods, and represent lived experience rather than simply stultified cultural practices. Tradition is thus intimately linked to notions of the common good; it is "necessarily transindividual and transgenerational," and can concern a variety of spatial constructs, from the local to the global. Likewise, the scale of the subject (and object) of the common good can also range from the local to the universal, as in the Islamic *umma* that encompasses all Muslims worldwide.

The contributors to this volume demonstrate an emphasis by religious actors on social justice as the primary articulation of the content of the common good. This is also the case for (primarily, though not exclusively) Western religious humanitarian groups, who currently move between an ethic of "charity" and one of "solidarity" in their work in various parts of the world (Lynch 2000). These groups also articulate the common good vis-à-vis an ambiguous relationship with the state, and a complex inter-twining of the local and the transnational. For the work of these religious humanitarians, moreover, taking into account tradition is critical. Local religious traditions must be respected, as must the global religious tradi-tions (Christian, Jewish, etc.), which motivate their own work. The growing awareness by Western-based religious groups of the need for understanding and respect of different religious traditions has resulted in a number of intra-faith and inter-faith dialogues (Ariarajah 1998).

But again, how do religious groups make decisions about how to act? Jonsen and Toulmin (1988) appeal to the concept of casuistry, advocating it as a normative goal for practical modes of moral reasoning, to be preferred over the resort to either universalism or relativism. They discuss the rise and decline of casuistry in the Christian West and the powerful critiques leveled against it during the reformation, when it was seen as an inherent component of the corrupt practices of some Catholic clerics and bishops. They also address Blaise Pascal's 17th repudiation of casuistry for breeding moral "laxity" (ibid.: 239). They argue, however, that we still have much to learn from the casuistic mode of moral reasoning, and in particular from its reliance on practical methods such as the use of analogy, the analysis of circumstances, and the use of cumulative arguments in arriving at a final resolution (ibid.: 251). They argue that casuistry can help us escape from overly dogmatic postures of various stripes.

It may be helpful to think of the work of religious groups analyzed in this volume, as well as elsewhere, as a type of "popular casuistry." That is to say, it may be helpful to think in terms of moral reasoning that incorpo-rates the voices of religious elites but is not limited to them, that relies on precedent and sacred texts, and that uses all these resources to debate and reason about the religious guides to action applicable in any concrete situ-ation. Thus we see that groups in Yemen appeal increasingly to *qanun* instead of shari'a, at least in part because the localized content of the latter is seen to have less and less connection to the legal and moral issues faced in a modernizing context. Conversely, in Pakistan, debates over interpre-tations of shari'a and their application to specific legal controversies is widespread, underscoring the discursive and contextual nature of shari'a in alternative contexts. Hamzah's critique of the debate about suicide bombing (versus martyrdom) adds an important qualification to casuistic methods, however. Those Egyptians who criticized the Saudi fatwa on judicial or extra-judicial grounds tended to engage in partial or misrepresentative argumentation. Severely circumscribed debate, or debate that refuses to acknowledge the main points of the adversary, can result in manipulat-ing morality rather than a deepening of ethical reasoning in concrete circumstances.

By using a concept such as casuistry in the context of Muslim majority societies, I do not at all intend to expose Islamic jurisprudential reasoning to the same criticisms as those leveled against Christian casuistic practices. On the contrary, it is interesting to note that the notion of *maslaha* in Islam, which incorporates concepts of practical reasoning and the protection of human interests in the achievement of the common good (Masud, this volume), bears multiple similarities to casuistry in the sense employed by Jonsen and Toulmin. Moreover, both have common temporal origins. One of the primary articulators of *maslaha*, Abu Ishaq al-Shatibi, lived and wrote during the high period of Christian casuistic methods (i.e., the 14th century).

Viewing casuistry as a helpful analytical concept rather than a normative goal may also help in understanding the various encroaching trajectories that shape the customary, sacred, humanly authored, and social concerns upon which moral reasoning and decision making are based. For example, the followers of an al-Sistani in Iraq must decide how to situate themselves vis-à-vis the seemingly contradictory goals of cooperating with the United States and fledgling Iraqi government for the common good of the nation, and insisting on institutional forms that can help realize Shi'a political power for the "common good" of a religious ideal. Likewise, Western religious humanitarians working in Iraq must make decisions regarding to what degree they should oppose U.S. occupational and military power, and demand the immediate exit of Coalition troops from the country. We can analyze these decisions as being based on a complex triangulation of engagement with moral concerns through the appeal to religious texts, understanding of local and translocal tradition, and interpretation of the political context.

I suggest, therefore, that we can compare more fruitfully casuistic methods in the Christian tradition with those of *maslaha* in Islam. Such methods of moral reasoning occur in practice in a variety of contexts. Sometimes such methods are formalized by religious elites, but at others, non-elites engage in their own, less formalized, casuistic practices, either when confronted with situations requiring new interpretations of religious beliefs, and/or in situations in which there is a gap between religious ethics and historical practice.

This volume analyzes a variety of problems and solutions engendered by the moral imperative to act for the common good in Muslim majority societies. In doing so, it provides a productive set of concepts with which to analyze religious belief and practice, locally and transnationally. We can obtain even more mileage from this set of concepts if we press theoretical and substantive comparisons with similar concepts (such as those of casuistry and *maslaha*) originating in multiple faith traditions.

References

Ariarajah, S. Wesley. 1998. *Gospel and Culture, An Ongoing Discussion within the Ecumenical Movement*. Geneva: World Council of Churches.

Asad, Talal. 1993. *Genealogies of Religion: Discipline and Reasons of Power in Christianity and Islam*. Baltimore and London: Johns Hopkins.

——. 2003. *Formations of the Secular: Christianity, Islam, Modernity*. Stanford: Stanford University Press.

Baker, Raymond (chapter 4 in this volume). "'Building the World' in a Global Age."

Chambers, Simone. 2002. "A Critical Theory of Civil Society." In *Alternative Conceptions of Civil Society*. ed. Simone Chambers, and Will Kymlicka, Princeton, NJ: Princeton University Press.

Comaroff, Jean, and John L. Comaroff, eds. 1999. *Civil Society and the Political Imagination in Africa: Critical Perspectives*. Chicago and London: University of Chicago Press.

Deeb, Lara (chapter 3 in this volume). "'Doing Good, Like Sayyida Zaynab': Lebanese Shi'i Women's Participation in the Public Sphere"

Dupret, Baudouin, and Jean-Noël Ferrié (chapter 5 in this volume). "Constructing the Private/Public Distinction in Muslim-Majority Societies: A Praxiological Approach."

Hamzah, Dyala (chapter 7 in this volume). "Is There an Arab Public Sphere? The Palestinian Intifada, a Saudi *Fatwa*, and the Egyptian Press."

Haynes, Jeff. 1997. *Democracy and Civil Society in the Third World: Politics & New Political Movements*. Cambridge: Polity Press.

Jonsen, Albert R., and Stephen Toulmin. 1988. *The Abuse of Casuistry: A History of Moral Reasoning*. Berkeley and Los Angeles: University of California Press.

Kalipeni, Ezekiel, and Paul T. Zeleza, eds. 1999. *Sacred Spaces and Public Quarrels: African Cultural and Economic Landscapes*. Trenton, NJ, and Asmara, Eritrea: Africa World Press.

LeVine, Mark, and Armando Salvatore (chapter 1 in this volume). "Socio-Religious Movements and the Transformation of 'Common Sense' into a Politics of 'Common Good'."

Lynch, Cecelia. 2000. "Acting on Belief: Christian Perspectives on Suffering and Violence." *Ethics & International Affairs,* vol. 14.

MacIntyre, Alasdair. 1984 [1981]. *After Virtue: A Study in Moral Theory*. Notre Dame, IN: University of Notre Dame Press.

Manoukian, Setrag (chapter 2 in this volume). "Power, Religion, and the Effects of Publicness in 20th Century Shiraz."

Masud, Muhammad Khalid (chapter 6 in this volume). "Communicative Action and the Social Construction of Shari'a in Contemporary Pakistan."

Messick, Brinkley (chapter 8 in this volume). "Cover Stories: A Genealogy of the Legal Public Sphere in Yemen."

Sajoo, Amyn B. 2002. *Civil Society in the Muslim World: Contemporary Perspectives*. London and New York: I.B. Tauris.

Schak, David C., and Wayne Hudson, eds. 2003. *Civil Society in Asia*. Hampshire, UK: Ashgate.

INDEX